DOUGLAS SOUTHALL FREEMAN
ON
LEADERSHIP

Edited with commentary
by
Stuart W. Smith

Foreword
by
James B. Stockdale

White Mane Publishing Company, Inc.

First Printing, 1990, 300 copies by the Naval War College Press

The following acknowledgment pages are incorporated by reference as part of this copyright page.

This White Mane Publishing Company, Inc. publication
was printed by
Beidel Printing House, Inc.
63 West Burd Street
Shippensburg, PA 17257 USA

In respect for the scholarship contained herein, the acid-free paper used in this book meets the guidelines for permanence and durability of the Committee on Production Guidelines for Book Longevity of the Council on Library Resources.

For a complete list of available publications
please write
White Mane Publishing Company, Inc.
P.O. Box 152
Shippensburg, PA 17257 USA

Library of Congress Cataloging-in-Publication Data

Freeman, Douglas Southall, 1886-1953.
Douglas Southall Freeman on leadership / edited with commentary by Stuart W. Smith ; foreword by James B. Stockdale.
p. cm.
Originally published: Newport, R.I. : Naval War College Press, 1990.
Includes bibliographical references and index.
ISBN 0-942597-48-6 : $25.00
1. Command of troops. 2. Leadership. 3. United States--History, Military. 4. United States--History--Civil War, 1861-1865--Campaigns. 5. Confederate States of America. Army--History. I. Smith, Stuart W., 1949- . II. Title.
[UB210.F68 1993]
355.3'3041--dc20 93-9260
CIP

PRINTED IN THE UNITED STATES OF AMERICA

Contents

List of Illustrations

Photographs

Maps

Credits

Page 2, National Archives; 32, 50, 216, Library of Congress; 60, U.S. Army Military History Institute; 192, Naval War College Museum; 20, 23, 27, 240, adapted from maps in *Atlas of American History* (New York: Charles Scribner's Sons, 1984).

Acknowledgments

Grateful acknowledgment is made to the following for permission to reprint previously published material:

CHARLES SCRIBNER'S SONS, an imprint of Macmillan Publishing Company: Excerpts from *George Washington* by Douglas Southall Freeman. Copyright 1948 by Charles Scribner's Sons, renewed 1976 by Mary Freeman Cheek, Anne Freeman Adler, James D. Freeman (Volume I). Copyright 1952 by Charles Scribner's Sons, renewed 1980 by Anne Freeman Adler, Mary Tyler Freeman Cheek, James D. Freeman (Volume 5). Copyright 1954 by Charles Scribner's Sons, renewed 1982 by Anne Freeman Adler, Mary Freeman Cheek, James D. Freeman (Volume 6). Excerpts from *Lee's Lieutenants: A Study in Command* by Douglas Southall Freeman. Copyright 1942, 1943, 1944 by Charles Scribner's Sons, renewed 1970, 1971, 1972 by Inez Goddin Freeman. Excerpts from *R. E. Lee* by Douglas Southall Freeman. Copyright 1934, 1935 by Charles Scribner's Sons, renewed 1962. 1963 by Inez Goddin Freeman. Maps adapted from *Atlas of American History*, Second Revised Edition, Kenneth T. Jackson, Editor. Copyright 1943, 1978, 1985 by Charles Scribner's Sons; renewal copyright 1971 by Charles Scribner's Sons.

METHUEN LONDON (incorporating Eyre and Spottiswoode): Excerpts from *George Washington* by Douglas Southall Freeman (7 volumes), United Kingdom and Commonwealth excluding Canada.

RUTGERS, THE STATE UNIVERSITY: Excerpts from *The Collected Works of Abraham Lincoln* by Roy P. Basler. Copyright 1953 by The Abraham Lincoln Association.

GALE RESEARCH, INC.: Excerpt from the *Dictionary of Literary Biography: Twentieth Century American Historians*, Volume Seventeen, Clyde N. Wilson, Editor. Copyright 1983 by Gale Research Inc.

THE NEW YORK TIMES CO.: Excerpt from "A Columbia Class of '39 Catches Up on the News," by Nadine Brozan, Saturday, May 6, 1989.

UNIVERSITY OF RICHMOND: Editor, *University of Richmond Magazine*: Excerpt from "Dr. Douglas Southall Freeman," by Guy Friddell, *Alumni Bulletin, University of Richmond*, July, 1953.

THE PUTNAM PUBLISHING GROUP: Excerpts from *Lee's Dispatches to Jefferson Davis, 1862-1865*, by Douglas Southall Freeman. Copyright 1915, 1957 by G. P. Putnam's Sons.

RANDOM HOUSE, INC.: Excerpt from *Lincoln and His Generals* by T. Harry Williams. Copyright 1952 by Alfred A. Knopf, Inc.

The remainder of the Douglas Southall Freeman lectures are in the public domain.

Foreword

Take a young man with a big heart and a lump in his throat for the Civil War cause and comrades of his Confederate soldier father; give him a topflight classical education with a history doctorate from Johns Hopkins; let thirty-plus years of his life be spent studying and writing from the private correspondence of Lee, Washington and Jackson; put him up before knowledgeable military audiences ripe for inspiration and insights into the past—and you get some words worth remembering. Today we would have it all on tape, but when Douglas Southall Freeman was making his stream of consciousness presentations to the war colleges of America in the thirties and forties, glancing only infrequently at his rough notes and occasional outlines, his colorful, rapid-fire deliveries were imprinted only on the minds of his rapt listeners and occasionally on their notepads. Thus, Lieutenant Commander Stuart Smith was on to a very good thing when he dedicated himself to researching the available sources to reconstruct the best of these messages Freeman imparted. To help bring out the "feeling for the past" the old gentleman exuded, our compiler has painstakingly constructed historical footnotes and maps to keep us in sync as we read.

Freeman on Leadership is the rub-off of Freeman's intimate grasp of the lives and private thoughts of his biographees, notably Robert E. Lee and George Washington. From his leadoff address herein, given in 1918 in celebration of the birthday of Abraham Lincoln, it is possible to say that he had a thorough grasp of the life and thoughts of that historical figure too. To know that a speaker is equipped to approach leadership from intimate glimpses of the lives of Washington, Lee and Lincoln, all essentially nation-builders and thus committed to common sense, compromise, and the art of the possible, is to prepare us for differences as well as likeness in their leadership styles. Moving people's souls to take unified actions of risk is an art, an art tied to the leader's intuitions regarding human nature and how best to develop focused power from it. In fact, Freeman has described the major lesson of his lifetime of scholarship as the reaffirmation of the influence of personality on history.

Freeman typifies George Washington the soldier with words he spoke as a young colonel serving the British in the French and Indian War: "Discipline is the soul of an army." Washington left that war disillusioned by the ineptness of his imperial masters in guerrilla warfare, but he never forgot how to fight: "I heard the bullets whistle, and believe me there is something charming in the sound." In the seventeen years that elapsed before he became commander of the

Continental army, biographer Freeman noted dramatic growth in his patience, judgment and an "essential sanity" that never left him, even in the heat of combat. But he was no prig. He was big and tough and he swore and he flirted. He backed up his General Anthony Wayne in the latter's harsh treatment of deserters. He was a great fan of the theatre and was so fascinated by the character of the Roman Republican Cato the Younger in Joseph Addison's play *Cato* that he made him his role model (some of Cato's lines can be recognized in Washington's Farewell Address). Washington had the play performed for his troops at Valley Forge despite a congressional resolution that plays were inimical to republican virtue. But the country might not have made it without him, as Freeman demonstrates in his lecture on "Leadership in Allied Operations."

Freeman characterizes Lincoln not with the metaphor of the log cabin or rail fence, but with the spirit of the rivers of the west—boisterous, moving, a force, a force accumulating a goal. He saw in young Lincoln's self-teaching, his drive for understanding, the makings of a teacher of a nation. He tells how the schoolboy Lincoln combed every book for ideas—and for expressions and quotations that "made things plain" to the common man. And throughout his life, he could reach back and pick out just the right expression to "make things plain" in his great speeches. Freeman comes across as a fair-minded man, *not* given to small-mindedness in matters concerning his father's Confederacy's enemies. He expresses regret that Lincoln's national profile was so narrow at the time of his election as president: "Scarcely a dozen lines of what Lincoln had uttered had found their way into the columns of the Southern newspapers." Without committing himself on partisanship, Freeman regrets that so much of the nation had no hint of the man's self-mastery, his growing confidence and emerging independence. "Save the Union" became Lincoln's watchword, and every decision was subordinate to that end. Lincoln had no time for the "party lines." In Peoria he had said, "Stand with anybody that stands right. Stand with him while he is right, and part with him when he goes wrong. Stand with the abolitionist in restoring the Missouri Compromise, and stand against him when he attempts to repeal the fugitive-slave law. In the latter you stand with the Southern disunionist. What of that? You are still right." And years later, as times got tough, he put saving the Union above the law. He expanded his army beyond the limits of the law, and when Southern sympathizers living in the North were obstructing the war effort, he gave that army the right to suspend the privilege of *habeas corpus* in areas where those sympathizers were active; and he ordered the spending of federal funds without writing for congressional appropriations. Freeman gives Lincoln full credit for his remarkable grasp of politics, and even his grasp of some aspects of military operations. (In 1911 Freeman had been the first historian to have access to the confidential wartime letters and telegrams flowing from Robert E. Lee to Jefferson Davis. From them he had concluded that Lincoln was more often right than wrong in overriding the proposed actions of his generals in the early war years; to have done otherwise would have played into Lee's hands.)

Of course Robert E. Lee is the most thoroughly analyzed of all the leaders Freeman mentions. And although he clearly reveres the memory of his father's most beloved general, he makes it clear that Lee could stretch a point here and there to make untenable procedures or customs workable, just like the rest of us. In the first place, the Confederacy's preoccupation with states' rights made a commanding general's job nightmarish. Not even Lee's boss Jefferson Davis could hire and fire like Lincoln and Grant. Lee could not even promote. That was a state's prerogative. Freeman states: "The Confederate army was the worst in the world on systems of promotion." Lee could only "ease out," or kick upstairs, but he did so with great graciousness. One of the old Confederate generals Freeman remembers seeing frequently as a boy was Jubal Early. From the sheaf of official Civil War papers the old gentleman had in his records, the document he was proudest to show off was the very nicely phrased letter to him from Robert E. Lee *relieving him of command.* Like Admiral E. J. King, our chief of naval operations during World War II, Lee spent the lion's share of his time assigning general officers. He treated generals as individuals, always giving thought to how to get the best performance out of each of them. (Lee was rather remarkably enlightened in his abhorrence of treating everyone like a number. When he was superintendent of West Point in the 1850s, he jumped all over War Department blather about "uniform treatment of all cadets": "I do not believe in treating cadets as though they were common soldiers. . . . I believe in treating them as gentlemen who are preparing for the profession of arms.")

General Lee was forced to take the colonels the states gave him, but once he knew them, he paid lots of attention to where they were assigned. On the battlefield, he never went by unit numbers, always by name: "What's that colonel's name on the flank?" Lee was very much a "person" man, and he paid particular attention to signs of personality quirks or emotional instability among his senior officers. He also paid a lot of attention to their alcohol consumption. Lee never drank whiskey and was suspicious of any person who did; Freeman suggests that some brilliant officers went out to pasture over this matter.

Freeman stresses how Lee, and some other generals, were objects of great affection among their men. They were spoken of like they were gods, even years after the war was over. One wonders if this was because of shared risks. One of the best books about the Vietnam War, *The Long Gray Line,* notes that in the Civil War, the risk of battle death to a general was twice that of a private. (Whereas in eleven years of fighting in the Vietnam War, only three general officers were killed in action.) The halo effect over Lee is centered on his concern for the lives of his troops, particularly in never ordering them to make unwarranted charges into death traps. Time and again Freeman stresses that the men knew he would never expose them to unwarranted risk. Likely the times when Lee took extremely long chances with his men were few, but the celebrated case of Pickett's charge up Cemetery Ridge at Gettysburg—the subject of many recent accounts which describe General Longstreet's opposition to Lee's plan as foolhardy and Lee's apologies for his mistake to Longstreet afterwards—raises questions of overstatement.

But overstatement of that sort takes little away from the Freeman phenomenon. As a bonus, we who read these reconstructed talks nearly fifty years after they were given can occasionally get history within history, as when Freeman compares happenings in 1862 to the current events of the day of his talk—November 5, 1936, for instance. In making the case for the high morale of Lee's Army of Northern Virginia on that day at the Army War College in Washington D.C., Freeman posed the question: "I wonder if there was ever great morale without a great commander?" He then contrasted the fortunes of Franco (villainous, as seen on that morning in 1936 Washington; rebuffed at the gates of Madrid the day before, November 4, 1936) to those of American General Winfield Scott (a great commander), who broke through Santa Anna's defenses into the gates of Mexico City on September 14, 1847. By stressing a "different morale" (in the army behind the villain as opposed to the army behind the great commander), a different "morale behind the morale" (vicious in the case of Franco, virtuous in the case of Scott), Freeman makes the case that breaking into city gates is a factor of morale and that morale is a factor of the overall virtue of the commander. No complaints there, but I wish he had gone on to say that another factor in Scott's entry was the greasing of the skids by the well-fought battle of Chapultepec the day before. And then maybe he would have reported the fact that a factor in the American success in the battle of Chapultepec was the courageous fighting of a U.S. Army officer "mentioned in the dispatches" the next day, a young man by the name of Lieutenant Ulysses S. Grant.

James B. Stockdale
Vice Admiral, U.S. Navy (Ret.)

Preface

This is a collection of speeches on leadership by Douglas Southall Freeman, who was perhaps the greatest American military biographer of this century. His four-volume study of *R.E. Lee* (1934-35) was awarded the Pulitzer Prize; his three-volume study of *Lee's Lieutenants* (1942-44) became "required reading" in military circles; and his seven-volume study of *George Washington* (1948-57) was also awarded the Pulitzer Prize. With these books, Freeman rendered an achievement stunning in its scope and scholarship, and earned for himself a permanent place in American letters.

During the course of his research, Freeman spent forty-two years "in the company" of Lee and Washington. As a result, the subject of leadership held a special fascination for him, and he became eminently qualified to discuss it.

An accomplished and popular public speaker, Freeman delivered hundreds of addresses and lectures throughout his long career, and many of these were on the subject of leadership. It is interesting to note that despite the number, quality, and variety of his speeches on leadership, no collection of these speeches has been published before.

The first two speeches in this collection—a Lincoln birthday address (1918) and a Lee birthday address (1926)—were prepared early in Freeman's career. During this period he was relatively well known in his native Virginia as the young editor in chief of the *Richmond News Leader*, the state's leading daily newspaper; but he was still working on the biography that would bring him to national prominence: *R.E. Lee*, published in 1934-35.

When the biography of Lee was awarded the Pulitzer Prize, Freeman was invited to deliver a lecture series at the Army War College. The eight lectures that comprise this series are unified by the central theme of leadership and appear here as the next section of this collection.

With the publication of *Lee's Lieutenants* in 1942-44, Freeman became very well known and respected in military circles. As a result, in the years following the Second World War, Freeman lectured on leadership at many service schools throughout the country. The four lectures that round out this collection—two at the Naval War College and two at the Armed Forces Staff College—are the ones I consider the best of those delivered at the "senior" service schools, i.e., those schools conducted (like the Army War College) at the graduate level.

Now, a brief word about the preparation of this material. The two early addresses, which are filed in Freeman's papers at the Library of Congress, were double-spaced roughs with handwritten corrections; and, since Freeman delivered lectures from notes or an outline, the service school lectures were preserved in the form of stenographic transcripts prepared by the schools themselves. The material, therefore, was fairly rough to begin with and required extensive editing. This I have done silently to avoid unnecessary distraction. My aim throughout has been to put these speeches in finished form for the contemporary reader. The endnotes and maps are, of course, my own, and have been inserted to enhance the understanding of the material presented.

During the preparation of this book I have frequently been asked, "Well, what does Freeman have to say about leadership?" This is not an easy question to answer, because Freeman approached this subject from many different angles and with a wealth of historical material at his command. However, for the reader searching for the "bottom line," I would recommend the lecture entitled "Leadership" as the closest thing to a distillation of his views on the subject.

Similarly, I have also been asked, "What does Freeman consider the most important quality in a leader?" That I can answer in one word: Character. And what is character? Freeman himself defined it in the epigraph that appears in the front of this book; and I think it remarkable that this definition was delivered extemporaneously following a lecture given at the Army's Command and General Staff College on March 7, 1949.

As a final note, I wish to express my thanks to the many people at the Naval War College involved in the preparation of this book, and particularly to John B. Hattendorf, Ernest J. King Professor of Maritime History, who supported this project from beginning to end, and Frank Uhlig, Jr., Editor of the Naval War College Press, who reviewed every page of the manuscript. Thanks are due also to the Naval War College Foundation, which provided the funds for the printing of the book, and to my wife Carol, my son Matthew, and my daughter Merryn, who lived with me and Freeman in the house for almost three years.

Stuart W. Smith

Naval War College
Newport, Rhode Island

"What is character? It is that quality of man which is going to make a man, in an hour of strain, do the just and if possible the generous thing. Character is that quality of mind which makes truth telling instinctive rather than strange. Character is the essence of all that a man has seen in life and regards as high and exalted. Character is like truth, the substance of the things that a man has forgotten but the substance of the things that are worth remembering in life. Character is the starting point from which we go on. When I say a man has character, I mean that when you go to that man and say, 'What are the facts in this case?' he will tell you the truth, justly, truly, and wisely as he knows, with the minimum of exhibitionism and the maximum of devotion to the common cause. Such character is the character of the American army."

Douglas Southall Freeman

Part One
The Man and His Work

DOUGLAS SOUTHALL FREEMAN

This photograph was taken in 1944, the year that Freeman completed the third and final volume of *Lee's Lieutenants*, thereby completing his history of the Army of Northern Virginia after a labor of twenty-nine years.

1

Douglas Southall Freeman

Douglas Southall Freeman was born on May 16, 1886, in Lynchburg, Virginia, the youngest of the four sons of Walker Burford and Bettie Allen Hamner Freeman. In 1891 the Freeman family moved to Richmond, Virginia, which would be Douglas' home for the rest of his life.

Freeman was raised in a stable family environment that emphasized religion, education, and hard work, and his childhood was set in the context of the Confederate experience. His father, who made his living as the Virginia agent of the New York Life Insurance Company, came from a long line of Baptist lay preachers. The Freeman boys all went to Sunday school and church on a regular basis, and all joined the Baptist church at about the age of ten. Since Douglas early on displayed a talent for speaking and academics, both his parents encouraged him to become a minister, and in preparation for this career he learned Greek in college. Although he found his true love in history in graduate school, religion continued to play an important role in Freeman's life.

Freeman received his early education at two private schools in Richmond: Miss Sye Roberts' School and McGuire's University School. Always an outstanding student, Freeman enrolled in Richmond College (later the University of Richmond) at the age of fifteen and graduated three years later with a Bachelor of Arts. During his college years he became interested in journalism and served as the college correspondent for the Richmond afternoon newspaper. In addition, under the influence of Professor S.C. Mitchell, chairman of the history department, he began to turn to history as his chief academic interest. Freeman later remarked that a statement made by this professor during a lecture on Martin Luther meant a great deal to him: "Young gentlemen, the man who wins is the man who hangs on five minutes longer than the man who quits."[1]

In his appreciation of this sentiment can be seen Freeman's reverence for work. Freeman said throughout his life that he regarded the wasting of time as a sin, and he lived his life accordingly.

Religion, education, and hard work—all were important in the growth of the young Freeman, but just as important was the backdrop of the Confederate experience. As the former capital of the Confederacy, Richmond was the center of the Confederate commemorative movement, with Confederate reunions, monuments, and funerals a vivid part of everyday life. Characteristic of this environment were men such as Mr. McGuire, headmaster of Freeman's university school, who would scold his boys for tardiness by reminding them that the battle of Gettysburg had been lost because General Longstreet stopped to give his corps breakfast. And as a forceful personification of the Confederate experience stood Freeman's father, who had fought in the ranks of the Army of Northern Virginia throughout the Civil War and had been present at the surrender of that army at Appomattox. As the youngest son, Douglas was particularly close to his father, who was an active member of Richmond's Robert E. Lee Camp of the United Confederate Veterans. In 1925-26, at the age of eighty-two, Freeman's father served as the commander in chief of the United Confederate Veterans.

As a result, then, of the Confederate setting and of his father's firsthand accounts of the war, Freeman developed a keen interest in Confederate military history. It is significant to note that this interest was not marred by bitterness. Like many Confederate veterans, Freeman's father regarded the surrender as the result of a fair fight and considered the abolition of slavery a good thing. In his view, the war was over, the issue decided, and it was now the job of the South to rebuild itself.

In the spring of 1903, during Freeman's second year at Richmond College, his father took him to a reenactment of the Battle of the Crater outside Petersburg, Virginia. Moved by the sight of the old Confederate veterans, many of them still showing the signs of their wounds, Freeman resolved that day that someone should write the history of the Army of Northern Virginia. In 1944, with the publication of the last volume of *Lee's Lieutenants,* he himself would complete this history after a labor of twenty-nine years.

Having graduated from Richmond College in 1904 at the age of eighteen, Freeman accepted a fellowship for graduate work at Johns Hopkins University in Baltimore, Maryland. He spent four years at Johns Hopkins, receiving his Ph.D. in history in 1908 at the age of twenty-two. By all accounts, these were very happy years for Freeman. He lived a simple life and worked hard (limiting himself to six hours' sleep a night, which would remain his standard). He developed a great respect for the head of the history department, the formidable Professor J.C. Ballagh, who reacted to Freeman's first research paper as follows: "Freeman, the research in this paper is excellent, indeed most exceptional. But you will never make a writer. Your purple prose is execrable."[2] Freeman resolved at this meeting to simplify his style.

While at Hopkins, Freeman wrote his parents every day. One of these letters provides a clear foreshadowing of his future career: "I aim at many things in this world, you know. I want to be a good scholar, one whose name will not be forgotten tomorrow; I want to be a keen thinker, the impress of whose mind will mold the thought of days that come after; I want to be a strong speaker, to carry conviction to the hearts of men in matters that concern their welfare most."[3] He would go on to achieve each of these objectives.

Having selected the Virginia Secession Convention as the topic for his dissertation, Freeman spent the summer of 1906 researching this topic in the archives of the Virginia State Library in Richmond.[4] The reference librarian there, who was a prominent member of the Confederate Memorial Literary Society, was so impressed with the young scholar that she asked him if he would be interested in preparing a catalogue of the society's holdings of books, documents, and pamphlets of the war years. Freeman jumped at the opportunity, and he spent the following summer in Richmond working on this catalogue. Published in early 1908, *A Calendar of Confederate Papers* displays the meticulous scholarship that would become Freeman's trademark. It describes five thousand miscellaneous documents and includes footnotes that identify all the people and places mentioned in the documents. The impressive work done by Freeman for this project provided him with an invaluable introduction to Confederate source material and led, three years later, to his next historical endeavor.

Freeman received his Ph.D. in the summer of 1908 and returned to Richmond to find work. Having been turned down for a teaching position at Richmond College, he spent the first year after graduate school teaching history at a private girls' school. In 1909 he was hired as an editorial writer for both Richmond newspapers (the *Times Dispatch* and the *News Leader*) but left this job in 1910 for a two-year stint as the secretary to the Virginia State Tax Commission.

One day in 1911 an unexpected visitor came to call at Freeman's office. He was Mr. Wymberley Jones de Renne of Wormsloe, Georgia, whose family collected Confederate papers and had made a valuable contribution to the Confederate Memorial Literary Society. Mr. de Renne explained that he had been impressed with Freeman's work on *A Calendar of Confederate Papers* and wanted him to examine two leather-bound documents. Freeman immediately recognized these documents as the confidential letters and telegrams sent by General Robert E. Lee to President Jefferson Davis—documents that had been lost since the evacuation of Richmond in 1865. When Freeman inquired as to the source of the documents, Mr. de Renne replied only that he had purchased them from "a well-known Southern writer," and he then asked Freeman if he would be interested in preparing them for publication.[5] Freeman readily agreed. Thus began Freeman's second historical work, which was published in 1915 under the title *Lee's Dispatches to Jefferson Davis, 1862-1865*. In this work Freeman once again proved a master scholar by using footnotes to construct a brief narrative of that part of the war covered by the 204 "dispatches."

In 1913 Freeman returned to newspaper work as the associate editor of the *News Leader*, Richmond's afternoon paper. Two years later, at the age of twenty-nine, he was appointed editor in chief of the *News Leader*, a position he would hold for the next thirty-four years.

His newspaper career begun, in 1914 Freeman married Inez Virginia Goddin, who was also from Richmond and was also the child of a Confederate veteran. This proved to be a wise and happy match, for his wife was devoted to his work and was willing to organize their home life around its ever-increasing demands.

During the next twelve years, Freeman's energies were primarily devoted to the newspaper and the family. His three children were born during this period: Mary Tyler in 1915, Anne Ballard in 1921, and James Douglas in 1923; and at the *News Leader*, the young editor in chief undertook to learn all facets of the business and quickly took charge. He put a sign beneath the clock in his office: "Time alone is irreplaceable. Waste it not." He promulgated *The News Leader's Twenty Fundamental Rules of News Writing*, which included the following:

- Above all, be clear.
- Therefore, use simple English.
- To that end, write short sentences.
- Try to end every story with a strong, and, if possible, a short sentence.

He became well known for the quality of his editorials on World War I and for his ability as a public speaker. He founded a Current Events Class for Men, which met weekly to discuss vital issues of the day, and in 1925 he began the practice of delivering two newscasts a day on the radio. These daily newscasts, although reduced to one a day in Freeman's retirement, continued until the day he died.

Freeman's main avocation during this period was his work on a biography of Robert E. Lee, which had been commissioned in 1915 by Charles Scribner's Sons as a result of the publication of *Lee's Dispatches*. Although the initial contract called for a one-volume study of seventy-five thousand words, Freeman quickly discovered that much of the original source material on Lee's life had never been consulted and that new source material was coming to light every day. He therefore became determined to write the "definitive" life of Lee, which resulted in a tug-of-war with his publisher over the scope and size of the book. This tug-of-war continued until 1923, when Scribner's assigned Maxwell E. Perkins to be Freeman's editor.[6] Perkins went to Richmond, met Freeman, and agreed to a biography based on all available source material. From this point on, their discussions centered on when the book would be ready rather than what the book would cover.

In 1926, with Scribner's firmly committed to the project and the *News Leader* by then the most popular daily newspaper in Virginia, Freeman decided to make his book his second vocation. He assigned himself a quota of fourteen hours a week to work on the book, and he kept track of the number of hours worked per day in his diary. As the work progressed, the quota increased to twenty-four hours a week. All of this work was done in his study at home, and he made time for it by greatly reducing his social engagements, carefully controlling the time spent with his family, and rising earlier and earlier. As a result of this rigorous system, which he continued to use for his later books, Freeman finally completed *R.E. Lee* in 1934, nineteen years after it was commissioned. Published by Scribner's in four volumes, the biography was met with great popular and critical acclaim and was awarded the Pulitzer Prize in 1935.

After completing "the Lee," Freeman began a preliminary investigation of source materials for a life of Washington but did not start another book until 1936. During this two-year period he became involved in a wide range of outside pursuits. He became chairman of the board of trustees at the University of Richmond, and a trustee of both the Rockefeller Foundation and the General Education Board; he accepted many speaking engagements, including a lecture series on leadership at the Army War College; and to finance his childrens' college education, he took a professorship in the School of Journalism at Columbia University, where he taught one day a week. At the fiftieth reunion of this school's class of 1939, Freeman was the faculty member "inspiring the most anecdotes." "He asked us to use whatever color paper we could write on the fastest, so I always used green," recalled one of his former students.[7]

The extent of Freeman's many activities is clearly indicated by his diary entry for Friday, December 31, 1937:

> For 1937:
> 30 regular trips to New York, with 3 hrs. lecture each
> 83 other lectures and addresses
> 22 formal meetings
> 22 journeys other than regular to N.Y.
> 25,960 miles total travel
> 771 hrs. research
> Wrote & ed. Bicentennial supplement
> ---and edited the *News Leader*.[8]

The research mentioned in this diary entry was conducted for Freeman's next book. In concentrating on the life of Lee, Freeman was concerned that he had placed in "undeserved shadow" the accomplishments of Lee's "lieutenants."[9] The story of the Army of Northern Virginia, he decided, was not yet complete. Accordingly, Freeman set aside his research on Washington and in June 1936 began work on his study of Lee's commanders. For this book, much of the source material had already been collected, and Freeman used the same rigorous system of working that he had developed for the Lee biography. Progress, therefore, was fairly rapid, and in 1942, with the United States at war, Scribner's published *Manassas to Malvern Hill*, the first volume of *Lee's Lieutenants: A Study in Command*. In the foreword to this volume, Freeman notes that the decision to publish his study piece by piece was made in the hope that "something, perhaps, may be gained by printing in the first year of this nation's greatest war, the story of the difficulties that had to be overcome in an earlier struggle before the command of the army became measurably qualified for the task assigned it. . . . The Lee and the 'Stonewall' Jackson of this war will emerge."[10]

Cedar Mountain to Chancellorsville, the second volume of *Lee's Lieutenants*, was published in 1943, and the final volume, *Gettysburg to Appomattox*, was published in 1944. Freeman recorded the completion of this work with this diary entry for Tuesday, May 30, 1944:

> At 6:05 P.M. in the presence of dear friends, I finished *Lee's Lieutenants* and concluded 29 years work to preserve the record of our fathers of the Army of Northern Virginia.[11]

During the summer of 1939, Freeman had devoted one month to the writing of a book entitled *The South to Posterity*. Based on his lectures earlier that year at the Alabama College for Women, this book was an informal survey of Confederate memoirs. He hoped that it would "create useful interest in Confederate history," but he did not regard it as a major work.[12]

In terms of single volumes sold, *Lee's Lieutenants* proved to be even more popular than *R.E. Lee.* The book was particularly well received in military circles. Admirals King and Nimitz and Generals Marshall, Eisenhower, MacArthur, and Bradley all expressed their admiration for the work; and some military leaders encouraged Freeman to write a history of the American command during World War II. Although nothing came of this suggestion, in late 1945 Freeman did serve as an adviser to Assistant Secretary of War John J. McCloy during a postwar tour of all major American military headquarters. Freeman enjoyed this tour immensely, for he was able to meet and talk at some length with many of the war's senior commanders, including Nimitz, MacArthur, Eisenhower, and Bradley.

In the fall of 1944, at the urging of friends and after an examination of the relevant source material, Freeman decided to embark upon his last great historical project: a biography of George Washington. He was fifty-eight years old, he had been editor in chief of the *News Leader* for twenty-nine years, and he had written ten books; but he was still determined to do more. At about this time he framed and put on the desk in his study these lines from Tennyson's poem "Ulysses":

> . . . something ere the end,
> Some work of noble note may yet be done,
> Not unbecoming men that strove with gods.
>
> * * *
>
> 'Tis not too late to seek a newer world.
> . . . My purpose holds
> To sail beyond the sunset and the baths
> Of all the western stars until I die.

For the Washington biography, Freeman received grants from the Carnegie Corporation and the John Simon Guggenheim Foundation that enabled him to hire the research and secretarial staff required to assemble and organize the vast amount of source material involved. With the assistance of this staff, Freeman resumed the grueling schedule that he had developed for his second vocation and plunged into a new century, a new war, and a new main character. The work proceeded rapidly, and in 1948 the first two volumes of the biography were published by Scribner's under the title *Young Washington.* In the introduction to these volumes, Freeman notes that Washington is "a more interesting young man to study because he was so much more complex a character than Lee."[13] Furthermore, the story of the Army of Northern Virginia was "drama played in the twilight. With Washington, the atmosphere is that of dawn."[14]

Despite the demands of his two vocations, Freeman still made time during the postwar years for other pursuits. He retained the board memberships that he had assumed in the thirties, and he continued an ambitious speaking schedule. Now well known and respected in military circles, he lectured at service schools throughout the country, primarily on the subject of leadership. In 1946 Freeman was elected to the fifty-member American Academy of Arts and Letters and in 1947 to the American Philosophical Society, which awarded him the Franklin Medal. He particularly valued the former honor, noting that he and William Faulkner were the only Southerners in the academy.

In June 1949, at the age of sixty-three, Freeman retired as editor in chief of the *News Leader* in order to devote himself full-time to the Washington biography. In his letter of resignation he wrote, "I have concluded that I can do nothing here at the newspaper and at the radio station that others cannot do readily and perhaps better. That statement may not hold so completely, perhaps, with reference to a task in which training in military history and the experience in biographical writing are requisite. There naturally are many more qualified newspaper editors than there are military biographers."[15]

Thus his historical work, which had started as an avocation in 1911 and had become a second vocation in 1926, finally became his only vocation. As usual, he set for himself a demanding pace: eight hours a day, seven days a week, for a total of fifty-six hours a week; but he loved the work and relished his newfound freedom. At the end of his first week of "retirement," having spent sixty-five hours on the Washington biography, he wrote in his diary, "Life is so beautiful now I'm afraid it is a dream from which I shall be awakened by a voice that says: 'Get up and go downtown and write two columns of editorial.'"[16]

As a result of this new schedule, the third and fourth volumes of the biography were published in 1951 under the titles *Planter and Patriot* and *Leader of the Revolution*; and the fifth volume, *Victory with the Help of France*, was published in 1952.

But even in "retirement," Freeman remained close to current events. His business and speaking pursuits continued unabated, and he still delivered a daily radio newscast from his home, where a teletype provided him with the Associated Press wire service.

A close look at the last week of Freeman's life provides a vivid sense of the man and his environment. On Saturday, June 6, 1953, exactly one week before his death, he made the following entry in his diary:

> By every test, this has been a bad week. I miscalculated the time [on the book] lost at Chestertown; I gave an hour to the coronation; the board meeting Thursday was long; to cap it all, a deaf old jackass came here today and took almost an hour to ask me when he should fly the Confederate flag on his confounded bank. Besides all this, I have the almost intolerable burden of a certain other man's utter laziness![17]

The "certain other man" must have been Freeman himself, for he was not feeling well. Four days later, on Wednesday, June 10, he typed a letter "to be opened immediately after my death." The letter began as follows: "Within the last fortnight, I have had two attacks which seem to me to be of angina pectoris or pseudo angina. I have not yet decided whether I shall talk of these with Dr. Higgins, because he may restrict my movements so severely that I had rather be dead." The letter then proceeded to give directions for his funeral, including the following inscription on his tombstone: "'Tis not too late to seek a newer world." "That," the letter concluded, "is my message to my wife . . . and to my children and grandchildren."[18]

On the morning of Saturday, June 13, the family butler inquired as to the "hymn of the day"—a custom in the Freeman household—and Freeman replied, "Today it will be 'Rest in Peace until We Meet Again.'"[19] Later that morning Freeman delivered his daily radio newscast, worked in the garden, then went to his study to put the finishing touches on the final chapter of the sixth volume of the Washington biography. He completed the chapter before lunch, revising the last paragraph to an extent uncharacteristic for this stage of the work.

After lunch Freeman became ill. His doctors were summoned, but he slipped into a coma and died late that afternoon.

Patriot and President, the sixth volume of the Washington biography, was published in 1954; and the seventh and final volume, *First in Peace,* was written by two of Freeman's research associates and published in 1957. In 1958 the seven-volume biography of Washington won for Freeman his second Pulitzer Prize.

* * * * *

In his four-volume study of *R.E. Lee,* his three-volume study of *Lee's Lieutenants,* and his seven-volume study of *George Washington,* Douglas Southall Freeman left us with an achievement perhaps unparalleled in twentieth century American biography; and in addition to the books themselves, he left us with an approach to biography and history that is worth remembering.

For Freeman, the aim of biography was "the faithful portrayal of a soul in its adventure through life."[20] This was the fundamental motivation underlying both his prodigious scholarship, which sought to establish exactly what happened in his subject's life, and his narrative technique, which told the story from the personal viewpoint of his subject.

This concentration on the individual reflected Freeman's view of history. He believed that one individual could make a difference, and that all would be right in the end. "I would say," he once remarked, "that the study of history is that which gives man the greatest optimism, for if man were not destined by his Maker to go on until the kingdom of heaven is attained, man would have been extinguished long ago by reason of all man's mistakes and frailties. Man was made to be immortal, else he could not survive being the fool he is."[21]

And when asked by a friend to identify the most important thing that he had learned from his work, Freeman replied, "The influence of personality on history."[22]

Notes

Although no book-length biography of Freeman has been written, there is an abundance of source material available on his life. Secondary source material exists in the form of numerous articles, many of them written by people who knew Freeman personally; and primary source material exists in the form of Freeman's personal papers, which by his direction are available to the general public. The bulk of Freeman's papers (70,000 items) are in the Manuscript Division, Library of Congress, Washington, D.C.; the papers relating to his work as editor of the *Richmond News Leader* are in the Alderman Library, University of Virginia, Charlottesville, Virginia; and the papers relating to his graduate school experience are in the Milton S. Eisenhower Library, Johns Hopkins University, Baltimore, Maryland.

1. Guy Friddell, "Dr. Douglas Southall Freeman," *Alumni Bulletin, University of Richmond* (July 1953): 18.

2. Mary Tyler Freeman Cheek, "Douglas Southall Freeman: My Father as a Writer," *Richmond Literature and History Quarterly* (Spring 1979): 35.

3. *Ibid.*, 36.

4. Several sources have reported that the only copy of Freeman's dissertation was destroyed in a fire at the Johns Hopkins University library. This is not true. The copy filed in the library was damaged by the fire but not destroyed; it is now filed in Freeman's papers at the Library of Congress (Container 126; Speech, Article, and Book File). Attached to it is a note signed by Freeman: "MS of Secession of Virginia—seriously damaged in fire Sep '08—fortunately, the original MS was in my possession."

5. John L. Gignilliat, "Douglas Southall Freeman," in *Dictionary of Literary Biography*, vol. 17, *Twentieth-Century American Historians*, ed. Clyde Norman Wilson (Detroit: Gale Research Co., 1983), 159. This is the most comprehensive biographical sketch of Freeman that I have come across, and the only source I have found that contains an account of Freeman's meeting with Mr. de Renne.

6. Maxwell E. Perkins is best known as the editor of F. Scott Fitzgerald, Ernest Hemingway, and Thomas Wolfe. Perkins was the basis of the character Foxhall Edwards in Wolfe's novel *You Can't Go Home Again* (1934). In 1950 Perkins' correspondence was published under the title *Editor to Author*.

7. Nadine Brozan, "A Columbia Class of '39 Catches Up on the News," *New York Times*, Saturday, 6 May 1989, p. 32.

8. Freeman diary, 31 December 1937, Douglas Southall Freeman Papers, Manuscript Division, Library of Congress, Washington, D.C. (Container 1; Diaries, Journals and Related Material File).

9. Douglas Southall Freeman, *Lee's Lieutenants: A Study in Command*, vol. 1, *Manassas to Malvern Hill* (New York: Charles Scribner's Sons, 1942), xv.

10. *Ibid.*, xxix-xxx.

11. Freeman diary, 30 May 1944, Freeman Papers, Library of Congress (Container 1; Diaries, Journals and Related Material File).

12. Dr. Malone, "Calendar of DSF Historical Works," Freeman Papers, Library of Congress (Container 123; Special Correspondence and Biographical File). These undated notes were apparently prepared by Dumas Malone, perhaps for his article "The Pen of Douglas Southall Freeman" (see note 16).

13. Douglas Southall Freeman, *George Washington*, vol. 1, *Young Washington* (New York: Charles Scribner's Sons, 1948), xxiv.

14. *Ibid.*, xxvi.

15. Freeman to D. Tennant Bryan, 3 May 1949, Freeman Papers, Library of Congress (Container 95; General Correspondence File).

16. Dumas Malone, "The Pen of Douglas Southall Freeman," in Freeman, *Washington*, vol. 6, *Patriot and President* (New York: Charles Scribner's Sons, 1954), xxviii.

17. Freeman diary, 6 June 1953, Freeman Papers, Library of Congress (Container 2; Diaries, Journals, and Related Material File). Freeman disguised the last sentence of this entry by using Greek letters to spell English words. My thanks to Professor Joseph G. Brennan of the Naval War College for deciphering this sentence.

18. Freeman to his family, 10 June 1953, Freeman Papers, Library of Congress (Container 244; General Miscellany File).

19. Geneva B. Snelling, "Douglas Southall Freeman" (unpublished reminiscence, October 1954), 7, Freeman Papers, Library of Congress (Container 123; Special Correspondence and Biographical File). Snelling served as Freeman's librarian for the Washington project in the early fifties. This warm, well-written reminiscence provides a vivid picture of Freeman in the last years of his life, including these gems:

o "This man of strong likes was equally vigorous in his dislikes. He abhorred laziness above all things. In this category also were loud-talking women, whistling, and barking dogs. His usual good humor vanished if someone stayed too long or had trouble breaking away. He regarded brevity as a desirable virtue."

o "He never carried a watch nor did I ever see him look at a clock, yet he always knew the time."

o "The side of his personality the public knew least about was his sense of humor. It was a delightful elfin humor, ever near the surface ready to bubble up. . . . A contemporary of Washington, William Gordon by name, was the only person given access to Washington's papers by Washington himself. He spent weeks at Mt. Vernon and produced an abominable history of the American Revolution. . . . When I found a reference in Dr. Freeman's hand to 'O. B.' Gordon, I spent hours trying to identify the gentleman. After a fruitless search, I appealed to Dr. Freeman's secretary for help and in great glee she told me that Dr. F. always referred to William Gordon as 'Old Bastard' Gordon."

20. *Ibid.*, 8.

21. Freeman, Untitled Lay Sermon (29 March 1925), 11, Freeman Papers, Library of Congress (Container 126; Speech, Article, and Book File). In 1924-25 Freeman delivered a series of 27 lay sermons to an adult Sunday school class at his church, the Second Baptist Church of Richmond, Virginia. This series, which he called "Parables of the City Streets," provides a revealing statement of Freeman's religion and his values. All of these sermons were transcribed and are filed together in Freeman's papers at the Library of Congress.

22. Mary Wells Ashworth (Historical Associate to Freeman), "Prefatory Note," in Freeman, *Washington*, 6:xliv.

2

Chronology of Life and Books

1886 May 16	Born in Lynchburg, Virginia, the youngest of the four sons of Walker Burford and Bettie Allen Hamner Freeman.
1891	Moved to Richmond, Virginia.
1892-1901	Attended private schools in Richmond.
1904	Graduated from Richmond College (later the University of Richmond) with a B.A.
1908	Published *A Calendar of Confederate Papers.*
1908	Awarded Ph.D. in history from Johns Hopkins University.
1909	Hired as editorial writer for the *Richmond Times Dispatch* and the *Richmond News Leader.*
1910-12	Served as secretary to the Virginia State Tax Commission.
1913	Appointed associate editor of the *Richmond News Leader.*
1914 Feb 5	Married Inez Virginia Goddin.
1915	Published *Lee's Dispatches to Jefferson Davis, 1862-1865.*
1915	Appointed editor in chief of the *Richmond News Leader,* a post that he held until 1949.

1915	Commissioned by Charles Scribner's Sons to write a biography of Robert E. Lee.
1934-35	Published *R.E. Lee* (4 volumes), which was awarded the Pulitzer Prize.
1939	Published *The South to Posterity: An Introduction to the Writing of Confederate History.*
1942	Published *Manassas to Malvern Hill,* volume 1 of *Lee's Lieutenants: A Study in Command.*
1943	Published *Cedar Mountain to Chancellorsville,* volume 2 of *Lee's Lieutenants: A Study in Command.*
1944	Published *Gettysburg to Appomattox,* volume 3 of *Lee's Lieutenants: A Study in Command.*
1946	Elected to the American Academy of Arts and Letters.
1947	Elected to the American Philosophical Society.
1948	Published *Young Washington,* volumes 1 and 2 of *George Washington.*
1949	Retired from the post of editor in chief of the *Richmond News Leader.*
1951	Published *Planter and Patriot* and *Leader of the Revolution,* volumes 3 and 4 of *George Washington.*
1952	Published *Victory with the Help of France,* volume 5 of *George Washington.*
1953 June 13	Died of a heart attack at his home in Richmond, Virginia.
1954	Published *Patriot and President,* volume 6 of *George Washington.*

1957 Published *First in Peace,* volume 7 of *George Washington* (based on Freeman's research and written by his assistants, John Alexander Carroll and Mary Wells Ashworth).

1958 Awarded Pulitzer Prize for *George Washington.*

3

Chronology of the Army of Northern Virginia

The first ten speeches of this collection are based on the research conducted by Freeman for his history of Lee and the Army of Northern Virginia. As a guide for the reader, it is therefore appropriate to close this section and to introduce the next with a chronology of Lee's army.

This chronology focuses on the leaders and battles discussed by Freeman. With regard to the battles, it is important to note that some of them have two names: the North used the name of a creek, and the South the name of a town. This applies, for example, to the battles of Manassas (known in the North as the battles of Bull Run) and the battle of Sharpsburg (known in the North as the battle of Antietam).

1861

March 4. Abraham Lincoln takes office as the sixteenth president of the United States, having been elected on a platform opposed to the extension of slavery into the territories. In the four months between his election and inauguration, seven Southern states have seceded from the Union, established the Confederate States of America at Montgomery, Alabama, and elected Jefferson Davis as president. In his inaugural address, Lincoln proclaims: "In your hands, my dissatisfied fellow countrymen, and not in mine, is the momentous issue of civil war. The government will not assail you. You can have no conflict, without being yourselves the aggressors. You have no oath registered in Heaven to destroy the government, while I shall have the most solemn one to 'preserve, protect, and defend' it."

April 12. The war begins at Charleston, South Carolina, when Confederate forces under Pierre G.T. Beauregard open fire on the Union garrison at Fort Sumter. Two days later Fort Sumter surrenders, and Lincoln issues a call for 75,000 militia.

April 17. Virginia convention approves ordinance of secession.

April 20. Robert E. Lee resigns from the United States Army. In his letter of resignation he writes, "Save in the defense of my native State, I never again desire to draw my sword."

April 22. Lee accepts command of Virginia's military forces.

May 23. In a public referendum, the people of Virginia approve secession. The next day, Union troops cross the Potomac and occupy Alexandria.

May 29. President Davis arrives in Richmond, the new capital of the Confederacy. Within ten days, Virginia's military forces are transferred to the Confederacy, and Lee becomes military adviser to Davis.

June 10. Union forces attack a much smaller Confederate force at Big Bethel, but are repulsed after a brief engagement.

June 11. Western Virginia refuses to secede and sets up its own state government.

July 11-13. Union forces under George B. McClellan win two battles in western Virginia (at Rich Mountain and Corrick's Ford).

July 21. Confederate forces under Beauregard and Joseph E. Johnston defeat Union forces under Irvin McDowell at the first battle of Manassas. McDowell retreats to Washington. (After the battle, McClellan replaces McDowell as commander of Union forces in and around Washington; and the Confederate forces at Manassas are combined under Johnston, with Beauregard second in command.)

July 28. Lee sent to western Virginia to coordinate Confederate military operations there.

October 31. Lee returns to Richmond, having halted the Union advance in western Virginia but having won no victories.

November 5. Thomas J. Jackson assumes command of the Confederate Army of the Valley at Winchester.

November 6. Lee sent to Charleston, South Carolina, to supervise the fortification of the southeast coast.

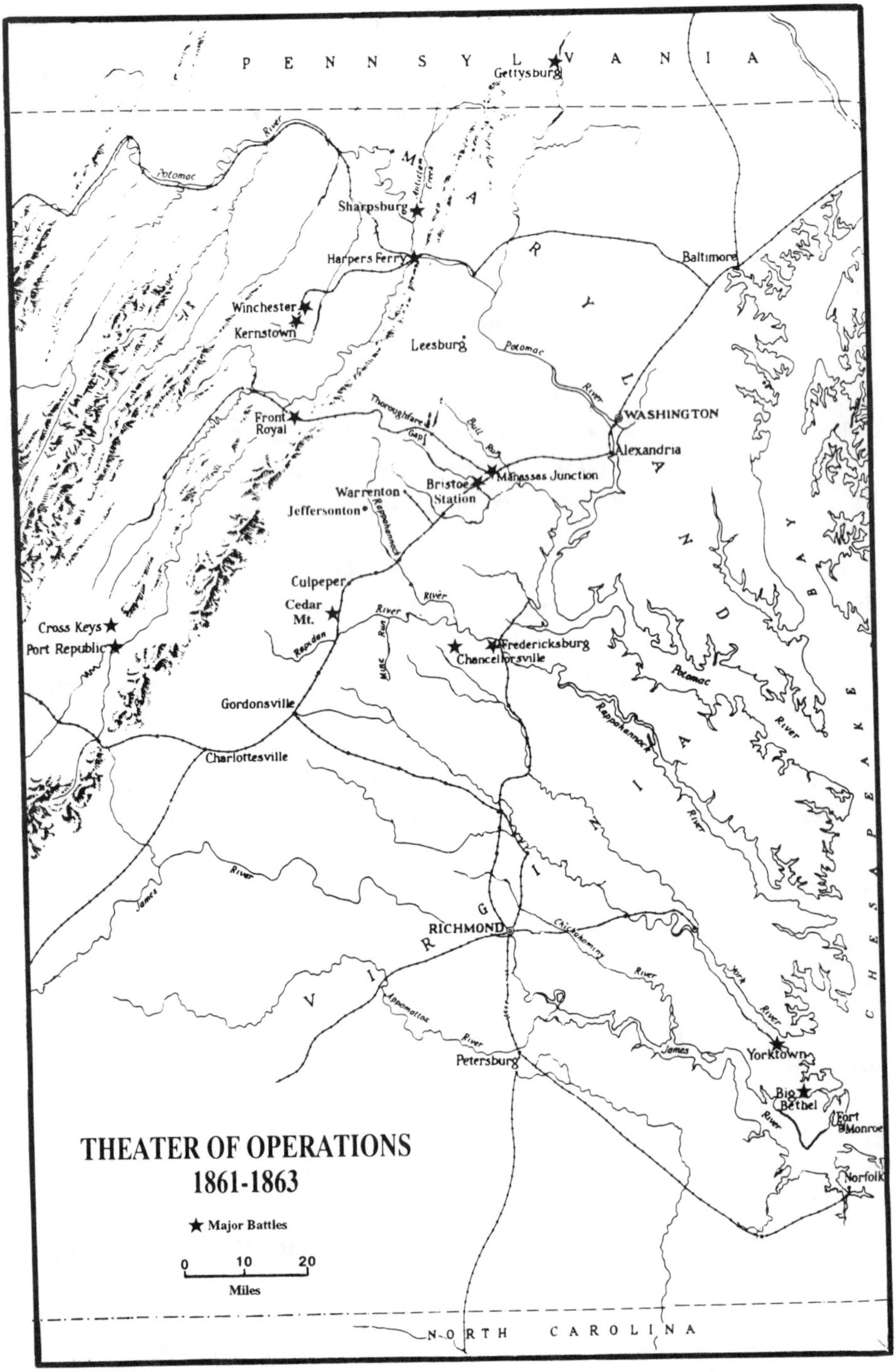

Adapted with permission of Charles Scribner's Sons, an imprint of Macmillan Publishing Company, from Atlas of American History, Second Revised Edition, edited by Kenneth T. Jackson. Copyright 1943, 1978, 1985 by Charles Scribner's Sons.

1862

January 30. Beauregard, never comfortable with his assignment as *second* in command to Johnston, is sent to the West, thus resolving a difficult situation.

March 6. Lee returns to Richmond.

March 17-May 2. The Union Army of the Potomac, under command of McClellan, is transported by water from Alexandria to Fort Monroe on the Virginia peninsula (that neck of land between the James and York rivers). In response, the bulk of Johnston's army reinforces the Confederate garrison at Yorktown, and Johnston's command is expanded to include the Confederate forces at Yorktown and Norfolk. McClellan thereupon begins a siege of Yorktown.

March 23-June 9. Jackson conducts his legendary Valley campaign, during which he fights six battles, winning all but the first: Kernstown (23 March); McDowell (8 May); Front Royal (23 May); Winchester (25 May); Cross Keys (8 June); and Port Republic (9 June). This campaign has the effect of pinning down a considerable number of Union forces—forces that otherwise could have reinforced McClellan on the Virginia peninsula.

May 3. Confederate forces evacuate Yorktown (before McClellan begins his major bombardment) and withdraw toward Richmond. McClellan follows them slowly up the Peninsula.

May 9. Confederate forces evacuate Norfolk and withdraw toward Richmond.

May 31. Johnston is seriously wounded at the battle of Seven Pines.

June 1. Lee assumes command of Johnston's army and christens it the "Army of Northern Virginia."

June 17. The bulk of Jackson's army leaves the Valley to reinforce Lee at Richmond (arriving in the vicinity of Lee's army on 24 June).

June 26-July 1. In the battles of the Seven Days, Lee drives McClellan from the outskirts of Richmond to the cover of gunboats at Harrison's Landing: Mechanicsville (26 June); Gaines' Mill (27 June); Savage

Station (29 June); Glendale (or Frayser's Farm) (30 June); and Malvern Hill (1 July).

July 13. Jackson is ordered to proceed to Gordonsville to meet the advance of a Union army under John Pope.

August 9. Jackson defeats a part of Pope's army at Cedar Mountain.

August 13. McClellan begins a general withdrawal from the James to reinforce Pope via the Rappahannock and the Potomac. In response, Lee and most of his army leave Richmond to reinforce Jackson.

August 25-26. In one of their most famous marches, Jackson's "foot cavalry" proceeds from Jeffersonton to Bristoe Station via Thoroughfare Gap, covering 54 miles in two days. This movement takes them around the right flank and behind the rear of Pope's army, thus setting the stage for the second battle of Manassas.

August 29-30. Lee defeats Pope at the second battle of Manassas. Pope's army retreats to Washington, where it is put under the command of McClellan.

September 4-7. Lee's army crosses the Potomac near Leesburg on its first invasion of the North.

September 9. Lee dispatches Jackson to capture Harpers Ferry.

September 15. Jackson captures Harpers Ferry then moves to reinforce Lee at Sharpsburg, Maryland.

September 17. McClellan attacks Lee at Sharpsburg in the bloodiest single day of the war.

September 18. Lee's army retreats across the Potomac into Virginia. To the consternation of Lincoln, McClellan does not pursue him. Lee sends Jackson to Winchester and masses the rest of his army at Culpeper.

September 22. Lincoln issues the Emancipation Proclamation (to take effect on 1 January 1863 in all states then "in rebellion against the United States").

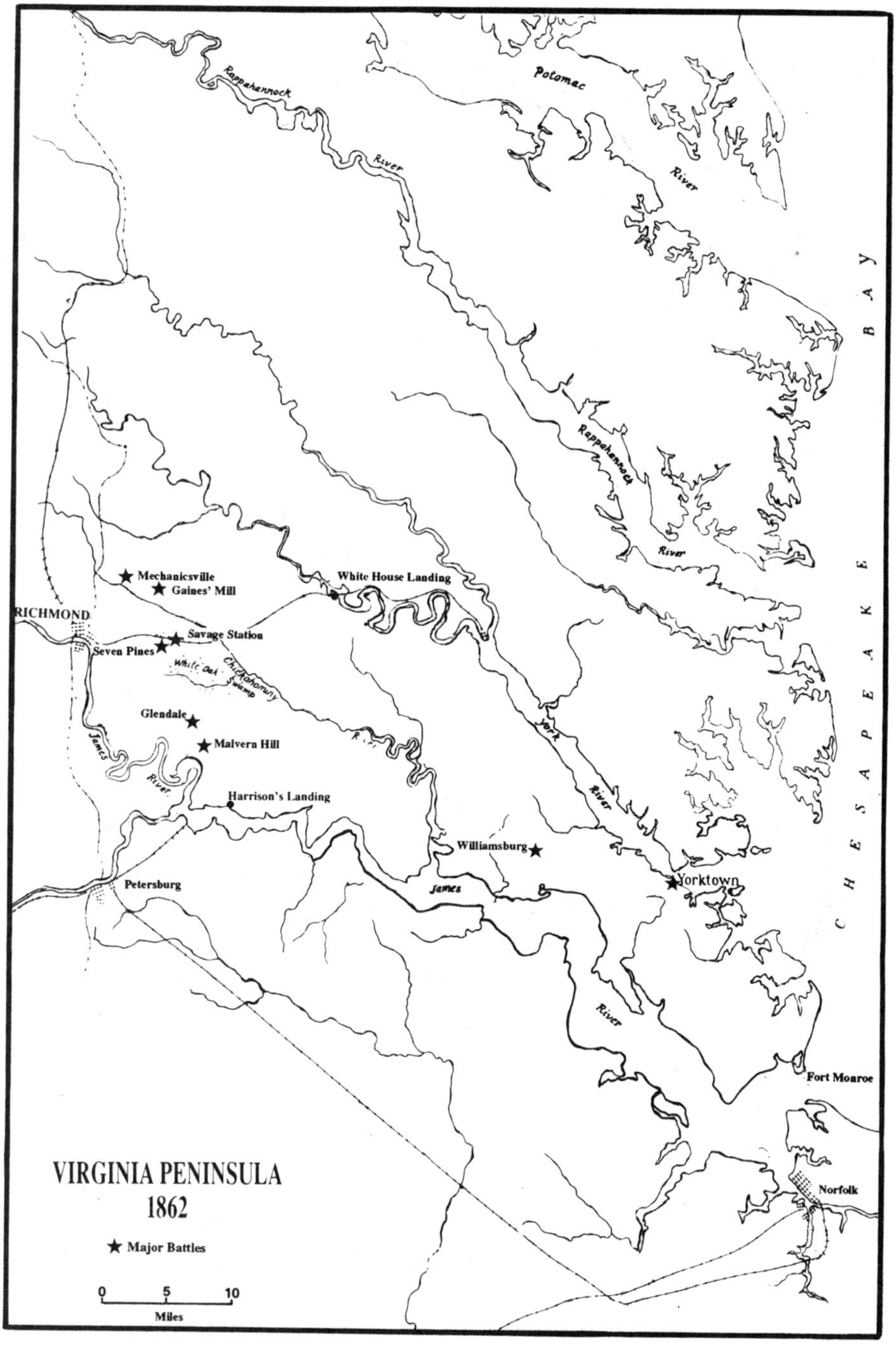

Adapted with permission of Charles Scribner's Sons, an imprint of Macmillan Publishing Company, from Atlas of American History, Second Revised Edition, edited by Kenneth T. Jackson. Copyright 1943, 1978, 1985 by Charles Scribner's Sons.

October 11. Lee's army is organized into two corps. James Longstreet is assigned command of the First Corps, and Jackson the Second.

October 25. Lincoln wires McClellan: "I have just read your dispatch about sore-tongued and fatigued horses. Will you pardon me for asking what the horses of your army have done since the battle of Antietam that fatigue anything?"

October 26. McClellan's army begins crossing the Potomac into Virginia.

November 7. Lincoln replaces McClellan with Ambrose E. Burnside.

November 15. Burnside begins the movement of his army from Warrenton to Fredericksburg. In response, Lee begins to shift his army to Fredericksburg.

December 13. Burnside attacks Lee's fortified positions at Fredericksburg and is repulsed with heavy losses. Burnside retreats to the north side of the Rappahannock.

1863

January 22. Burnside's second attempt to assault Fredericksburg breaks down due to heavy rains in the "Mud March."

January 25. Lincoln replaces Burnside with Joseph Hooker.

May 1-3. Lee defeats Hooker at the battle of Chancellorsville, but Jackson is mortally wounded. Hooker retreats to the north side of the Rappahannock.

May 30. With Jackson gone, Lee's army is reorganized into three corps. Longstreet retains command of the First, Richard S. Ewell is assigned to command the Second, and Ambrose P. Hill the Third.

June 3. Lee's army begins to leave Fredericksburg for its second invasion of the North.

June 10. Hooker writes Lincoln that now is the time to move on Richmond. Lincoln replies, "I think Lee's army, and not Richmond, is your true objective."

June 13. Hooker's army leaves Fredericksburg and heads north in a movement designed to keep itself between Lee's army and Washington.

June 28. Lincoln replaces Hooker with George G. Meade.

July 1-3. Battle is joined at the village of Gettysburg, Pennsylvania. On the first day the Confederates drive the Union forces out of the village; the Confederates occupy Seminary Ridge (to the south of town) and the Union forces occupy Cemetery Ridge (to the southeast of town). On the second day Lee attacks the Union flanks but the Union line holds. On the third day Lee attacks the Union center, but once again the Union line holds.

July 4. Lee's army begins a withdrawal to the Potomac, where its retreat is halted by high waters. Meade does not pursue Lee immediately.

July 13. Lee's army crosses the Potomac into Virginia before Meade is ready to attack him in force.

July 14. In a letter he did not send, Lincoln writes Meade, "Your golden opportunity [to destroy Lee's army] is gone, and I am distressed immeasurably because of it."

July 19. Meade's army crosses the Potomac but is unable to strike the main part of Lee's army before it reaches Culpeper. Meade concentrates his forces at Warrenton.

July 31. Lee writes Davis of Gettysburg: "No blame can be attached to the army for its failure to accomplish what was projected by me, nor should it be censured for the unreasonable expectations of the public—I am alone to blame, in perhaps expecting too much of its prowess & valor."

August 8. In a letter to Davis, Lee writes: "The general remedy for the want of success in a military commander is his removal. . . . For, no matter what may be the ability of the officer, if he loses the confidence of his troops disaster must sooner or later ensue. . . . I have seen and heard expression of discontent in the public journals at the result of the [Gettysburg] expedition. I do not know how far this feeling extends in the army . . . . It is fair, however, to suppose that it does exist, and success is so necessary to us that nothing should be risked to secure it. I therefore, in all sincerity, request Your Excellency to take measures to supply my place." Davis , of course, denied this request.

October 9-November 7. Meade's army having been reduced by two corps (to reinforce the Union Army of the Tennessee), Lee marches his army around Meade's right flank and heads north toward Washington. Meade quickly withdraws to the north, where Lee attacks him at Bristoe Station (14 October) without significant effect. Lee then withdraws to the south, first to the Rappahannock and then, under pressure from Meade, to south of the Rapidan.

November 26-December 1. Meade crosses the Rapidan and Lee blocks this movement at Mine Run. Unable to find a weak spot in Lee's line, Meade withdraws to north of the Rapidan and goes into winter quarters.

1864

March 10. Ulysses S. Grant is appointed commanding general of the Union armies. Two weeks later Grant makes his headquarters with Meade's army in Virginia.

April 9. Grant issues Meade orders for the Virginia campaign: "Wherever Lee goes, there you will go also."

May 4 - June 3. The Army of the Potomac crosses the Rapidan, beginning the Virginia campaign of 1864. In the course of five battles, Grant is unable to turn Lee's right flank but drives him south by relentlessly sliding the Army of the Potomac to the left: The Wilderness (5-6 May); Spotsylvania Court House (8-19 May); North Anna (23-24 May); Totopotomoy (30 May); and Cold Harbor (3 June). On 9 May Lincoln says to his secretary, John Hay: "How near we have been to this thing before and failed. I believe if any other general had been at the head of that army it would have been now on this side of the Rapidan. It is the dogged pertinacity of Grant that wins."

May 5. The Union Army of the James, under Benjamin Butler, lands at Bermuda Hundred to attack Richmond from the south. This attack is blocked by the Confederates, and Butler is "bottled up" between the James and Appomattox rivers.

June 13. Lee detaches the Second Corps under Jubal Early to deal with a Union offensive in the Shenandoah Valley.

June 14. Grant crosses the James River at Wilcox's Landing in a move toward Petersburg that surprises Lee.

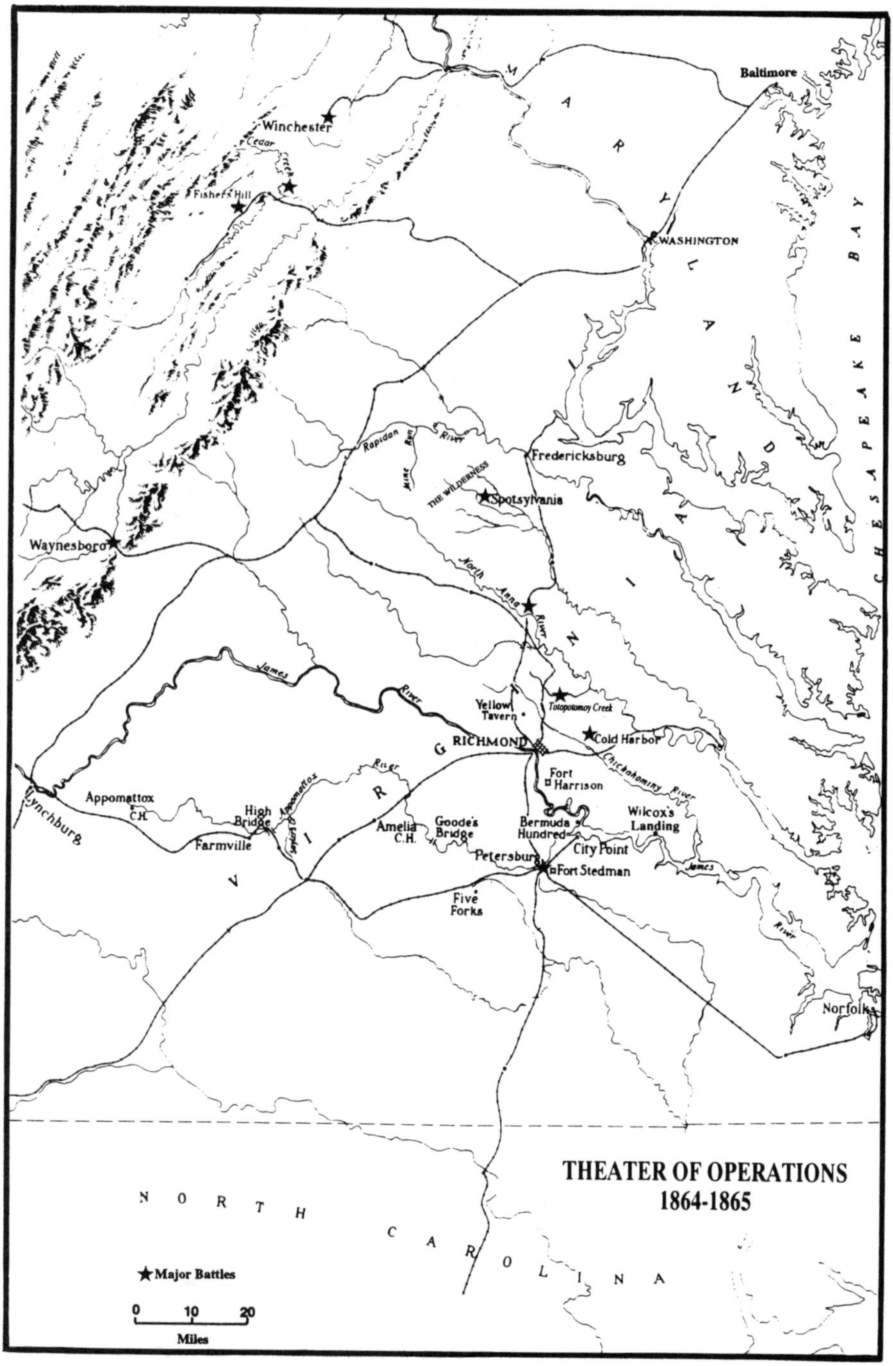

Adapted with permission of Charles Scribner's Sons, an imprint of Macmillan Publishing Company, from Atlas of American History, Second Revised Edition, edited by Kenneth T. Jackson. Copyright 1943, 1978, 1985 by Charles Scribner's Sons.

June 15-18. Grant's attack on Petersburg fails, and the siege of Petersburg begins.

June 23. The Union army in the Valley having withdrawn to West Virginia, Early's Second Corps heads north on a raid that takes it to the outskirts of Washington before withdrawing across the Potomac on 14 July.

July 30. Having constructed a 586-foot-long tunnel under the siege lines at Petersburg, a Pennsylvania regiment blows a hole in the Confederate line, and the Battle of the Crater begins. The Confederates rally quickly, and within a few hours this attack is repulsed.

September-October. A Union army under Philip Sheridan decimates Early's Second Corps in battles at Winchester (19 September), Fisher's Hill (22 September), and Cedar Creek (19 October).

1865

March 2. Sheridan captures most of Early's remaining troops in the battle of Waynesboro.

March 25. Confederate forces under John B. Gordon capture Fort Stedman (opposite Petersburg) but are forced to withdraw under heavy fire.

April 1. Grant finally turns Lee's right flank at the battle of Five Forks.

April 2. Grant orders a general assault and breaks through Lee's line. Lee's army begins a retreat from Petersburg and heads west to the railroad at Amelia Court House.

April 5. Sheridan blocks Lee's escape route south from Amelia Court House, forcing Lee to head for the railroad at Lynchburg.

April 6. Grant cuts off and captures Lee's rear guard at Sayler's Creek.

April 7. Lee repulses a Union attack at Farmville. Lincoln wires Grant: "General Sheridan says, 'If the thing is pressed I think that Lee will surrender.' Let the *thing* be pressed."

April 8. Sheridan reaches Appomattox Station to cut off Lee's retreat.

April 9. At 5 o'clock in the morning, Gordon leads the last attack made by Lee's army in an unsuccessful attempt to break through the Union lines. "I have fought my corps to a frazzle," reports Gordon, "and I fear I can do nothing unless I am heavily supported by Longstreet's corps."

Since Longstreet's corps is already committed to the defense of the army's rear, Lee says to his staff, "Then there is nothing left me to do but to go and see General Grant, and I would rather die a thousand deaths." To this one of his colonels responds, "Oh, General, what will history say of the surrender of the army in the field?" And Lee replies, "Yes, I know they will say hard things about us. They will not understand how we were overwhelmed by numbers. But that is not the question, Colonel. The question is, Is it right to surrender this army? If it is right, then I will take all the responsibility."

Lee then discusses the situation with Longstreet, who asks Lee if the sacrifice of the army would help the Confederate cause. When Lee says no, Longstreet remarks that the situation speaks for itself.

Edward Alexander, Longstreet's chief of artillery, suggests that the men be dispersed with orders to report to the governors of their states to continue the fighting. To this Lee replies, "If I took your advice, the men would be without rations and under no control of officers. They would become mere bands of marauders, and the enemy's cavalry would pursue them and overrun many sections they may never have occasion to visit. We would bring on a state of affairs it would take the country years to recover from." Years later Alexander writes, "I had not a single word to say in reply. He [Lee] had answered my suggestion from a plane so far above it, that I was ashamed of having made it."

That afternoon Lee surrenders to Grant at the village of Appomattox Court House.

14 April. Lincoln is shot by an assassin and dies the next morning. At Lincoln's passing Secretary of War Stanton remarks, "Now he belongs to the ages."

Part Two
Early Addresses

ABRAHAM LINCOLN

This photograph, one of the best known pictures of Lincoln, was taken on November 8, 1863, eleven days before the Gettysburg Address.

4

The Key to Lincoln's Greatness

Lincoln Birthday Address
February 12, 1918

Ten months after America's entry into the First World War, Freeman delivered this address to the soldiers of the 159th Infantry Brigade, Eightieth Division, Camp Lee, Virginia. Although only thirty-two years old, Freeman at this time had been editor of the Richmond News Leader *for three years, had published two books* (A Calendar of Confederate Papers *and* Lee's Dispatches to Jefferson Davis, 1862-1865), *and had begun work on his biography of Lee.*

In this address, Freeman sees the key to Lincoln's greatness as his self-mastery of mind and spirit. Freeman states that he will discuss three expressions of this self-mastery, but only two of these are included in the unfinished text: first, Lincoln's extraordinary grasp of both political and military issues; and second, Lincoln's fixity of purpose.

The third expression of self-mastery is, of course, a matter of speculation, but it may well have been Lincoln's absence of malice in dealing with the South; for one of the most remarkable things about Lincoln was his determination to remain dispassionate during a time of great passion. Listen to him in 1854, addressing a Northern audience on the subject of slavery in the South:

> *. . . I have no prejudice against the Southern people. They are just what we would be in their situation. If slavery did not now exist amongst them, they would not introduce it. If it did now exist amongst us, we should not instantly give it up. . . . I surely will not blame them for not doing what I should not know how to do myself. If all earthly power were given me, I should not know what to do, as to the existing institution.*[1]

And again in 1862, writing to a Louisiana Unionist in the midst of civil war:

> *I shall do nothing in malice. What I deal with is too vast for malicious dealing.*[2]

And in 1865, at the end of the war, on the question of whether the seceded states were in or out of the Union:

... that question is bad, as the basis of a controversy, and good for nothing at all—a merely pernicious abstraction.[3]

In a letter written in 1926, Freeman recalled this address as follows: "He [Lincoln] has been much maligned and misunderstood. I recall with great pleasure that when we had some twenty thousand young Virginians and Pennsylvanians at Camp Lee, I was invited to make the address on Lincoln's birthday, and I was glad, as a Southern man, that I could pay him warm and honest tribute."[4]

Happy auguries attend this hour. No such audience as this has ever assembled in America on the twelfth of February. We are met in a building whose foundations rest in the ashes of old camp fires. We have as our senior officer the distinguished son of a Federal officer of the sixties. We number in this throng many of similar stock and some whose fathers read, across the seas, the troubled story of a divided nation. But we have as honored guests the General Assembly of the Commonwealth of Virginia, and most of us are the sons of men who fought against the host of which the mightiest leader was Abraham Lincoln.

We owe these auguries of brother in part, of course, to time and in part to circumstance. When the Eightieth Division was formed of Pennsylvanians, West Virginians, and Virginians, it was certain that the commingling of these men would give America the strength of unity after the healing of wounds. Understanding and appreciation were bound to come, and they have been both fostered and evinced by the celebration within these walls of the birthdays of the two greatest Americans of the nineteenth century, Lee and Lincoln. Had we of the South known more of Lincoln, and had our brothers of the North known more of Lee, we would not have had to wait for war to give us this understanding, this appreciation. And with this, I have done for this hour with North and with South, for we are met not as Southerners to honor a former foe, nor as Northerners to hear that tribute paid. To do homage to the spirit of America, we are met as Americans!

* * * * *

A nation's rivers are its first highways. Down them pass its first adventurers. From them radiate its first explorers. About them develop its traditions and its mysteries. There was mystery in the Nile, mystery in the Tigris, mystery in the Maeander, mystery in the Tiber. Why were they the first settlements of great states, and why had the sons of those streams a distinctive spirit? Why did they cradle each a civilization, and why was each different? These questions, asked of the ancient, we may apply to our rivers of mystery, our James, our Potomac, our Hudson, our Ohio, and our Mississippi. From the James grew Virginia; from the Potomac came the wonderful group of Westmoreland[5] statesmen; from the Hudson came that daring spirit of trade; from the Mississippi came daring voyagers and men with mind of a stamp; from the Ohio came Abraham Lincoln.

Why, we may not pause to answer. We may suffice by saying that even as Washington, Monroe, the Masons, and the Lees were in a sense the creatures of their environment, the Potomac, so Lincoln incarnated the spirit of the western rivers, the affluents of the Ohio. Until after he was twenty-one, all that he had seen of life had been on the banks of the Ohio, the Wabash, the Illinois, and the Sangamon. To the end of his days he retained the spirit of the rivers—boisterous sometimes, cutting new channels, freighted with the quaint store of the woods, yet moving, ever moving, with a force men might not reckon to a goal they could not see.

I dwell upon this because the rivers, rather than the log cabin and the rail fence, typify the Lincoln of history. Fact and gossip alike of his humble origin and his youthful hardships are of interest only as they show the depth of his democracy and the height of his achievement. Had Lincoln died in a cabin, men would not have thought it remarkable that he had been born in one. Had he not mauled Stephen A. Douglas,[6] they would not have reminded the world that he had mauled rails. The manger grows in significance only as we approach the open tomb.

There is no mystery of Lincoln's birth, and there is no mystery of Lincoln's rearing. He was of the line of the restless, unsuccessful pioneer, driven steadily westward before advancing civilization; but in him atavism showed itself, and he returned the way his fathers had gone. And there is the mystery—that he came back so surely and so perfectly equipped.

Take the cold facts. In all his life, he enjoyed scarcely a single full year's schooling. At seventeen, we know of scarcely a dozen books he had read. At twenty-one, he was without a dollar and had to maul four hundred rails for each yard of cloth wherewith to emulate Adam (according to the version of the Breeches Bible).[7] At twenty-five, he had been riverman, storekeeper, surveyor, and aspirant for office, and still was barely earning a living. At thirty-five, he had a brief record as a state legislator, a small law practice, a reputation for humor, and a modest home as his chief tangible assets. At forty-five, he was an ex-congressman with one term as his crown, had a reasonably profitable law practice and a wide circle of friends. But even then, when he reentered public life and boldly met Judge Douglas on the great issue of the hour, many of his friends trembled to think of the fall the Tall Sucker was destined to receive at the hands of the Little Giant. That was in 1854.[8] Striking the mean between the estimates of those who wish to make him appear utterly inconspicuous and those who wish to have him full-grown ere he really developed, we may safely say that Lincoln, when forty-five, was of the goodly company who are known and unknown. Illinois knew him fairly well; Indiana probably knew his name; in the East he had few acquaintances and practically no personal friends. Yet in six years he had been elected president in one of the noisiest and most bitterly contested campaigns of American history.

The mystery, I repeat, is how he achieved it. And yet, like the mysteries of the rivers' source and course, it is reasonably plain if we follow it back, or move with it, turn by turn. The wellspring of Abraham Lincoln's greatness was his self-mastery. I would not have you think that this came with a single struggle or that it was complete until nearly the end of his career. I would have you keep rather the figure of the river—to find the thin beginning of that self-mastery in the woods, to follow it as it grew through the years, to see where the mastery of mind was mingled with the mastery of spirit until the two swept, full-powered, through the muddy banks of the slavery agitation, to be lost at length in the sea of lasting fame.

Lincoln's struggle for self-mastery is first to be seen in his childish efforts to conquer his own mind. History shows us few more pathetic figures than that of the lank, unformed boy, sitting with the wooden shovel in his hand before the fire of his father's cabin, struggling to master the "sum" he had been given at school or had devised for himself. Nothing made him more wrathful than to be told something he could not understand. Pacing restlessly through the woods, sometimes tearing his hair, he would never rest content until he had placed in language his humble family could understand the problem he sought to solve. In his passion for "making things plain," as he put it, all but the blind can see that mental mastery that made a slogan for the Illinois farmer of those issues in the Douglas debates[9] which the historian of today finds difficulty in stating intelligently for educated readers.

In this self-mastery of his mind, no proper place has been given Lincoln's tremendous powers of absorption. Every book he ever read he combed clean of useful ideas. Every fertile thought he incubated. Thus it was that the language of the Northwest Ordinance,[10] which he found in a well-thumbed copy of the statutes of Indiana, became a veritable part of him. Thus, too, he read and studied Aesop as a child until he was himself a nineteenth century reincarnation of the beloved old Greek of myth. Thus, again, when he read an address that contained a sentence that stirred him, he tucked away the words in some corner of his mind and used them, slightly modified, years after, in the magnificent peroration that concludes the Gettysburg Address.[11] Thus, above all, he remembered from Holy Writ those phrases he used to clinch his arguments in his most masterful addresses.

Whoever knows himself, knows man. When Lincoln had mastered himself, he was able to move men. Quite naturally, this aspect of self-mastery came after the days of his earliest and hardest study. The stove in his store at New Salem was as important a factor in his education as the open fire by which he ciphered when a lad in Indiana; and those rough debates and arguments along the Sangamon gave him a command of himself in dealing with others that accounts in no small measure for his rise in politics, his capacity to win and hold friends, and for his ability to keep amicably in the same cabinet such volatile compounds as Chase, Seward, and Stanton.[12] He knew and shared the mind of the average man as had no statesman before him, except Jackson, and none since him, except, perhaps, Roosevelt.

Developing slowly, laboring patiently and always under handicaps that must never be underestimated, Lincoln came to his forty-fifth birthday with his mind mastered and his power over other men developed, if not fully realized. That year marked his great decision. Kansas was being settled; whether she should or should not recognize slavery was being argued wherever two men met. To the North, the freedom of Kansas seemed essential to the maintenance of the Missouri Compromise; to the South, it represented a condition not covered by the Compromise and should be opened to slaveholding settlers.[13] Lincoln's views prior to that time had been those of the average Northern Whig.[14] He believed slavery an evil recognized by the Constitution and restricted by the Compromise of 1820. He did not believe it could be extinguished in the states where it existed, except with the consent of those states; and he did not believe it should be extended. The Fugitive Slave Law,[15] in his opinion, should be enforced, and so definitely was he of this opinion that he had appeared on one occasion—unsuccessfully as it happened—as counsel for the owner of a slave who had fled into Illinois. Yet he was on record in the legislature of his state as declaring slavery unjust, and he had supported the Wilmot Proviso.[16]

How, then, are we to explain the Lincoln of the next six troubled years? How are we to reconcile our ideas of this quiet conservative with the familiar picture of the enthused radical leading the hosts of abolition in the conquest of the South? What made Lincoln the Whig, Lincoln the abolitionist? I cannot answer, but this I know: Lincoln was led into the fight against slavery not for the sake of the slaves but for the sake of the Union. I repeat: Lincoln became an abolitionist because he believed that the abolition of slavery was essential to the Union, and not because he was obsessed by any great desire to free from bondage Africans of whose estate he knew little. This does not mean that Lincoln was without sympathy for the slaves. He had that sympathy, profound and growing through the years, and it played no small part in his change from Whig to abolitionist. Yet this was small compared with the desire of the man to do that which he believed essential to the safety of the Union.

There was about Lincoln from the very hour he spoke at Bloomington[17] something that won the confidence of men, something that satisfied them that slavery could not be settled in the halls of Congress, something that made the preservation of the Union as profoundly moral a question as the abolition of slavery itself was esteemed by many. In all American history there is no story more astounding than that of Lincoln's rise to fame, immortal fame, in six brief years.

Take for example his showing in the debates with Judge Douglas. This brilliant Illinois Democrat was recognized throughout the country as one of the ablest men of his day. He was as diplomatic as he was adroit, and he was as experienced as he was clever in rejoinder. Lincoln was regarded no match for such a man as this. As earnestly as they might, Lincoln's friends sought to dissuade him from joint debates with Judge Douglas. But Lincoln was obdurate. Douglas had voted for the Kansas-Nebraska bill; Douglas proclaimed the doctrine of popular sovereignty, which Lincoln regarded, in the circumstances, as inapplicable. The hour had come to strike; Lincoln would not hold back. He left little to chance in that series of debates. He prepared himself as adequately as he could before he appeared for the first time on the platform with Judge Douglas; and he planned out in detail the speeches he would deliver, the questions he would ask, and the attitude he would assume before the voters. There can be no mistaking his purpose, and there can, in my opinion, be no doubting his absolute sincerity. For when his friends criticized as too sectional and as too partisan his speech on "the house divided,"[18] Lincoln said this in justification: "If I had to draw a pen across my record and erase my whole life from sight, and I had one poor gift or choice left as to what I should save from the wreck, I should choose that speech, and leave it to the world unerased."

Douglas was elected senator, but he was defeated for the presidential nomination.[19] That was plain as soon as the vote was counted. It was likewise apparent that as Lincoln's speeches had been epochal and had been studied by the leading abolitionists in the North, he might be considered as presidential timber in 1860. But this had not been his object in undertaking the campaign, and to it, even now, he gave little thought. "What's the use of talking of me for the presidency?" he said. "We have such men as Seward, Chase, and the others, who are so much better known to the people and whose names are so intimately associated with the principles of the Republican party. Everybody knows them; nobody, scarcely, outside of Illinois, knows me. Besides, is it not, as a matter of justice, due to such men, who have carried this movement forward to its present status in spite of fearful opposition, personal abuse, and hard names?"

The salient facts of the presidential campaign are known to you; the rest are unimportant. Election day came, and over a divided democracy and a respectable Democratic opposition, Abraham Lincoln was elected. He had a clear majority of the electoral college, but he was, in one sense, a minority candidate, in that the combined vote of the opposing candidates exceeded his by almost one million. Fifteen states of the Union gave him no electoral votes, and in ten states he had not received a single popular vote.[20] This was ominous in the extreme. Yet curiously enough, Lincoln himself did not realize the extent of dissatisfaction at the outcome of the election. This was due in part to the fact that Lincoln did not know in any way the sentiment of a great part of the Union. He had never been south of Washington, except when, as a young man, he had made two trips down the Mississippi; and even of the East he knew little except what he had learned during his one term at Washington and during his visit to the New England states. Such ideas as he had formed at the time when he came to New York and delivered his address at Cooper Union[21] were not calculated to give him any insight into the mind of the opposition. As he knew little of the South, so was he little known.

A second factor—and a most serious one—was Lincoln's settled belief that as the policies of the Republican party had been definitely stated in the Chicago platform, it was neither necessary nor becoming for him to elaborate thereon. "I know," he said, "the justice of my intentions and the utter groundlessness of the pretended fears of the men who are filling the country with their clamor. If I go into the presidency, they will find me as I am on record, nothing less, nothing more. My declarations have been made to the world without reservation. They have been often repeated. And now self-respect demands of me and of the party that has elected me that when threatened, I should be silent." One can understand this readily, and yet, as one ponders these words, one is apt to wonder how different it might have been if at that time Lincoln had spoken and had shown himself to the South as he was.

Do you say he had already spoken? I answer that scarcely a dozen lines of what Lincoln had uttered since 1854 had found their way into the columns of the Southern newspapers. Misunderstood from the first—inevitably misunderstood—he was never given a hearing until it was too late for his voice to make itself heard above the roar of cannon.

When Lincoln came to Washington, the clouds had never been so dark and the danger so acute. And to the despairing, it seemed that during the whole history of the Union never had there come to the presidential chair a man less adequately equipped than was this stranger from Illinois. Little wonder it seemed so, for measured by the cold standard of service rendered and office held, Abraham Lincoln was the least qualified man who ever became president of the United States. He had served in the general assembly of his state and he had seen two years' duty in Washington, but in all his life he had never held a single executive office and had never had men in any number under his direction. Withal, he came as silently as though he had been a humble spectator of a great scene rather than as the central actor in a coming drama of blood and division.

But Lincoln was ready. The stream of his strength was flowing full-banked. It had passed the meadows of doubt. It was flooded with high purpose, and soon it was to be joined with that other stream to make his self-mastery complete—the conquest of his own spirit. Let me say here that I have never understood why some of Lincoln's biographers seem to think it necessary to conceal or else to apologize for the spiritual struggles through which the man passed. We may regret, of course, that he never was affiliated with a church, and we may still more profoundly regret that at one time he was so far in the forest of doubt that he sought to blaze his way back to hope and to faith with the cold steel of destructive criticism. We know that these experiences are common to many men. Instead of seeking to conceal them, we should rather rejoice that after so much of doubt there came so strong a faith, that after a night of anguish came the day of patience and of prayer. It is generally assumed that the strong spiritual influence in Lincoln's life began to assert itself after the death of his son William, who died in the White House. I do not doubt that there was more than this crisis. In fact, I can reconcile with any just estimate of Lincoln any view but that the spirituality of the man was being steadily aroused through the years and that it needed only some spur—even the roweling spur of the death of his son—to arouse him to be in fact before the world what he must long have been in his heart of hearts.

I shall not attempt this afternoon so much to sketch the crowded events of those anxious years. I shall not seek to trace the influence of Lincoln's broader spiritual life upon his administration. I shall rather, with your permission, limit myself to three expressions of the great power, mental, yes, and moral, of Abraham Lincoln, the commander in chief of those armies against which our fathers fought.

The first of these expressions was, to my mind, Lincoln's remarkable grasp of the essential issues both of politics and of military operations. It has been a commonplace of history to say that the Union armies won in spite of Lincoln and not because of him. It has been customary for some writers to select Lincoln as the grimmest example of that executive interference which is fatal to the prosecution of war. I know that for this there is a certain foundation in fact, yet by no means so complete a foundation as some of you may believe. It was, in truth, pathetic that Lincoln took from his crowded hours time to study books of strategy he could not hope to master. It was not less pathetic that when he summoned Grant to take command of the armies, he thought that his own plan of operations warranted his laying it before Grant. But if he erred in these things, it was because of his zeal; and if he hurried McClellan in his preparations, or gave orders that some commanders found it difficult to execute, it was because he wished to hasten the end of war, with its wastage and its slaughter. And against these errors, I would have you balance just three examples of Lincoln's rare insight into the essential issues.

The first was his appreciation of what the blockade could accomplish in ending the war. You will recall that after the Confederate victory at First Manassas, Lincoln drew up a plan for future operations. Parts of that plan were amateurish, some parts were impractical, and some were debatable. But remember, if you please, that at the head of the list he placed the absolute necessity of a strict blockade of the Southern ports. He had no Mahan[22] among his advisers, and he was ignorant of the part sea power had played in the Napoleonic wars; but he saw the far-flung coasts of the Confederacy, and he knew that if behind them a battling Confederacy could be confined, the war must end in victory for the North. Throughout the war, Lincoln remained unostentatiously but nonetheless assuredly the staunchest supporter that Secretary Welles and the navy had.[23]

Take again Lincoln's appreciation of the place Kentucky had in the war. Perhaps it was because that was the state of his birth which he wished to save if possible from the tramp of armies, but whatever the cause, Lincoln realized as did none of his commanders that Kentucky must be kept safe for the Union; and though his advisers bewailed his strange regard for the border states, and though they asked themselves how many times he would hazard the Union to save Kentucky, Lincoln nevertheless adhered to his purpose. I shall ask gentlemen who are better advised of such matters than am I to figure for themselves what the plans of campaign might have been had the Federals been on the northern rather than on the southern banks of the Ohio, and had they not been able to use the fertile fields of Kentucky as a base for their flanking operations against Virginia and for their drives against Tennessee, Alabama, and Georgia.

Once again. McClellan claimed that he lost the Seven Days fight when Lincoln kept at Washington McDowell's corps. In the anguish of his retreat, McClellan contended that if he had had only ten thousand more troops, he could have turned disaster into victory. Historians, though they may not have agreed, have nevertheless condemned the action of Lincoln. Lee certainly, with his marvelous mastery of the minds of men, played consistently upon Lincoln's fears for the safety of Washington. Yet when we remember what a large part Richmond played in the psychology of the war, can we doubt that Washington would have played at least an equal part, and can we question, after all, the fundamental accuracy of Lincoln's judgement that Washington had to be saved, let the cost be what it might? I am now about to make another explanation on this point—an explanation which may seem strange coming from the son of one of Lee's soldiers. Yet for its accuracy I can vouch. At the time when McClellan was clamoring most for reinforcements, and at the time Lincoln in the face of McClellan's opposition kept McDowell around Washington, Lee in reality was seriously contemplating that which Lincoln most dreaded. Instead of permitting McClellan to keep him in the trenches around Richmond, whence by siege tactics he might ultimately be driven, Lee was planning or at least was considering a withdrawal from Richmond and a concentration in the valley of Virginia that would have enabled Jackson to move northward and perhaps to capture Washington. I cannot speak with absolute assurance on this point, but I am satisfied that the retention of McDowell's corps around Washington did more to upset this bold plan than any other factor with which I am familiar. Thus, fifty years after the war, Lincoln's judgement is vindicated from the newly discovered dispatches of Lee.[24]

The second expression of this full self-mastery of Lincoln you will find in that patient fixity of purpose that characterized every movement in the deep stream of his stalwart soul. Victories had not been easily won with him, whether as a lad in Indiana, a lawyer in Springfield, or a pleader before the people. That which he gained, he won. And well it was that he had learned not to weary of the battle! For when he came to Washington, he found himself opposed not merely by gallant armies, most brilliantly led, but badgered and opposed, misunderstood and maligned by men of his own nation and often of his own party. Factional feeling ran higher in the North, during the

War between the States, than it did in the South. Republicans and Democrats there were—but Republicans of many hues and Democrats of a dozen dyes. Among those whom Lincoln might have expected to give him unfailing support were many who regarded him as too conservative, some who regarded him as too radical, and some who held him right but weak. His it was to reconcile these as far as might be, and to make them work together—not for Lincoln but for the task to which he had set himself, that which he styled the preservation of the Union.

I shall not attempt to show how this patient fixity of purpose showed itself in the negotiations over Sumter, for upon those North and South can never be expected to agree. Nor shall I attempt to trace the tangled story of his relations with Cameron,[25] with Stanton, with Chase, and with Seward—bitter though that story seems in retrospect. I think I shall rather rest the case upon Lincoln's attitude toward the Emancipation Proclamation.[26] Freeing the slaves was deemed by the North the great reserve weapon it could employ when all else failed. Some viewed it as justifiable; others regarded it much as the better class of Germans viewed unrestricted submarine warfare when it was first proposed—a desperate remedy for a desperate evil. Few saw that the weapon was worthless where the negroes were faithful. Lincoln had not advocated emancipation. He hesitated long after others were convinced in the North. He countermanded Hunter's emancipation ordinance as quickly as he had cancelled the proclamation of Fremont.[27] His one object—how I wish I could drive this home to North not less than to South—was to do what was necessary, and only what was necessary, to save the Union. Upon this, his own cold words are the best expression of his purpose: "If I could save the Union without freeing any slave, I would do it; if I could save it by freeing all the slaves, I would do it; and if I could save it by freeing some and leaving others alone, I would also do that. What I do about slavery and the colored race, I do because I believe it helps to save the Union; and what I forbear, I forbear because I do not believe it would help to save the Union." Why need posterity search any further when every act of the man is in honest accord with this purpose? Why need we question, when here is the answer?

I may be pardoned if, in this connection, I say another word of his patience in dealing with his generals.[28]

[The typed text ends at this point and is followed by two handwritten words: *Whiskey* then *Pre-Election.*]

Notes

This address is filed in Freeman's papers at the Library of Congress (Container 126; Speech, Article, and Book File). The original text is an unfinished double-spaced rough with handwritten corrections. The draft title for this address was "The Leadership of Lincoln in the Light of the Present War"; the title that appears here is mine.

1. Speech at Peoria, Illinois, 16 October 1854, *The Collected Works of Abraham Lincoln*, ed. Roy P. Basler, 9 vols. (New Brunswick, N.J.: Rutgers University Press, 1953-55), 2:255.

2. Lincoln to Cuthbert Bullitt, 28 July 1862, *The Collected Works of Lincoln*, 5:346.

3. Last Public Address, 11 April 1865, *The Collected Works of Lincoln*, 8:403.

4. Freeman to Judge Edgar J. Rich, 2 December 1926, Freeman Papers, Library of Congress (Container 8; General Correspondence File).

5. Westmoreland, a county in northeast Virginia situated between the Potomac and Rappahannock rivers, was the birthplace of George Washington, Richard Henry Lee, and James Monroe.

6. Stephen A. Douglas was the powerful Democratic senator from Illinois who in the 1850s became the leading proponent of the doctrine of popular sovereignty, under which the question of slavery in the territories was to be decided not by Congress but by the territories themselves. It was the arguments of Lincoln, more than any other man, that exposed the moral and political problems presented by this doctrine. Before his election to Congress, Douglas was a judge on the Illinois Supreme Court; hence he was commonly referred to as Judge Douglas.

7. The Breeches Bible was the popular name for the Geneva Bible of 1560, which described Adam and Eve as having made "breeches" to cover themselves.

8. In 1854 Congress passed the Kansas-Nebraska Act, which applied the doctrine of popular sovereignty to the territories of Kansas and Nebraska—territories where slavery had formerly been prohibited by the Missouri Compromise of 1820. This act aroused the opponents of slavery, including Lincoln, as never before, and brought the issue of slavery to the forefront of American politics. In response to the Kansas-Nebraska Act, its opponents joined forces to form the Republican party, the Whig party split over slavery and disintegrated, and the Democratic party split over slavery in the election of 1860. Lincoln, who joined the Republican party in 1856, emerged as the leading spokesman for those opposed to the extension of slavery into the territories. The physical contrast between Lincoln and Douglas was striking: Douglas, short and stout but of great ability, had long been known as the Little Giant; Lincoln, tall, lean, and slow and rather awkward in manner, came to be known in Illinois as the Tall Sucker. For a superb account of this period, see David M. Potter's *The Impending Crisis 1848-1861* (New York: Harper & Row, 1976).

9. In 1858 Lincoln was the Republican nominee for the Senate seat held by Douglas. During the campaign the two men engaged in a series of seven formal debates that provided the American people with a magnificent discussion of the slavery issue. Although Lincoln lost the election, these debates brought him to national prominence. For a detailed account of these debates, see Saul Sigelschiffer's *The American Conscience: The Drama of the Lincoln-Douglas Debates* (New York: Horizon Press, 1973).

10. Passed by Congress in 1787, the Northwest Ordinance established procedures for the organization of the old Northwest Territory (that area west of Pennsylvania, north of the Ohio River, and east of the Mississippi River). Among other things, the Northwest Ordinance prohibited slavery from this territory.

11. In his biography of Lincoln, William Herndon (Lincoln's law partner) recalls that Lincoln read, re-read, and underlined the following sentence from a sermon delivered by Theodore Parker in Boston in 1858: "Democracy is direct government, over all the people, by all the people, for all the people." Lincoln's Gettysburg Address concludes with these words: ". . . and that government of the people, by the people, for the people, shall not perish from the earth."

12. Salmon P. Chase was Lincoln's secretary of the treasury until 1864; William H. Seward was Lincoln's secretary of state; and Edwin M. Stanton became Lincoln's secretary of war in 1862. Chase and Seward were leaders of the Republican party, and Stanton was a Democrat.

13. The Missouri Compromise of 1820 admitted Missouri to the Union as a slave state but barred slavery from the rest of that area of the Louisiana Purchase north of latitude 36-30 (this included both the Kansas and Nebraska territories). As noted earlier, the Kansas-Nebraska Act of 1854 opened these territories to slavery under the principle of popular sovereignty.

14. The Whig party was organized in 1834 in opposition to the policies of President Andrew Jackson. Under the leadership of men such as Henry Clay and Daniel Webster, the Whig party generally appealed to those in the South who advocated "states' rights," those in the West (like Lincoln) who favored internal improvements, and those in the East who supported the establishment of a national bank. In the early 1850s the Whig party split over the slavery issue and then disintegrated, its members for the most part gravitating to the Democratic party or to the new Republican party.

15. The first Fugitive Slave Law was adopted by Congress in 1793 pursuant to the following passage in Article IV of the Constitution: "No person held to service or labour in one State under the laws thereof, escaping into another, shall, in consequence of any law or regulation therein, be discharged from such service or labour, but shall be delivered up on claim of the party to whom such service or labour shall be due." The original law left its enforcement chiefly to the states. In 1850, in response to Southern demands, a new Fugitive Slave Law was adopted that provided for enforcement by federal authorities.

16. Introduced by Congressman David Wilmot of Pennsylvania in 1846, the Wilmot Proviso sought to prohibit slavery in the territory acquired from Mexico as a result of the Mexican War. This measure passed the House of Representatives in 1846 and 1847 but was defeated in the Senate. In the end, the issue of slavery in the Mexican territory was resolved by the Compromise of 1850, under which California was admitted to the Union as a free state and the remainder of the territory organized according to the new principle of popular sovereignty.

17. In September 1854 Douglas returned home to Illinois to defend the Kansas-Nebraska Act. On 25 September Lincoln followed him to Bloomington, where the next day Lincoln spoke in opposition to the act. This was the first of many face-to-face confrontations between Lincoln and Douglas over the issue of slavery in the territories.

18. This was the speech with which Lincoln accepted the Republican nomination for the Senate seat held by Douglas. Delivered in Springfield, Illinois on 16 June 1858, the speech begins as follows:

> If we could first know *where* we are, and *whither* we are tending, we could then better judge *what* to do, and *how* to do it.
>
> We are now far into the *fifth* year, since a policy was initiated, with the *avowed* object, and *confident* promise, of putting an end to slavery agitation.
>
> Under the operation of that policy, that agitation has not only, *not ceased*, but has *constantly augmented*.

In my opinion, it *will* not cease, until a *crisis* shall have been reached, and passed.

"A house divided against itself cannot stand."

I believe this government cannot endure, permanently half *slave* and half *free*.

I do not expect the Union to be *dissolved*—I do not expect the house to *fall*—but I *do* expect it will cease to be divided.

Either the *opponents* of slavery, will arrest the further spread of it, and place it where the public mind shall rest in the belief that it is in course of ultimate extinction; or its *advocates* will push it forward, till it shall become alike lawful in *all* the states, *old* as well as *new*—*North* as well as *South*.

19. During his debates with Lincoln, Douglas proclaimed his moral and political indifference to slavery, and asserted that under the doctrine of popular sovereignty a territory could exclude slavery by choosing not to adopt the police regulations necessary for its protection. This position was not acceptable to the Democrats of the South, who sought the extension of slavery into all the territories. As a result, the Democratic party split into two factions in the election of 1860: the Northern faction nominated Douglas for president, and the Southern faction nominated John C. Breckenridge.

20. In the election of 1860, Lincoln was opposed by Douglas, Breckenridge, and John Bell of the new Constitutional Union party (which adopted no platform, but simply declared itself in favor of the Constitution and the Union). Lincoln received 1,838,347 votes in the free states and only 26,388 in the slave states, for a total of 1,864,735; his opponents received 1,572,637 in the free states and 1,248,520 in the slave states, for a total of 2,821,157. However, Lincoln won all of the free states except New Jersey, giving him a total of 180 electoral votes (27 more than the number required for election). The polarization of the country along sectional lines over the issue of slavery can be seen clearly in the fact that Lincoln was not even on the ballot in the following ten Southern states: North Carolina, South Carolina, Georgia, Florida, Tennessee, Alabama, Mississippi, Arkansas, Louisiana, and Texas. Furthermore, Lincoln received no electoral votes in the following five states: Virginia, Kentucky, Missouri, Maryland, and Delaware.

21. This speech, delivered before the Young Men's Central Republican Union on 27 February 1860, was Lincoln's first major address in the East. In the first part of the speech, Lincoln demonstrated that 23 of the 39 signers of the Constitution had at one time or another voted on the issue of slavery in the territories, and that of these 23, 21 had voted to prohibit slavery in the territories. He concluded this analysis with these words:

> As those fathers marked it [slavery], so let it be again marked, as an evil not to be extended, but to be tolerated and protected only because of and so far as its actual presence among us makes that toleration and protection a necessity. Let all the guarantees those fathers gave it, be, not grudgingly, but fully and fairly maintained. For this Republicans contend, and with this, so far as I know or believe, they will be content.

Lincoln then directed his remarks to the Southern people, appealing for an understanding of this Republican position on slavery but responding to threats of secession as follows:

> But you will not abide the election of a Republican President! In that supposed event, you say, you will destroy the Union; and then, you say, the great crime of having destroyed it will be upon us! That is cool. A highwayman holds a pistol to my ear, and mutters through his teeth, "Stand and deliver, or I shall kill you, and then you will be a murderer."

And finally, Lincoln had this to say to his fellow Republicans:

> The question recurs, what will satisfy them [the South]? Simply this: We must not only let them alone, but we must, somehow, convince them that we do let them alone . . . . what will convince them? This, and this only: cease to call slavery *wrong*, and join them in calling it *right* . . . . but, thinking it wrong, as we do, can we yield to them? Can we cast our votes with their view, and against our own? In view of our moral, social, and political responsibilities, can we do this? . . . . can we, while our votes will prevent it, allow it [slavery] to spread into the National Territories, and to overrun us here in these Free States? If our sense of duty forbids this, then let us stand by our duty fearlessly and effectively . . . . LET US HAVE FAITH THAT RIGHT MAKES MIGHT, AND IN THAT FAITH, LET US TO THE END, DARE TO DO OUR DUTY AS WE UNDERSTAND IT.

This address, one of Lincoln's best, was very well received, and played no small part in his securing of the Republican presidential nomination three months later.

22. Alfred Thayer Mahan, an American naval officer, was the author of *The Influence of Sea Power upon History 1660-1783* (1890). This and his subsequent studies of the 1792-1805 period are still regarded as a classic exposition of the importance of sea power "upon the course of history and the prosperity of nations."

23. Gideon Welles was Lincoln's secretary of the navy. In a letter to James C. Conkling of 26 August 1863, Lincoln noted the achievements of the navy as follows: "The signs look better. The Father of Waters again goes unvexed to the sea. . . . And while those who have cleared the great river may well be proud, even that is not all. It is hard to say that anything has been more bravely, and well done, than at Antietam, Murfreesboro, Gettysburg, and on many fields of lesser note. Nor must Uncle Sam's Web-feet be forgotten. At all the watery margins they have been present. Not only on the deep sea, the broad bay, and the rapid river, but also up the narrow muddy bayou, and wherever the ground was a little damp, they have been, and made their tracks."

24. See Dispatch No. 2 (dated 5 June 1862) in Freeman's *Lee's Dispatches to Jefferson Davis, 1862-1865* (New York: G. P. Putnam's Sons, 1915; reprinted by Putnam's in 1957 with additional dispatches and foreword by Grady McWhiney).

25. Simon Cameron, Lincoln's first secretary of war, resigned in January 1862.

26. Lincoln discussed the draft of the Emancipation Proclamation with his cabinet in July 1862, just after McClellan's failure to capture Richmond. At Secretary Seward's recommendation, Lincoln waited for a Union victory to issue the proclamation so that it would not be perceived as a last desperate measure. Accordingly, Lincoln announced the proclamation on 22 September 1862, four days after Lee's retreat to Virginia following the battle of Antietam. The key section of the Emancipation Proclamation read as follows: "That on the first day of January, in the year of our Lord, one thousand eight hundred and sixty-three, all persons held as slaves within any state, or designated part of a state, the people of which shall then be in rebellion against the United States shall be then, thenceforward, and forever free. . . ."

27. On 30 August 1861 Major General John Charles Fremont, commanding the Union's Western Department, issued a proclamation putting Missouri under martial law and ordering that the slaves of rebels there be seized and "declared freemen." Lincoln countermanded this order on 2 September. On 9 May 1862 Major General David Hunter, commanding the Union's Department of the South, issued a proclamation freeing all the slaves in the states of Georgia, Florida, and South Carolina. Lincoln countermanded this order on 19 May.

28. With regard to this subject, Lincoln's famous letter to General Joseph Hooker deserves to be quoted here in full:

Executive Mansion
Washington, January 26, 1863

General.

I have placed you at the head of the Army of the Potomac. Of course I have done this upon what appear to me to be sufficient reasons. And yet I think it best for you to know that there are some things in regard to which, I am not quite satisfied with you. I believe you to be a brave and a skilful soldier, which, of course, I like. I also believe you do not mix politics with your profession, in which you are right. You have confidence in yourself, which is a valuable, if not an indispensable quality. You are ambitious, which, within reasonable bounds, does good rather than harm. But I think that during Gen. Burnside's command of the Army, you have taken counsel of your ambition, and thwarted him as much as you could, in which you did a great wrong to the country, and to a most meritorious and honorable brother officer. I have heard, in such a way as to believe it, of your recently saying that both the Army and the Government needed a Dictator. Of course it was not *for* this, but in spite of it, that I have given you the command. Only those generals who gain successes, can set up dictators. What I now ask of you is military success, and I will risk the dictatorship. The government will support you to the utmost of its ability, which is neither more nor less than it has done and will do for all commanders. I much fear that the spirit which you have aided to infuse into the Army, of criticising their Commander, and withholding confidence from him, will now turn upon you. I shall assist you as far as I can, to put it down. Neither you, nor Napoleon, if he were alive again, could get any good out of an army, while such a spirit prevails in it.

And now, beware of rashness. Beware of rashness, but with energy, and sleepless vigilance, go forward, and give us victories.

Yours very truly A. Lincoln

(This letter is displayed in a glass case in the reading room of the Manuscript Division, Library of Congress, Washington, D.C.)

5

Robert E. Lee: Maker of Morale

Lee Birthday Address
January 19, 1926

Freeman wrote this address for his father, Walker B. Freeman, who was the commander in chief of the United Confederate Veterans organization in 1925-26. It was delivered to the annual "camp fire" of the Confederate Veteran Camp of New York. The elder Freeman, who was seventeen years old at the beginning of the Civil War, served in the ranks of the Army of Northern Virginia throughout the entire war and was present at the surrender of the army at Appomattox on April 9, 1865.

In this address, Freeman takes as his theme the morale of the Army of Northern Virginia in its relation to Lee. He attributes the high morale of that army to three factors: the confidence of victory; Lee's faith in the army; and the army's faith in Lee. Ten years later, in his lectures at the Army War College, Freeman was to explore this theme in much greater detail.

It was in 1926, the year of this address, that Freeman put himself on a strict weekly schedule for the research and writing of his biography of Lee. This approach, which he continued to use for his later books, resulted in the completion of the Lee biography in 1934, nineteen years after he had begun it.

You are very gracious in your welcome. I thank you for your cordial greetings, and I count myself fortunate to be able to celebrate this nineteenth of January, this "Saint's Day" of the South, among those who have not forgotten the land of their fathers' love.

In one of the volumes of reminiscence by an officer of high rank in the war with Germany, I recently read a critical estimate of his general in chief, a man well known in fame to all of you. His superior, this soldier wrote, was admirable but not magnetic, a man to inspire respect but not a man to arouse enthusiasm.

It seems to me that these phrases very fairly represent the opinion most of the ex-servicemen have of the generals under whom they fought

ROBERT E. LEE

This photograph was taken in Richmond in early 1864. In keeping with his simplicity of manner, Lee wore the three stars of a Confederate colonel without the encircling wreath of a general officer.

in France. I have heard these young soldiers praise their captains often and their colonels frequently, but never their generals, and I have heard other veterans of earlier wars note the same fact. How deeply significant this may be, I cannot say. Much of the lack of enthusiasm of these fine fighting men for their chiefs doubtless is due to the size of the armies engaged in the World War. A single corps of the American Expeditionary Force was larger than the Army of Northern Virginia ever was, except for a short time in 1863. There was one brigadier general of infantry to every ten thousand infantry in France, whereas in "our" war, comrades, the brigade was four thousand men at full strength and, after the bloody battles of 1864, seldom actually numbered more than one thousand effectives. I have seen Confederate brigades, in the last dreadful days of our struggle, with fewer enlisted men than were counted in a full company of the AEF. Very naturally, officers in those days were closer to their men and better known to them than in 1917-18.

Even so, I cannot but contrast the difference between the ex-serviceman of the World War and the Confederate soldier in his opinion of the general whose orders he obeyed. It is a constant amazement to me to perceive how high a morale the American Expeditionary Force displayed, when I reflect that the morale of that army was based on enthusiasm for a cause, whereas in the Confederate army there was enthusiasm for a cause plus enthusiasm for the men who were the chief exemplars of it. With these boys, our sons and grandsons, the cause was America; with us "old boys" it was the South—and Lee.

The contrast suggests a theme I do not think has ever been treated in any of the books on the war, except as it may have been hinted by Swinton and by Henderson.[1] That theme is the morale of the Army of Northern Virginia in its relation to him whose birthday we are here to observe.

When Swinton came to describe Appomattox as it appeared to a man who greatly admired the Army of the Potomac, he had praise for those bluecoats who followed us from Petersburg through the mud and rain of that torrential spring. You and I join in that praise, for the Army of the Potomac was a great army. It had patience. It acquired the very quality of high morale about which I am speaking. It was, in fact, at that time a magnificent host. I often caution my sons, and I warn you, young gentlemen, you sons of Confederate veterans: Never speak lightly of the Army of the Potomac. After it became seasoned, it was the *second best* army in the world. Modesty forbids us Confederates from suggesting which was the best army then in existence.

Swinton, I say, had high praise and natural partiality for Meade's army, but when he told of the ninth of April, when we marched out into that field near Appomattox Courthouse,[2] even Swinton was moved. And in an unforgettable passage he apostrophized the "incomparable infantry"—incomparable he called it—of the Army of Northern Virginia.

I well remember a still higher tribute paid us that day. We were coming on that dreadful field under General Gordon, and we were passing through the open ranks of a superb brigade of infantry. We were ragged and we had no shoes. The banners our army had borne to the heights of Gettysburg were bloody and in shreds. There were less than eight thousand of us with arms in our hands, though they were bright and burnished still. Great divisions, the very names of which had once spread terror in the North, were reduced to small regiments, and regiments to squads. We were only a shadow of an army, a ghost of an army, and as we marched in tattered, hungry columns between those magnificent straight lines of well-fed men, faultlessly armed and perfectly equipped, most of us wished, as our great chief did, that we might have been numbered with the fallen in the last battle. But, as we marched forward with heads up—no Confederate soldier ever held his head any other way and no Southerner ever should—as we marched forward in the silence of that sodden field, suddenly I heard a sharp order sent down that blue line, and on the instant I saw that whole brigade present arms to us—to us, the survivors of the Army of Northern Virginia. It was a Maine brigade, comrades, and I confess to you that though more than sixty years have passed since that gray April noon, I never hear the name of that state but that I feel a certain swelling pride as I reflect that there was an army good enough to deserve that salute—and another army magnanimous enough to give it!

What made Swinton call us the "incomparable" infantry of the Army of Northern Virginia? What made Chamberlain's brigade present arms that day in that field by Appomattox Courthouse? It was, I think, primarily because of that army's accomplishments. And what made those accomplishments possible? The morale of the army, I say, and its leadership. The two were bound up together. I doubt if even General Lee could have won so many battles for three unforgettable years, and against such odds, if he had not had the material he did. I am sure the army would not have gained the plaudits it has ever since received if it had not had a Lee to lead it and to inspire its morale. The process, I say, cannot be divided. An army is seldom better than the general who has commanded it through an open campaign. A general is never greater than the troops he leads. It was so with Caesar and his legions. It was so with Richard the Lion-Hearted and his crusaders. It was so with Lee and the Army of Northern Virginia, and Grant and the Army of the Potomac. It was true of Pershing and the AEF, and it will be true, I suspect, of the army that fights the last Armageddon and ends forever the bloody strife of a race led away at last from selfishness.

Victory, of course, was responsible for much of the high morale of Lee's army and of the other Confederate forces, whose deeds were as valiant and oftentimes were performed in the face of greater difficulties than we encountered. All honor to our comrades in Tennessee and in the Gulf states, at Vicksburg[3] and on that stubborn resistance to Sherman's march![4]

Yet see how quickly that morale was attained, and how few were the victories necessary to develop it! The army that faced McClellan in front of Richmond in June 1862 consisted largely of recruits brought together under a system of elective command, which is about the worst system that can be devised. That army had not passed through the test that weeds out those general officers who are unsuited for the field. General Lee was not popular then. His campaign in West Virginia had not been successful, and he was regarded as a desk-soldier or as an engineer.[5] Within less than four weeks after he assumed command, he led that green army against a force that was far better equipped and outnumbered him in the ratio of five to three. He took the offensive, fought five battles within seven days, lost 23 percent of his army, and finally saw his adversary get away to the cover of gunboats at Harrison's Landing with fewer losses than he himself had sustained. Within two months thereafter, he had the morale of the army at such a pitch that he was able to divide his forces, to converge on the field of battle with Jackson desperately engaged when Longstreet arrived, and to win a victory there at Bull Run as brilliant as any he ever gained, except perhaps at Chancellorsville. He not only did this, but he was absolutely confident of his army. When it seemed that day at Second Manassas that Jackson's lines would certainly break before Longstreet went into action, Lee never showed by so much as the quivering of an eyelash that he doubted the arrival of Longstreet's troops. An officer who stood nearby him—the story has never been printed—was atremble with excitement during those tense moments, and when at last he heard the roar of Longstreet's guns and knew that the troops that had come through the gap were there to relieve the pressure on Jackson, he could scarcely control his enthusiasm. General Lee heard the guns open, of course, but he sat where he was without the slightest gesture or change of expression. Do you wonder we had confidence in a man who had that much confidence in us? And do you not agree that there was something besides victory to give the army such morale that it could win so difficult a victory as that before Lee had been in command three months?

What else was there in the relations of general and subordinates, and what was there in the heart of men and leader that made possible not only that campaign but also those that followed through the months, till hunger wrecked us and our horses there in the trenches of Petersburg in the winter of 1864-65? I am not sure any man can ever give the full answer to that question, for in seeking it we are carried into subtleties of spirit that defy the analyst. We were a peculiar lot, we Southerners of 1860. I think we were never characterized better than by an old comrade of mine, a cavalry captain and long a congressman,[6] who often said that no man could ever understand the exploits of the Army of Northern Virginia unless he realized that we were a voluntary association of gentlemen organized for the sole business of driving out the Yankees. Nothing else mattered greatly—of privation or of hardship, of long marches or of lonely vigil. We *were* volunteers and we tried to be gentlemen, in camp and in battle, and it *was* our business to drive out the Yankees. We were rather intent upon discharging that business.

"Marse Robert" knew that and knew that he could trust us to the limit of human endurance. He did not have to ask whether we *would* do a thing. You will not misunderstand when I say that he had only to inquire whether the thing *could* be done—whether it was humanly possible for the numbers he assigned to the task. If it *could* be done, he knew it *would* be done! Hence the extreme daring of his campaigns, as in that awful time in June 1864 when he ordered General Beauregard to take those of us who were on the south side of the Appomattox and to hold Petersburg, no matter at what cost. Our line was so thin that in the night, as the bullets kept raining into the stump behind which I crouched, there was not another soldier in sight. The issue was so close that when the artillery was rushed through Petersburg at the gallop, the dust from its dash had not settled on the streets before the anxious people heard the guns open on the enemy. But we held Petersburg. General Lee had told us to.

If he knew he could count on us, we knew we could rely on him, and in our faith in him you have, I think, the third component in the morale of the Army of Northern Virginia. We knew that whatever generalship could accomplish, he would do. We knew he never told us to make a charge unless it had to be made. We knew he never said "hold" unless failure to hold meant disaster to our homes. We were often hungry, but we knew he tried to find us food. We were nearly naked, but we knew he was doing his best to get clothing for us. We were weary oftentimes from the marches he set before us, but were satisfied that he did not call on us to make good his delinquencies. He came daily among us—always the ideal figure of a soldier—and though he never sought popularity by ostentation, when he spoke to us it was with as much of affection as of dignity. I see him now as he looked that awful morning of the seventh of April, 1865, on a hill above Farmville. He had seen all his plans go wrong and all his hopes destroyed. The day before, Ewell's corps had been captured at Sayler's Creek and Gordon's had barely escaped destruction. He must have foreseen what was just two days ahead, but there he sat, composed and reassuring, on his horse. You could see from his manner that his thought was of us, not of himself—of the army's distress and not of its commander's defeat. There was not a tremor in his tones as he told us to form across the hill and to collect the stragglers. Nor was there a word of reproach for those good men whose strength had failed them after five days of hard marching.

All that went into making the morale of the army—the confidence and the memory of victory, the general's faith in the army, the army's faith in Robert E. Lee—all three were exhibited more dramatically at Appomattox than anywhere else in the whole history of the army. As he rode back through Gordon's command, the men thronged about him, as you know, until the road was blocked and he had to speak to them.[7] And what was his message? All about them and nothing about himself! "I have done the best I could for you, men," he began—and I think he need scarcely have gone on and told us we could go home on parole. If he had done his best, that sufficed. His best was enough for us, even in the hour of the death of the Confederacy.

I think our answer to that statement of his was best given by one of the men about sundown, after General Lee had left the apple orchard and while he was on his way to headquarters.[8] The boys all crowded about him, as they had when he came from the McLean house[9] to the apple orchard. They started to cheer, and after a little they wept as they looked into his face and saw his anguish for them. And then, one man—a bearded private who doubtless had followed him through it all—cried out to him in words that ought always to be remembered. "General Lee," he said, "General Lee, I love you as much as ever." In that warm pledge, the Army of Northern Virginia, on the scene of its last engagement, did homage to the leadership of Robert E. Lee. He has been dead these fifty-five years, and we who were "his boys" are now old men. We represent an age that has ended, and we speak for a society that has been well-nigh submerged among alien millions who know not of our yesterdays. Men speak now of another struggle when they refer to "the war." Some of them are so mistaken as to say we should no longer talk of

"Old, unhappy, far-off things
And battles long forgot."

But whatever may have been taken and whatever may have been denied, thank God we have our memories—of the civilization that is no more, of the army whose rear guard we are, of the days when the name of that army made Southern hearts beat up. Nothing in life can take those memories from us, and I doubt if death does. And always in the center of the picture, as radiant as in life, our old chieftain sits astride his horse. Always he rides at the head of the mighty column that memory brings back from the grave, and we acclaim him still as we did in those distant days: General Lee, we love you as much as ever!

Notes

This address is filed in Freeman's papers at the Library of Congress. The original text, a double-spaced rough with handwritten corrections, is in the Speech, Article, and Book File (Container 127). The finished version, a brochure apparently printed for the occasion, is in the Special Correspondence and Biographical File (Container 123). Freeman did not assign a title to this address; the title that appears here is mine.

1. William Swinton was the author of *Campaigns of the Army of the Potomac* (New York: C. B. Richardson, 1866; revised and reissued by Charles Scribner's Sons, 1882). G. F. R. Henderson was the author of several books on the Civil War, the best known of which was *Stonewall Jackson and the American Civil War*, 2 vols. (London, New York, etc.: Longmans, Green & Co., 1898; new impression published 1904). In the introduction to *Lee's Dispatches*, Freeman noted this book as follows: "Where the careers of Lee and Jackson run together, this book is and will doubtless remain the one best account of their campaigns, and this apart from the fact that as a literary biography it is a masterpiece."

2. "The ninth of April" was the day Lee signed the surrender terms. The surrender ceremony, during which the Confederate army "marched out into that field near Appomattox Courthouse," took place on 12 April. Neither Lee nor Grant was present at the ceremony. Accepting the surrender for the Union was Brigadier General Joshua L. Chamberlain; at the head of the Confederate column rode Major General John B. Gordon. Chamberlain was commissioned in the Twentieth Maine Infantry in the summer of 1862 and took command of that regiment in June 1863, one week before the battle of Gettysburg, where he won the Congressional Medal of Honor for his defense of Little Round Top. In the summer of 1864 Grant promoted Chamberlain to brigadier general as a result of his performance at the battle of Petersburg (this was the only field promotion Grant made for gallantry in action). For a marvelous portrait of Chamberlain, see Michael Shaara's *The Killer Angels* (New York: David McKay Co., Inc., 1974), a superb novel of the battle of Gettysburg as told through the eyes of some of the principal commanders there.

3. Vicksburg, Mississippi, a Confederate stronghold high on a bluff overlooking the Mississippi River, fell to Union forces under Grant on 4 July 1863. The fall of Vicksburg combined with the Confederate defeat at Gettysburg marked the beginning of the end of the Confederacy. The Mississippi River was now in Union hands, the Confederates had lost men that they could not replace, and the stage was set for the major events of 1864: the assignment of Grant to command all the Union armies, his movement against Richmond, and Sherman's movement against Atlanta.

4. William Tecumseh Sherman assumed command of the Union armies in the West in succession to Grant, who in March 1864 was called east to take command of all the Union armies. During the next few months Grant moved against Richmond and Sherman moved against Atlanta, which fell in September 1864. On 15 November Sherman's forces left Atlanta on their "March to the Sea," which ended with the capture of Savannah on 21 December. Sherman was a proponent of "total war," and this march was characterized by the widespread destruction of civilian property.

5. Lee's service reputation rested on the following foundation:

o He graduated second in the West Point class of 1829, having served as adjutant of the corps during his senior year. In his four years at West Point, he had not received a single demerit.

o He spent the next twenty-six years in the Corps of Engineers. During the Mexican War he served with great distinction on the staff of General Winfield Scott. He displayed great skill and bravery during the invasion of Veracruz and the subsequent advance of Scott's army to Mexico City, rising in rank from captain to brevet colonel. Scott later referred to Lee as "the very best soldier I ever saw in the field."

o From 1852 to 1855, Lee served as the superintendent of West Point (a position then required by law to be filled by an engineer officer).

o In March 1855 Lee transferred from the staff to the line when Secretary of War Jefferson Davis appointed him second in command of the newly established Second Cavalry regiment. These duties took him to the frontier (primarily Texas), where he was involved in many courts-martial and an occasional skirmish with Indians or bandits. In October 1857 Lee began an extended period of leave to return to his home in Arlington, Virginia and settle the complicated estate of his father-in-law. He was concluding this leave in October 1859 when he was assigned to command of the forces hastily assembled to capture John Brown and his men, who had seized the Federal arsenal at Harpers Ferry, Virginia.

o During the first year of the Civil War, Lee served briefly as the commander of Virginia's forces and then as military adviser to President Davis. In late July 1861, Davis sent Lee to western Virginia to coordinate Confederate operations against two Union armies. During the next three months, Lee reorganized the Confederate forces and managed to halt the Union advance, but the only offensive operation of the campaign failed when Lee's forces became bogged down on rain-slickened mountain slopes. From November 1861 through February 1862, Lee supervised the fortification of the Georgia and South Carolina coasts. He returned to Richmond in early March 1862.

As a result of this background, Lee was regarded as a staff officer rather than a field commander; and his appointment to command the Army of Northern Virginia was greeted with skepticism in many quarters.

6. Identified in later lectures as Captain John Lamb. Lamb commanded a Virginia cavalry company during the war and served in the House of Representatives from 1897 to 1913.

7. This scene occurred just after Lee's surrender to Grant (their meeting having concluded at about 4 o'clock in the afternoon).

8. After speaking to Gordon's men, Lee retired to a nearby apple orchard, where he clearly wanted to be left alone. He departed the orchard just before sunset to ride back to his headquarters, about a mile away.

9. Grant and Lee negotiated the surrender of Lee's army at the home of Wilmer McLean in the village of Appomattox Court House. McLean's former home in Manassas had been occupied by the Confederate army and seriously damaged by Union

artillery fire during the first battle there. In the spring of 1862 McLean had moved to Appomattox to escape the war, but to no avail. The war in Virginia ended as it had begun: in McLean's parlor.

Part Three
The Army War College

THE OLD ARMY WAR COLLEGE, WASHINGTON, D.C.

This photograph, taken in 1938, shows the old Army War College as it appeared while Freeman was lecturing there. Located at Fort Lesley J. McNair, the building now houses the National War College.

In May 1935, Freeman was awarded the Pulitzer Prize for his four-volume biography of Robert E. Lee. One month later the Army War College (then located in Washington, D.C.) invited him to present a lecture on Lee, which he delivered there in January 1936. Thus began a series of lectures at the Army War College that would run until February 1940, with Freeman lecturing each autumn on the morale of Lee's army, each winter on Lee as a leader, and concluding the series with a lecture on the objectives of the Union and Confederate armies.

Of the nine lectures that comprise this series, all except the first were preserved. Those eight are all included here and are grouped by subject (i.e., morale, Lee, and objectives). For four of these lectures, I have included some of the remarks made by Freeman during the discussion period because these remarks pertain directly to the topic of leadership.

Although there is some repetition within this series, Freeman deliberately varied his approach for each lecture so that each is distinctive—an achievement facilitated by the fact that throughout this period Freeman was working on *Lee's Lieutenants,* his study of the high command of the Army of Northern Virginia, which was published in three volumes in 1942-44.

In June 1940, eighteen months before America's entry into the Second World War, the gravity of the international situation resulted in the suspension of classes at the Army War College, which remained closed throughout the war and for a five-year period thereafter. In August 1950 the college was reestablished at Fort Leavenworth, Kansas, then moved to Carlisle Barracks, Pennsylvania, in July 1951.

6

Morale in the Army of Northern Virginia

Lecture of November 5, 1936

Robert E. Lee was thrust into command of the Army of Northern Virginia on June 1, 1862, when General Joseph E. Johnston was wounded at the battle of Seven Pines, just outside of Richmond, Virginia, capital of the Confederacy. When Lee assumed command, the Union Army of the Potomac, under General George B. McClellan, was within seven miles of Richmond. In this lecture, Freeman first discusses why Lee was forced to quickly create morale in an army where little discipline existed. He then traces the steps that Lee took to establish morale, dividing these steps into three stages: "corrective," "aggressive," and "progressive."

The discussion period features a look at Lee's relationship with his personal staff, an analysis of the difference in leadership style between Lee and Stonewall Jackson, and a colorful sketch of Confederate General Richard S. Ewell.

I am to lecture to you this morning on the creation of morale in the Army of Northern Virginia during the period that army was under the command of General R.E. Lee. Morale and discipline are so closely related, of course, in all military organization that we often use the two terms as synonymous. Discipline, we say, creates morale. Where there is morale, there is discipline. Here, however, is one instance where morale, for four interesting reasons, had to be created where little discipline existed. The lesson of the creation of morale in the Army of Northern Virginia is therefore a matter of profound interest to you as military men. At least some of the conditions that existed in Virginia in 1862 might be created in the contingency of another war. It is conceivable that we might be compelled to put troops in combat when they have as little discipline as the Army of Northern Virginia had then. Accordingly, I think it is worth your while to know what that situation was, what were the four reasons why discipline had not been created, and how, out of a condition approaching chaos, morale was created.

First, there was no background of a regular army. One of the great advantages of the North in the War between the States was the fact that though it lost some of its ablest soldiers, it kept the organization of the army of the Union. It kept the background of a small corps of trained NCOs. None such existed when the Army of Northern Virginia was organized. There was no background, I repeat, of regular military organization.

Second, there was no time for the creation of discipline by drill and routine military service before combat began. As you may remember, the Confederacy was organized in February 1861. The state of Virginia, which gave so large a part of its force to the Army of Northern Virginia, did not secede until April seventeenth. Hostilities began, in effect, on the twenty-third of May. By July eighteenth, combat was joined in front of Bull Run.[1] In many instances, therefore, troops had not more than two months in which to prepare for combat; some went into action at Bull Run with less than one month's experience in camp. Further, that condition was complicated by the fact that even where they were put in "camps of instruction," as they were called, there often were no arms with which to drill them.

Still again, the third reason why morale had to be created in this army without discipline was the fact that the company officers, in the main, and in large part the line and field officers of higher command—the majors, the lieutenant colonels and colonels—were poor military material. That fact must always be understood. The Army of Northern Virginia was best at the top. The corps commanders were excellent, with perhaps one or two exceptions; the divisional commanders were probably above the average; the brigade commanders, as I shall try presently to show you, became better; the colonels were fair; but the company officers as a rule were distinctly poor. The condition this created for the commanding general was due primarily to the system by which the army was enlisted. Companies could elect their own commanding officers; the personnel of a battalion could elect its major; a whole regiment could elect its colonel. It is inconceivable that a worse setup for an army could have been established. Men who owed their commissions less to their government than to the men in the ranks certainly were not men who could be enabled to exercise firm and disciplinary command. The Confederacy suffered throughout its history from that condition. It is one which I pray God will never be created again in any American war.

The fourth reason why morale had to be created without a firm foundation of stable discipline was, of course, the individualism that dominated that army. It very seldom liked to have itself styled an army; it preferred to consider itself a voluntary association of gentlemen organized to drive out the enemy. Individualism was a barrier throughout the war to efficiency in the Confederate army. Every man considered himself not only a competent commander of his own action, but a strategist certainly as good as his brigadier and perhaps second only to the general in chief. Individualism, often in many respects admirable—for example, in making men scouts, in making them sharpshooters, in making them excellent artillerists—was almost fatal, at some periods of the war, to discipline. It had, however, its contrary effect: that contrary effect was a confidence on the part of the individual soldier that he was at least twice as good as his adversary. He had that feeling when he entered the ranks; perhaps if he hadn't had that feeling, the politicians would never have been foolish enough to provoke a war. But he believed he was twice as good as the man on the other side of the hill, that he could dispose of two adversaries. That was the reason why they were not afraid to have a smaller force meet a more numerous adversary.

To sum up, then, morale had to be created without discipline because there was no background of a regular army, because there was no time for the creation of discipline before combat, because the subordinate officers were, in the main, incompetent, and because there was this strong tradition of individualism.

In addition to these circumstances, such morale as had been created in the Army of the Potomac (for thus the Army of Northern Virginia was first styled) had largely been destroyed by the events of the winter of 1861-62. High morale of a sort had been created by the Confederate victory at First Manassas. That morale was largely lost, first, by friction between the army and the War Department—a sad, sad story in itself, one upon which I have not time to dwell. Secondly, such morale as had been created under Generals Johnston and Beauregard was impaired further by the reorganization of the army in the spring of 1862. I don't believe we have ever realized the full effect of this on the Army of Northern Virginia. Some of the colonels—though perhaps a minority of them—had developed well during the fall and winter of 1861-62; many of the most incompetent men had resigned from the army; the field officers were, on the whole, better by far than they had been in July 1861. The army, however, had, in the main, been enlisted for a twelve-month period. There was little disposition on the part of many of the units to reenlist. Wherefore in the winter of 1861, the Confederate Congress passed a succession of laws, beginning with the so-called "Bounty and Furlough Act,"[2] under which various concessions were made to the soldiers in return for their reenlistment for the period of the war. This whole policy proved a failure.

Before the opening of the spring campaign, it became necessary to introduce conscription. Prior to that, however, one of the concessions held out to the men was that upon reenlistment, they could reorganize.

In other words, if they so chose they could throw out the company officers, the battalion officers, and the regimental officers, and reelect them or elect men in their places. The inevitable result, of course, was the choice of many politicians in the places of men who had become, in some instances, fairly competent soldiers. A greater piece of folly never marred the pages of Upton's *Military Policy of the United States.*[3] To reorganize the army in the face of the enemy meant the elimination of those men who, by good discipline, had acquired the animosity of these marked individualists. To think that this was done, in the main, in April 1862, and then to think that before the year was out this army had fought the Seven Days, had fought Second Manassas, had fought Sharpsburg, and had fought Fredericksburg makes one have a feeling of positive amazement. It seems that every chance that could be taken to ruin the army was taken, and then by some miracle the army acquired this amazing morale.

Furthermore, there was a third factor in impairing what morale had been created. That was the wretchedness of the medical service of the army. At one time the average soldier of the Army of Northern Virginia considered that if he was admitted to a hospital, he had, by that very fact, received his death warrant. Hospital mortality at that time was almost 50 percent. You must remember also that at the time the Southern soldiers (most of them rural-born) were enlisted, a period of at least three months had to be allowed for those men to pass through what we now would regard as children's diseases. Those men, living in isolated communities, had never had measles, chicken pox, and mumps. They had to have those diseases, recover from them, regain their full strength, and then they were ready for duty. Fancy having to assume that after you enlisted this army, from 30 to 40 percent of it was going to be in the hospital constantly for a period of three months! Yet that was what happened. If the great state of West Virginia ever wants to erect a monument that will really explain what I believe is the major factor in its success, if it wants to find the true reason why the Confederacy lost West Virginia so soon, the reason and the monument should be measles. It might be difficult to erect a monument to measles, but after all, measles was the real explanation for the failure of the Confederate offensive in the late summer of 1861 in West Virginia. Nothing could do more to demoralize an army than a condition of that sort. Typhoid was rampant; malaria was everywhere; the heart of men was taken out by most of these diseases and by the wretchedness of the medical service.

Still again, the morale of Manassas was impaired by the mismanagement of the quartermaster and commissary under General Johnston. You may form what opinion you will of General Johnston, but in 1861-62, no man who reads the evidence can fail to conclude that General Johnston was an exceedingly poor military administrator. I could cite a hundred examples of the manner in which, even in some of the regimental matters such as the preparation of winter quarters, he failed to use the ordinary diligence you would expect of a military administrator.

Nevertheless, the morale of the army was still further impaired by the wounding of General Johnston on the thirty-first of May, 1862, in the battle of Seven Pines (or Fair Oaks). The army's morale was impaired by the reason that there existed at that time in the Army of the Potomac (which the next day became the Army of Northern Virginia)[4] a feeling that Johnston was a great soldier. There had been built up around General Johnston—I shall not say a clique for that would be an unfair term—but there had been built up around him a crowd of men who believed profoundly in him and who did not, at the outset, believe in his successor. You can take the history of the Army of Northern Virginia and can carry it down as far as Sharpsburg, and you will find there a community of interest, a similarity of outlook on the part of those officers who had held high command under General Johnston and who, at that late date, looked upon General Johnston's successor as an outsider. That is very definitely shown in the records.

Now then, to recapitulate, for the four reasons I first gave, they had to create morale without discipline. In the second place, the Army of Northern Virginia lost, during the winter of 1861-62, such morale as it had acquired. The reasons were friction between the army and the War Department; this wretched reorganization; the poor medical service; the mismanagement of the quartermaster and commissary services under General Johnston; and the wounding of General Johnston, who was regarded by so large an element of the high command as the one great soldier of the South.

How did General Lee meet this situation when, from a position analogous to that of the chief of the general staff,[5] he was called on the first of June, 1862, to take command of the army in the face of the enemy? You can trace as far as Sharpsburg three successive stages in the establishment of morale within the Army of Northern Virginia. The first such I would call "corrective," the second I would style "aggressive," and the third I would term "progressive." Let me explain.

The first thing General Lee did was to establish order within the army. I may say for the comfort of some of you that General Lee in those difficult days received his reward for the patience with which he had performed court-martial duty. From 1855, when he returned to active service as lieutenant colonel of cavalry, until his resignation, more than half his time in the field was spent on court-martial duty. There seemed to be something judicious about the man that made department commanders seize upon him for court-martial detail. More unpleasant duty could hardly have been given him, yet there was no duty that gave him so clear an insight into the mind of the private soldier. You may remember that prior to that time he had been exclusively a staff officer; he had never been with troops in command. Court-martial duty was for him an education in the psychology of the men in the ranks. It was with General Lee that began that famous story which, after all, explains much of discipline. When a sergeant who had been drunk and engaged in sundry escapades that disgraced the Second Cavalry was brought before Colonel Lee in Texas, the colonel, knowing the man had been a good soldier, said to him, "Sergeant, you shall have justice." "Yes, Colonel," said the sergeant, "that is just exactly what I am afraid of, that I will get justice."

Court-martial duty had given him an understanding of the mind of the soldier. He also knew how much an army travels on its stomach. He was very soon to discover the important fact that the quality of a ration is by no means as vital in the eyes of the soldier as the regularity of issue. The Army of Northern Virginia lived on next to nothing. As you know, one of its wags remarked that there were two armies fighting in America—the fed and the corn-fed. General Lee saw to it at the very start that the quartermaster and commissary services were reorganized, so that if men were due clothes and the clothes were available at the depots, they were issued; and above everything else, that the men were fed regularly, however poor the ration that had to be issued. The effect of that on the army was immediate. It was noted by a number of observers at the time.

The second corrective step he took was to put an end to favoritism in details. The army at that time was in front of Richmond. Every man who had a pull with a captain whom he had helped to elect three months before, if desirous of getting into Richmond, would get a detail. The army was reduced by details most seriously, but worse than the reduction in combat strength was the feeling on the part of the enlisted men that favoritism figured in these details behind the line. General Lee stopped that. One of his first orders to the army was that all details had to be ended, the men called in, and all details reorganized.

Then General Lee did something that must perhaps always be kept in mind by a good soldier. Of course, in the United States Army, if we ever have to go to war again in your lifetime, it will be possible to break an incompetent man, I hope, with ease. It could not be done in the South. Politics, individualism, a thousand considerations made it almost impossible to relieve the army of an incompetent regimental or company officer other than by a long and difficult trial for incompetence. Charges had to be preferred, and this, that, and the other thing had to be done before the man could be relieved of command, or at least before his commission could be taken away from him. General Lee had to accept the condition as it was and not as he wanted it to be. What was his solution? Unable to rid himself of incompetent company and regimental officers, he concentrated his effort on getting good brigade and divisional commanders.

The reorganization of the Army of Northern Virginia shows quite plainly that Lee had to reconcile himself to many incompetent regimental officers, but that deliberately and constantly he labored to get the best possible men for his brigades and his divisions. All that he knew of human nature was put to work there. Many of the most amusing episodes of the old man's career were in the manner in which, quietly, tactfully, thoughtfully, without hurting anybody's feelings, he eased out of command those who were incompetent. Quite often men never knew it until it was done. There was one notorious brigadier of cavalry, one of the most incompetent men that the Army of Northern Virginia ever had. General Lee was determined after the operations at Cedar Mountain that that cavalryman should never command a brigade in action, but he was of high connection and great station. Whenever General Lee sent him off on detached service, which he always did, he put in orders that this general's services were imperatively needed in the state of South Carolina (or elsewhere) in order to organize the cavalry there. How good a job this general did of it you may judge when D.H. Hill said he had four regiments of cavalry and would trade them at any time for three companies of good infantry.[6] General Lee had to accept a measure of incompetence, but he was determined that this incompetence should be limited to the smallest possible scope. If he had to have poor company officers, he wanted the best of them to be the regimental officers; if the lives of two or three hundred men in a brigade were at stake, he certainly wanted to get the best brigadiers he could. One time a half-dozen different dispatches written by General Lee to President Davis after he took command of the army related to the choice of competent brigadiers.

The fourth thing he did in this corrective period of his work was to put his soldiers digging dirt. There was nothing they hated more. The Confederate soldier of 1862 considered that the work of entrenchment was labor suited for slaves, not for gentlemen. Besides that, it was not becoming to valiant men, under any circumstances, to get behind a pile of dirt: soldiers had to stand out in the open and fight. It was with the greatest difficulty that General Lee made them dig the entrenchments, which he knew to be absolutely necessary to protect the right wing of his army when he struck with the left. He put them to work not only because he needed the fruits of their labor, but because he knew they needed the labor themselves. That was a very essential part of what I have called his "corrective" first labors to restore the morale of this army.

Then began what might be termed the "aggressive" period of his struggle for morale. He went into the Seven Days distrusted by nearly all his subordinates (save perhaps Jackson),[7] regarded by them as a paper soldier, a man whose strategic combinations looked fine when put in an order of battle but certainly would not work out. Not one, in that staff organization of incompetents he had in many cases, possessed belief. When I have the pleasure of carrying men over the battlefields of the Seven Days, I don't dwell much on the tactics, for tactics change every ten years. I dwell comparatively little on the general strategy, because that is reasonably familiar. I labor on the defects of staff work more than anything else. There, perhaps, is one place where we have to take our lesson for the future. Few armies are better than their staffs. General Lee took this army, with its wretched staff, with men distrusting him, and he created morale by successful aggressive action. The history of the Seven Days battles from the Southern point of view is essentially a story of what can be achieved by sound strategy despite clumsy and defective staff work. The change in the army in the month of June alone was incredible. At the end of May it had seen itself hurled against Seven Pines, marched backwards and forwards to no purpose; it had seen its quartermaster and commissary services utterly disorganized. It saw this new man come into the field; it saw those faults corrected; and when he had been in command exactly one month and one day, it saw the threat to Richmond virtually removed by one great sweep from Mechanicsville to Malvern Hill.

There are many things that enter into the morale of the Army of Northern Virginia, but I am not sure that the most obvious factor is not the most important. What created morale above everything else? Victory! What made victory? In the case of that army, strategy. To be sure, in that campaign the strategy was very elaborate, entirely too elaborate for the incompetent staff to handle. Think of the convergence of five columns on one objective to be handled by a staff that was wholly inexperienced![8] Nonetheless, the basic strategy was sound, the strategy made victory, and the victory made morale.

Then began what I have termed the third stage in the creation of morale—the "progressive" stage. It meant simply doing better what had been done before. It meant the continuation of a vigorous and victorious offensive. It meant the promotion of those men who were competent not only to lead with minimum loss but also by their own victories to contribute to morale. Put a little more simply, the first factor in the morale of the Army of Northern Virginia was R.E. Lee, the second factor was Stonewall Jackson, the third factor was probably Jeb Stuart, and Old Pete Longstreet is not to be left altogether out of the picture.[9] You will find it well worth your while in studying the morale of the Army of Northern Virginia to see how the achievements of corps commanders contributed to sustain the example, the influence, the prestige of the commanding general.

You will find, I think, on the other hand, that no small part of the failure of morale in the Army of the Potomac was due to the bickerings in the Army of the Potomac, especially during 1862. It is well worth studying. It is almost impossible to have morale where the general in chief does not draw the support of his corps commanders. One of the mysteries in the history of the Army of Northern Virginia, the disappearance of a brilliant figure, is to be explained by the fact that that particular man, though thoroughly qualified, though able to get as much offense out of a given number of men as any general of the army, was so carping, so critical, that he got to be regarded only as a disorganizer.[10] If any of you commands the new AEF, whatever else you have, have corps commanders who are going to contribute to morale and not destroy it.

If you study the history of the Confederate artillery, you will find that the Confederate artillery, while it had some superb units and some magnificent battalions, nonetheless suffered in comparison with the Federal artillery because it did not have a chief who commanded the confidence of the men.[11] I know the Confederate ordnance was inferior to the Federal. I know also that while the North had in Hunt a man who commanded the admiration of everyone who knew breech from muzzle,[12] the Confederates had a chief of artillery who was regarded by some of his most competent assistants as a man who really was a jest on what an artillery commander should be. If some of you gentlemen are going to undertake historical studies in the field of artillery, I beg you study that. It is one of the most monitory examples I know. Everyone realizes that the greatest superiority of the Army of the Potomac was in its artillery. I say the greatest factor in the superiority of the Federal artillery was not in the range of the guns but in the direction of that corps. Of course, when I say that, I do not for one minute mean to reflect on some of the magnificent artillery officers. I could take a day to talk to you of the work of such men as Alexander, Young, Walker, McIntosh, Poague, Pelham, Breathed—but I must stop or you will say I am calling the roster of the artillery of the Army of Northern Virginia. But at the head there was not a commander who could contribute to the morale of the army, and the artillery of the Army of Northern Virginia suffered throughout on that score. Take in contrast the cavalry: a magnificent contribution was made there by Stuart. Some of these days I would like to talk to you for a whole morning on the problems of cavalry morale as indicated in the Army of Northern Virginia. It is a very interesting problem and one worth your study.

These three stages carried the army through the battle of Sharpsburg.[13] That battle, September 17, 1862, presented a new test to the army because Confederate straggling and the vigorous Federal attack led to heavy losses, to retreat, and, though they did not admit it publicly, to a feeling on the part of the army that for the first time it had failed. I have recently made a new study of Sharpsburg, and you may be interested to know that I am forced to revise downward my estimate of Confederate strength at Sharpsburg. If I remember correctly, I have stated that Lee carried thirty-seven thousand bayonets into that fight, that all his infantry were engaged. Straggling, I now discover, had reached such proportion that at full tide on the seventeenth, Lee did not have more than thirty thousand men engaged. Straggling in that campaign was incredible. The reasons for it I have tried to outline, but I am not sure I have laid as much emphasis on them as I should.

Anyway, here we are back in Virginia, the great invasion of Maryland a failure; fifteen thousand men out of ranks—dead, wounded, captured, straggling; the army not demoralized but by no means of the same spirit it had displayed in August. God, what a contrast! Take McLaws. When McLaws moved from Maryland Heights through Harpers Ferry to join Lee at Sharpsburg, there never was a poorer march in American history—incredibly bad; and yet those troops were virtually as good as those who, under Old Jack and A.P. Hill, had covered fifty-two miles in forty-eight hours a month before.[14] Something had happened.

How did Lee meet that situation? He met it first by resting his men. A tired army needs nothing so much as it needs rest. That is an ABC fact that often is forgotten. I don't know how much time you gentlemen have had to carefully investigate the subject of fatigue in the army. I don't know how the factor of fatigue has changed, but I know that in the Army of Northern Virginia the men could stand almost anything for four days, but the fifth day in almost every instance they would crack. Beware of the fifth day, if the experience of the Army of Northern Virginia is applicable to the modern American. Lee gave his men rest, all the rest he could, and he increased their ration. In the face of opposition of the commissary general, Lee simply disregarded the ration law and fed his men. He reorganized them as rapidly as he could, and in particular he reorganized his artillery. He broke up eighteen batteries of manifest incompetence and distributed the men, guns, and horses. He then proceeded to promote the competent men, and he added a fourth factor for the reestablishment of morale.

General Lee said, "One of the chief troubles of this army is that punishment is not prompt. We must punish the delinquent promptly. It is the speed of punishment rather than its severity that counts." The result, as some of you know, was that he organized a military commission. He did not rely on courts-martial; he organized a military commission, which we might call a military police justice. The military commission moved along with the army always, and if a man was guilty of an offense, he was tried immediately. He was not left in the guardhouse and kept comfortable for three weeks during the winter, while a good soldier marched outside in the rain and cold to keep guard over him. He was punished immediately.

I was justified in saying that the morale of the army had not been destroyed, else the morale of the army could not have been recovered so soon after Sharpsburg. By these four steps I have outlined, the morale of the army was recovered, and the army thereafter showed its recovery by Fredericksburg and Chancellorsville. If you ever get discouraged, gentlemen, about the morale of troops, remember that morale which had sunk from the Groveton level of August twenty-ninth[15] to what might be called the October level after Sharpsburg, and rose again in so short a time that in all the reports of the removal of the Army of Northern Virginia to the Fredericksburg front at the end of November 1862, there is not one report of straggling. That was how quickly morale had been restored.

By the spring of 1863, Lee's system had been in operation nearly a year. He had organized and reorganized and systematized. He was a great military administrator, and little by little his hands had been lifted up by the support of his loyal lieutenants, and then came Chancellorsville. An army that could do what Lee's army did at Chancellorsville considered itself invincible. That army believed it could do anything. Unfortunately, General Lee took the army's estimation of itself. In all the studies I have made of Gettysburg, the most illuminating of all is General Lee's own explanation: "I thought the army was invincible; I expected too much of it." Well, it was not; it fell back.

There was no shock after Gettysburg comparable to the shock after Sharpsburg, and with the campaign of 1864, three new conditions developed. First, there was no successor to Jackson in the creation of morale.[16] Second, the brigade command was distinctly better by reason of the promotion of competent men, but broadly speaking, the divisional and corps command was not so good. Casualties were responsible. In the third place, the horse supply had failed, and with the failing of the horse supply and the great improvement of the Federal cavalry, Stuart's command no longer believed itself invincible. As a result of these three conditions, General Lee himself had to undertake to fight the army. You cannot understand the campaign of 1864 unless you realize that General Lee himself fought that campaign. Longstreet was wounded at its very outset.[17] Ewell was scarcely able to keep going.[18] General Lee himself handled the army in combat. That had a curious effect on morale. At a time when attrition was beginning to claim its toll, General Lee's contact with the soldiers changed his admiration for them into a deep affection. He was always sympathetic with the individual. He was always accessible. He was completely indifferent himself to danger, yet he demonstrated to the men that he was always willing to do what he could to protect them.

Nothing should be more interesting to an American soldier than to go down where the battlefields of First Cold Harbor and Second Cold Harbor join and to study there the wild valor with which the assault was made at First Cold Harbor and the trained, careful discipline displayed by that same army on the same ground two years afterward.[19] The effect of Lee's training showed. The men believed General Lee. He had convinced them that he would call on them only to do the necessary things and to do that with a minimum loss. I am not sure but what that is the final expression, dynamically, of morale—that when men are convinced that their commander is an able soldier, that he will call on them only to do the necessary things and to do them with a minimum loss and with every promise of success by reason of his intelligence, then you have a fighting machine.

Then began the twilight of the army, but such was its morale that for ten months it kept its position against an enemy 2½ times its size and subsisted on one-third rations in the face of superior artillery. This army also accepted the difficult duty of guarding both sides of a river with an exceedingly small mobile reserve. There are many, many instances that illustrate this. This same army recovered the Crater and fought its way with its Second Corps within sight of Washington. And that, of course, when all who would look could see that the doom of the Confederacy was sealed. Morale kept that army going when men knew that it could not hope to win.

When the end approached, the breakdown came with only three classes of troops: the late conscripts failed; those who were closest to the enemy often deserted; those whose homes in other states were threatened for the first time likewise increased the ranks of the deserters. The rest of the army stood firm. It is worth knowing that those divisions whose commanders, through four years of war, had proved themselves less capable in combat were those from which there were the heaviest desertions at the end. There was only one exception, and that was Pickett's division.[20] Pickett's division was well led up to Gettysburg, but thereafter it was demoralized by its proximity to Richmond and by the fact that it received an exceedingly large number of late and poor conscripts. With that exception, the divisions that had good commanders were the divisions that held their own all the way to Appomattox.

I have tried, gentlemen, in fifty minutes to epitomize what ought to go into a long series of lectures or into a book, for there is a book in the morale of the Army of Northern Virginia. I fear I have covered so much ground that I may have confused you by the number of points I made. In the end the picture stands out very clearly. Morale was built around the man in the ranks and around a great commander. I wonder if there ever was an army that had great morale that did not have a great commander. Probably the most neglected man in American military history is General Winfield Scott; he ought almost to be called the "father of the American army."[21] Scott was a first-class soldier of his day, and I have been thinking the last few days what a different prospect lies before Madrid, compared with that which was before Mexico City when Scott marched in. His army was six thousand; I doubt if Franco has ten thousand. See the difference between what happened in Madrid and what happened in Mexico City.[22] There is the different morale and behind the morale, the character of the men.

My father has often told me in his lifetime how when he got to Appomattox on the night of the eighth, the sky was lowering, the clouds close to the ground, the camp fires of the Federals plainly visible.[23] Men could stand on the hill within the Confederate lines and looking out could see the Federal camp fires on three sides of them. Only to the north was there an open space, dark against the North Star. He said, "For the first time we knew that the end had come." They knew it, and yet the next morning Gordon went forward; the army became almost a hollow square, only about 2½ miles from front to rear; and when the order came to charge, Gordon charged just as gallantly as he had on the second day in the Wilderness, or at the Bloody Angle.[24] The white flag passed. General Lee went to the McLean house, and when he came back there occurred that unforgettable scene in which the army showed its reverence for him. However poorly I have told the tale, their morale must have been great because when he came back, these ragged boys, unfed for six days, came running up to him, and what did they say above everything else? "General, is it true we have surrendered? General, General, say the word and we will go at them again!"

I am not sure but what I would be willing to have that left as the final tribute to the Army of Northern Virginia. Not, of course, with any thought of a renewal of domestic war. But never was its spirit better displayed than in that last hour when, with only eight thousand men with muskets in their hands and the artillery reduced to two little battalions with only enough ammunition for two hours' fighting, something that had been done to them by their officers had so stirred them that the cry went up, "General, say the word and we will go at them again!"

Discussion Period

Q. In your *R.E. Lee* you have discussed at considerable length General Lee's relations with his official family, that is, his immediate staff. I gathered from that discussion that General Lee was not a warm personality in the commonly accepted sense of that word, that is, his relations were somewhat austere, even at times cold in such matters as denial of promotion and a slight disinclination to advance their interests. I was wondering if you have given consideration to the proposition that General Lee was a great Virginia gentleman and was so recognized by these individuals in the Southern army, and that a great part of their regard for him was the regard that Americans seem to have for personages who are recognized as outstanding. An example of that quite recently was the election of Mr. Lodge in Massachusetts,[25] and numerous others. I should like to know if that particular proposition has been considered.

A. That is very interesting and up to a certain point I think is true. General Lee had that prestige of family and station and of gentle bearing when he entered the war. He largely lost prestige by the unsuccessful West Virginia campaign. He was very warmly criticized as being entirely too much of a theorist, but he had no reputation other than that of being a fine gentleman when he took command of the Army of Northern Virginia.

In his relations with his staff, this is to be said: He regarded economy of force as one of the absolute essentials of Confederate later success, that not one man was to be wasted, and that it was incumbent upon him to set an example of economy of force, even to the extent of economizing in staff officers. He was wrong in that. Beyond question he would have been better served if he had had two or three more staff officers, but it was his idea that it was for him to set an example of simplicity, of self-sacrifice, and disregard for rank. It was incumbent upon his staff officers to do the same thing. He held them, in respect to the volume of service they performed and their disregard of rank and their simplicity of life, to precisely the same standards that he set for himself. It was only when the war was over that they got over these little things and had for him the admiration and affection that they later cherished. They admired him as a magnificent man, but they did not love him. I think I can say that with some fair claim to authority because I knew personally three of General Lee's staff officers and have talked with them many times about their attitude toward him.

Q. I wonder if you would draw a thumbnail sketch of Jackson's method of maintaining morale in his outfit as compared with General Lee.

A. One day a Confederate soldier was very close to the Federals, and they were firing with some very mean sharpshooters. It happened to be the old Stonewall Brigade, which was Jackson's own command. This man said, "I wish all those damn Yankees were in hell." The man who was loading his gun said, "I'll be damned if I do, because if they were in hell, Old Jack would be within a half a mile of them and he would say that the Stonewall Brigade would have to charge them." There, in essence, is the morale of the old Stonewall Brigade and of Jackson.[26]

Jackson, however, started out right. When he was sent to Harpers Ferry he had a lot of militia officers—major generals commanding regiments, brigadier generals commanding battalions, and so on. He rid himself of most of them very promptly. About the first thing he did was to send back to Richmond and say, "Send me ten of the cadets of the Virginia Military Institute." The Virginia Military Institute boys had gone down to Richmond and were acting as drillmasters at Camp Lee, a Virginia artillery camp. Jackson took ten of those boys and during the quiet days when he was first in command at Harpers Ferry, he drilled his men. The Stonewall Brigade started out with more rudimentary instruction in drill than almost any other unit in the army.

In dealing with his troops in the creation of morale, Jackson, like Lee, relied very much on his officers. As you know, Jackson cared very little about his colonels; it is surprising how few of Jackson's colonels ever became brigadier generals. He relied on his brigadiers, relied on his division commanders, but most of all he relied on Jackson and God. It is remarkable how few of his colonels ever became eminent men. He looked to his brigadiers to maintain discipline, and he maintained discipline himself with a very firm hand, much firmer on his officers than on his men. He held that if he disciplined his officers, his officers would discipline the men. Of course, the result of it was that he was constantly quarrelling with one or another of his officers. He had a run-in early in the war with General W.W. Loring;[27] he arrested A.P. Hill and Garnett. He believed that the responsibility for discipline rested on the officer; if the officer himself was disciplined, the army would be.

He believed in feeding his men and in resting his men, and above everything else he believed in keeping his column closed up on the march to prevent straggling. You have plenty of pictures of Old Jack, but if you want to get the correct one of Old Jack in dealing with his army, remember him on the march. I have often said that the epitome of Jackson was the cry that he raised so often: "Close up, men, close up!" They had a fanatical admiration for him.

Ewell said, "I never rest easy when I am with Old Jack. I am firmly persuaded he is crazy. I expect any time to get an order from him to charge the North Star." It ought to be added that a good deal of the credit that belongs to Jackson for the creation of morale also belongs to Ewell. "On a march," Ewell said, "you don't need anything but your ammunition and your ambulances. The road to glory isn't covered with a wagon train." That is worth remembering.

I ought to add this: In the matter of final court-martial decisions, especially for desertions—and I have turned over a great many of these—Jackson was more lenient than Lee. Jackson reversed more court-martial death sentences, relatively, than did Lee.

Q. I would like to hear something about Ewell. There is quite a famous Civil War picture showing Lee and his staff, but Ewell is absent. Why was he left out?

A. I don't know the picture to which you refer. I know that Ewell is in the great mural at Richmond. If you have not seen it, there is an interesting book just out by Dr. P.G. Hamlin; I think he calls it *Letters of a Soldier Officer*.[28]

Ewell was a man of abilities well above the average man, one of the most amusing and diverting men of the war. I could entertain you for hours with stories about Ewell. He had been in the West as a dragoon and had great confidence in himself as a forager. When he was in command of a brigade at Manassas in 1861, they came and told Ewell they were out of fresh meat. Ewell said, "That is absurd; there must be meat in this army. If you all can't go out and forage, I will." He went out and by and by came in leading a decrepit old cow that nobody had thought worth taking. Ewell said, "There you are, got it with very little effort." One man said, "General, how far will that poor lean cow go in feeding this brigade?" Ewell said, "I forgot—I thought I was still commanding a squadron of cavalry."

Ewell's failure, relatively, in high command was due to his inability to adjust himself from Jackson's system of command to Lee's system of command. Jackson left no discretion whatever: "Here are the orders"—usually in writing—"obey them. Don't rely on anybody; do what I tell you." On the other hand, Lee's orders to his corps commanders almost always were discretionary. By one of the ironies of war, Ewell had just come under Lee's command when in the little town of Gettysburg rode up a young officer who said, "General Ewell, General Lee sends you his compliments and says take that hill, if practicable." That "if practicable" cost the Confederates Cemetery Hill, and Cemetery Hill cost them Cemetery Ridge, and Cemetery Ridge cost them Gettysburg. What Gettysburg cost them, you know.

Ewell was a man who, if left with discretionary orders, always consulted anybody at hand—his subordinates, his brigade commanders. He preferred peremptory orders; Lee never gave peremptory orders if they could be avoided. Ewell never made the adjustment. In the Valley, Ewell was influenced by a man whose name probably none of you have heard—General Arnold Elzey.[29] At Gettysburg and throughout, he was influenced more by General Early than anybody else. There are one or two instances where we are almost justified in saying Early was Ewell.

Ewell, as you know, late in the war married his cousin. Her name was "Miss Brown." He was wooden-legged, and whenever he would hobble up to introduce her, he would say, "Gentlemen, I want to present you to my wife, Miss Brown." He never would call her Mrs. Ewell.

At Gettysburg he was riding along and suddenly cried, "I am shot!" His staff officer said, "My God, General, shot again after all the wounds you have received?" "Yes," said Ewell, "shot again. I would be obliged if you would look at the back of my saddle and take off that other wooden leg and let me use that one." He had been shot that time in the wooden leg.

Notes

The stenographic transcript of this lecture is filed in the archives of the U.S. Army Military History Institute, located adjacent to the Army War College at Carlisle Barracks, Pennsylvania. The lecture was originally entitled "Methods Employed by General Lee to Maintain Morale in the Army of Northern Virginia."

1. The "combat" of 18 July 1861 was a small skirmish; the major engagement occurred three days later, on 21 July.

2. Passed by the Confederate Congress on 11 December 1861, this act authorized a $50 bounty and a 60-day furlough for every soldier who reenlisted for three years (or for the duration of the war). It also provided for the election of officers upon the reenlistment of the army.

3. Emory Upton was graduated from West Point in May 1861 and became one of the most capable Union commanders of the war, rising to command of a battalion of infantry, a battalion of artillery, and a division of cavalry in succession, and attaining the rank of brevet major general. After the war Upton wrote numerous military treatises, the best known of which was *The Military Policy of the United States* (Washington, D.C.: Government Printing Office, 1904). This study, which Upton was still working on at the time of his death in 1881, was published at the direction of Secretary of War Elihu Root, and it became required reading at West Point and the Army War College. In tracing American military policy from the Revolution to midway through the Civil War, this work argued forcefully for the maintenance of a strong standing army, well organized, well trained, and well equipped. In the introduction Upton noted that "all of our wars have been prolonged for want of judicious and adequate preparation," and, with respect to the Civil War, he asserted that "twenty thousand regular troops at Bull Run would have routed the insurgents, settled the question of military resistance, and relieved us from the pain and suspense of four years of war."

4. On 1 June 1862, in his first order to his army, Lee addressed it as the "Army of Northern Virginia."

5. In March 1862, Lee (then serving as military adviser to President Davis) was assigned responsibility for "the conduct of military operations in the armies of the Confederacy." However, due to Davis' determination to direct military operations himself, Lee's duties remained essentially the same.

6. This "notorious brigadier of cavalry" was Beverly H. Robertson, who was selected by President Davis to command Stonewall Jackson's cavalry brigade in succession to Turner Ashby (killed in battle in June 1862). Following Robertson's lackluster performance at the battle of Cedar Mountain (9 August 1862), his cavalry brigade was placed under Jeb Stuart for the second battle of Manassas (29-30 August 1862). After this battle Robertson was sent to North Carolina. He returned to Virginia in May 1863 for the Gettysburg campaign, but was soon relieved and sent to South Carolina. D. H. Hill commanded the Confederate forces in North Carolina from February to July 1863.

7. Thomas Jonathan ("Stonewall") Jackson had just completed his magnificent Valley campaign (23 March - 9 June 1862) when his army joined Lee for the battle of the Seven Days. As military adviser to President Davis, Lee had played a key role in the development of the strategy of the Valley campaign, and Jackson had great respect for him. After the Seven Days, Jackson said to a member of his staff, "So great is my confidence in General Lee that I am willing to follow him blindfolded."

8. Lee launched the Seven Days offensive with an attack on the Union right flank (north of the Chickahominy River). For this attack Lee divided his forces into five separate columns, four of which were to guide on Stonewall Jackson's column. On the first day of the attack (Mechanicsville) things went awry when Jackson, for once, did not appear as scheduled; however, Jackson's column did arrive on the second day (Gaines' Mill) and the combined Confederate forces broke the Union line, thereby beginning the Union retreat south that ended at Harrison's Landing (on the James River) four days later.

9. Stonewall Jackson and James ("Old Pete") Longstreet emerged from the battles of Seven Days, Second Manassas, and Sharpsburg as Lee's best division commanders. In October 1862 the Army of Northern Virginia was organized into two corps: Longstreet was given command of the First Corps and Jackson the Second. James Ewell Brown ("Jeb") Stuart was Lee's commander of cavalry.

10. This "brilliant figure" was Jubal A. Early, who was given command of the Second Corps in May 1864. In March 1865, following the defeat of that corps in the Shenandoah Valley at the hands of a much larger Union force, Lee relieved Early of command and sent him home to "await further orders" because Lee believed that Early no longer had the support of his soldiers or the public.

11. Lee's chief of artillery was William N. Pendleton, who was graduated from West Point in 1830 but resigned from the army in 1833 and became an Episcopal minister. Although Lee became aware of Pendleton's military deficiencies, the two men were close friends, and Lee could not bring himself to remove Pendleton.

12. Henry J. Hunt was the chief of artillery for the Union Army of the Potomac. Hunt was graduated from West Point in 1839 and spent his entire army career as an artillerist. He served with distinction in the Mexican War, and in the 1850s he served on a board whose recommendations resulted in a new system of light artillery tactics.

13. For an excellent account of this battle, see Stephen W. Sears' *Landscape Turned Red* (New York: Warner Books, Inc., 1983).

14. Lafayette McLaws, then in command of two divisions, left Harpers Ferry on the afternoon of 16 September but did not arrive at Sharpsburg (about 16 miles away) until the next morning. On 25-26 August forces under Stonewall Jackson and A. P. Hill (commanding a division) had marched completely around the Union right flank and then down in the Union rear in a movement that set the stage for the second battle of Manassas.

15. The second battle of Manassas was fought near the small crossroads village of Groveton.

16. Jackson was mortally wounded at the battle of Chancellorsville (1-3 May 1863).

17. Longstreet was seriously wounded on 6 May 1864 at the battle of the Wilderness, and Richard H. Anderson was chosen to succeed him in command of the First Corps. Longstreet returned to command of this corps in October 1864.

18. Richard S. Ewell, who succeeded Jackson in command of the Second Corps, became ill in late May 1864 and was transferred to Richmond to supervise the defenses there. Command of the Second Corps was assigned to Jubal A. Early. In addition to the loss of Longstreet and Ewell, Jeb Stuart was mortally wounded at the battle of Yellow Tavern on 11 May 1864. Lee selected Wade Hampton to succeed Stuart as the head of the Cavalry Corps.

19. The Confederate assault at First Cold Harbor was part of the Seven Days battle of Gaines' Mill (27 June 1862), during which the Union line was broken and the retreat of Union forces south to the James River begun. At Second Cold Harbor (3 June 1864), Grant launched an unsuccessful assault on the Confederate line in which he lost over 6,000 men in one hour.

20. George E. Pickett, who commanded a division in Longstreet's First Corps, is best known for leading the unsuccessful assault on Cemetery Ridge on the third and final day of the battle of Gettysburg (1-3 July 1863).

21. Winfield Scott became commanding general of the U.S. Army in 1841. During the Mexican War he commanded a seaborne invasion of Mexico that captured Veracruz (March 1847) then proceeded inland to capture Mexico City (September 1847) after an unbroken series of victories. Too old and feeble for active service in the Civil War, Scott retired as commanding general of the army in November 1861.

22. Francisco Franco was the Spanish general who overthrew the Spanish democratic republic during the Spanish Civil War (1936-39) and ruled Spain until his death in 1975. Franco's forces arrived at Madrid in November 1936 (just before Freeman gave this lecture), but Madrid did not fall until March 1939.

23. This was the night of 8 April 1865, the Confederate retreat from Petersburg having begun on 2 April. Lee surrendered to Grant on the afternoon of 9 April.

24. As a brigade commander, John B. Gordon turned the right flank of a Union corps on the second day of the battle of the Wilderness (5-6 May 1864). On 9 May he was given command of a division, and on 12 May this division launched a successful counterattack to restore the Confederate line at the Bloody Angle during the battle of Spotsylvania (8-19 May). In late March 1865, just before the Confederate retreat from Petersburg, Gordon succeeded Early in command of the Second Corps. On the morning of 9 April, Gordon launched the last attack made by Lee's army in an unsuccessful attempt to break through the Union lines. Lee surrendered to Grant that afternoon.

25. Henry Cabot Lodge was elected to the U.S. Senate in 1936. Lodge was the product of two prominent Massachusetts families (the Cabots and the Lodges) just as Lee was the product of two prominent Virginia families (the Carters and the Lees).

26. Jackson was graduated from West Point in 1846 and served with distinction in the Mexican War, rising to the rank of brevet major. In 1852 he resigned from the army to become an instructor at the Virginia Military Institute. In the spring of 1861 Jackson entered Confederate service as a colonel and was assigned to command of the Confederate forces at Harpers Ferry. As noted earlier, during the next eighteen months Jackson rose to command of the Second Corps of Lee's army, becoming the most famous of Lee's commanders. In the first volume of *Lee's Lieutenants,* Freeman introduces Jackson as follows: "Mediocre teacher at the Virginia Military Institute and a former professional soldier, age 37, profoundly and, some say, fanatically religious, with a precise regard for discipline and army regulations. A man he is of contrasts so complete that he appears one day a Presbyterian deacon who delights in theological discussion and, the next, a reincarnated Joshua. He lives by the New Testament and fights by the Old."

27. The details of this "run-in" deserve to be noted. In the fall of 1861 Jackson was assigned to command of Confederate forces in the Shenandoah Valley. In January 1862 Loring, commanding a brigade under Jackson, sent a petition to the War Department objecting to Jackson's assignment of his brigade to the occupation of the small town of Romney. When the secretary of war thereupon ordered Jackson to relocate Loring's brigade, Jackson replied as follows:

> Your order requiring me to direct General Loring to return with his command to Winchester has been received and promptly complied with.
>
> With such interference in my command I cannot expect to be of much service in the field, and accordingly respectfully request to be ordered to report for duty to the superintendent of the Virginia Military Institute at Lexington. . . . Should this application not be granted, I respectfully request that the President will accept my resignation from the Army.

When Jackson's letter reached Richmond, the governor of Virginia and several powerful Confederate congressmen immediately interceded on his behalf. In the end, Jackson remained with his army in the Valley, Loring and his brigade were transferred elsewhere, and, most importantly, the secretary of war never again intervened in the operation of Jackson's army.

28. The actual title of the book was *The Making of a Soldier: Letters of General R. S. Ewell* (edited by Percy Gatling Hamlin and published in Richmond, Va. in 1935). Ewell served as a division commander under Jackson during the Valley campaign, the battle of the Seven Days, and at Second Manassas, where he was seriously wounded. He lost a leg as a result of these wounds and was out of action for the next nine months.

Ewell returned to the army in May 1863 and assumed command of the Second Corps in place of the fallen Jackson.

29. Elzey commanded a brigade under Ewell during the Valley campaign.

7

Morale in the Army of Northern Virginia

Lecture of November 4, 1937

Freeman begins this lecture by stating that General Lee viewed the problem of morale in terms of three factors: supply, discipline, and command. After first reviewing the limits on Lee's control of these factors, Freeman proceeds to show how Lee employed them in developing and maintaining the morale of his army through its various campaigns, from the battle of Seven Pines in June 1862 to the surrender at Appomattox in April 1865.

In the discussion period, Freeman addresses two topics: first, the loyalty of the commander to his subordinates, and second, Lee's method of relieving those commanders whose performance in the field had proved inadequate.

Since last I had the pleasure of addressing you in the spring of 1937, my military researches have been directed to a close study of General Lee's lieutenants. Of them, I propose next fall to issue a rather elaborate study. I cannot say that examination of these men in their temperamental peculiarities, their excellencies, and their deficiencies has changed essentially my judgement of General Lee. It would be proper to say, however, that in this, as I believe in every case of a great commander, he is himself interpreted by his lieutenants. You see his problems magnified in some instances and in others simplified by the men who executed his orders. In no aspect of the work of General Lee has this been more apparent to me than in a study of his methods of promoting morale. That is better interpreted from every angle if one knows the peculiarities of the men through whom General Lee's orders were carried out. Oftentimes, the problems of morale were simplified by a great lieutenant. How could it be otherwise with Jackson? In some instances, all that the commanding general sought to do in establishing and in maintaining morale was offset by an incompetent officer.

I think General Lee himself realized this. He held that the material in the Army of Northern Virginia was as good as that which could be had in any army. In a very familiar letter written to General John B. Hood in 1863, he said, "I quite agree with you that our men are capable of doing anything and of going anywhere if they have competent officers. But, how are those officers to be had? That is the question."[1]

General Lee, I think, believed, to put it in another form, that the problem of morale was essentially that of supply, of discipline, and of command. May I repeat, essentially a problem of supply, of discipline, and of command. The manner in which these three factors played their part in the Army of Northern Virginia will be the subject of my remarks this morning.

At the outset, I must ask you to remember that General Lee's control of his army in these essential respects was limited in several ways, some of which have been forgotten. In the first place, you will remember that if a battalion, a company, or a regiment offered its services to the Confederacy as a unit, it was authorized to elect its own officers. Fortunately for the Confederacy, most of the tenders of service in 1861 and in the early part of 1862 were tenders of companies. Therefore, only the company officers were elected. In a good many instances, however, regiments were offered, and their regimental officers were elected by the men—a system as vicious as could well be conceived. Until the summer of 1862, it made the officer essentially the subject of his own soldiers; it was impossible for him in many instances to procure proper discipline other than by risking his command.

Remember again that General Lee had no power whatever of promotion. He might tell his soldiers that each of them had a baton, a marshal's baton, in his knapsack, but he could not himself raise a sergeant to a second lieutenancy or for any feat of valor promote even a second lieutenant to the next grade above. All the great incentive of morale that is offered by promotion on the field of battle was denied him under the laws of the Confederacy.

Furthermore, if an officer was wounded and there was any prospect of his returning to command, that officer could not be taken from the roster. He might be a brigadier general who had as his senior colonel a very capable man, a man more capable than he himself; if there was any prospect that the general officer would return to duty at any time, the colonel commanding the brigade could only command as a colonel. The result of this was that by the winter of 1863-64, half the brigades of the Army of Northern Virginia were commanded by colonels. In many instances they were admirable men—some of them were promoted in the summer of 1864—but many of them were by no means as good as the men who were disabled and absent, nor were they as good in any respect as the qualified brigadiers who at that time were without commands.

Still again, General Lee could not remove incompetent officers until the third year of the war other than by court-martial. It was with great difficulty that he prevailed on Congress to enact a law by which a board of examiners could remove incompetent officers. You would be very much interested if you had an opportunity to examine the proceedings of some of these boards. I am sure the incompetence, even in the smallest tactical details, disclosed by some of these examinations is unbelievable. Yet, these were the men who, until this complicated machinery was employed, had under the laws of the Confederacy to be kept in command.

Finally, the whole process of promotion was complicated by that singular provision of Confederate law regarding the vacation of a commission. A great combat brigade, even the Stonewall Brigade itself, that matchless brigade of Jackson's—the Grenadier Guards of the Confederacy, I have always called them—might be so depleted numerically by combat that their organization as a brigade would cease to exist. Indeed, that very condition did arise with the Stonewall Brigade after the twelfth of May, 1864. Whenever that happened, no matter how competent might be the officers of the brigade, on the dissolution of the brigade they lost their commissions and had to be recommissioned ere they could see field service again.

I think that to study these difficulties, gentlemen, is to put in a new light the problems that General Lee faced. Granting his major premise that command was one of the essentials of morale, you realize how difficult it was for him to have competent commands.

Before I proceed more specifically to analyze the method by which he built up command and morale despite these problems, let me explain that I would not have you assume that General Lee, in the creation of morale, relied exclusively on his officers. He had close contact with his own army. He had that presence and person that inspired awesome respect on the part of his soldiers. Moving among them, pausing at their camp fires, exchanging greetings with them on the road, answering their inquiries—these things, the inevitable and inescapable incidents of a day's work, were in themselves great factors for morale.

As we proceed, I hope you will see how General Lee labored, as it were, simultaneously with his officers and no less with the men in the ranks. I think it necessary to emphasize that point, gentlemen, because those factors must be taken into account in any war. No matter how vast an army, it still is built on the individual soldier. The implementation of the army is through its officers. The officer cannot forget, as your general remarked in introducing me, the human equation of the individual soldier.

Now then, let's begin to trace the development of morale in the Army of Northern Virginia until it reached what was, to General Lee, a satisfactory condition. We have a process of development from the first of June, 1862, to the first of May, 1863—in short, from the end of the battle of Seven Pines to the battle of Chancellorsville. Then we have the great peak of morale, a peak that was responsible in large measure for some of the strategic combinations at Gettysburg. That morale was not greatly impaired by the defeat at Gettysburg, and to a surprising extent it was maintained until the summer of 1864. Then, little by little, as the nature of the inevitable end was revealed to the soldiers, the morale of a great part of the Army of Northern Virginia declined.

You might, therefore, say that so far as that army was under the command of General Lee, there were these periods of morale: the period of upbuilding, June 1, 1862 to May 1, 1863; the peak of morale, the Chancellorsville-Gettysburg period, May 1 to July 3, 1863; thereafter, the maintained period, which I sometimes call the period of "the momentum of morale," that carried the army through the Mine Run campaign at the end of November 1863; and thereafter, the decline.

When General Lee, on the first of June, 1862, took command of the Army of Northern Virginia, its problem of morale was an exceedingly difficult one. Three armies had just been combined. The first was the Army of the Potomac—broadly speaking, the command of General Johnston, which had been moved from the most central sector to the Peninsula and then back to the Richmond front. The second army was the Army of the Peninsula, which had been commanded by General John B. Magruder. This command had been organized on the lower Peninsula in May 1861, had fought the engagement of Big Bethel on the tenth of June, 1861, and thereafter had been engaged in semi-siege operations until the retreat from Yorktown in May 1862. With these was combined the army from Norfolk, generally known as Huger's command (so far as I know it never had a distinct army name). You will recall also that by some classifications, after General Lee took command and Jackson came down from the Valley, there might have been said to be present a fourth army: the Army of the Valley. That army, however, was not on the Richmond front when, following the wounding of General Johnston on the thirty-first of May, 1862, the president assigned General Lee to command of the army. You will recall that General Lee at that time had been military adviser to the president, a position tantamount to that of chief of staff today.

Remember, in the second place, that when General Lee assumed command of the Army of Northern Virginia, the divisions were entirely unrelated; there was no corps organization. The military law of the Confederacy did not even contemplate the organization of corps. Not only were these divisions unrelated, but in some instances they were jealous. There was not that measure of cooperation that should have been desired between, say, the divisions that had fought in northern Virginia in 1861 and those that had spent a like period in the swamps of the lower Peninsula; neither was there a feeling on the part of the troops from the Peninsula or of northern Virginia that the forces that had come up the south side of the James with General Huger were exactly their peers in valor or achievement.

There was again, at that time, a wretched service of supply. If I might interrupt my general narrative, I want to say that I have been engaged during the last year in a rather careful study, among others, of General Joseph E. Johnston's period of command in Virginia. I remain convinced of the strategical capacities of General Johnston, however, I must confess that I believe him during this period a wretched military administrator. I cannot see in any of his organization the work of a good army administrator. When General Lee took command, the service of supply in all its branches was disorganized, feeble, and confused. Among other things, the men detailed for this service were far too numerous for an army as limited in personnel as was the Army of Northern Virginia.

Still again, you must remember that this army had just passed through a reorganization. Most of its regiments had been recruited for one year, and that year had expired. A succession of very bad laws, including the Bounty and Furlough Act, had culminated at length in the Conscription Act.[2] Under the terms of the Bounty and Furlough Act, regiments that reenlisted for the war were authorized to elect their officers up to and including regimental rank. It happened—I doubt if it ever happened elsewhere in a war—that on the very day when Longstreet's division was engaged in a very difficult rearguard action at Williamsburg, the fifth of May, 1862, some of the regiments of that army, in the face of the enemy, were holding elections and were replacing colonels with nine months' experience with officers who, in some instances, that day had been raised from captains. The reorganization of the army had, in fact, not been actually completed at the time General Lee assumed command on the first of June.

Finally, when General Lee took command, the morale of the army could not be said to have been impaired materially by anything that had happened, but the overconfidence of Manassas was gone. You see, the army had had an accidentally easy victory at Manassas, a victory which goes to show that sometimes, no matter how bad the strategy may be on the part of GHQ, the tactics of the brigadiers and of the regimental commanders may be good enough to save the day. That happens. The reverse also happens: Sometimes the strategy of GHQ has to compensate for the poor tactics at brigade and regimental headquarters.

That overconfidence had been very costly to the Confederacy. It led to an underestimate of the valor of the Army of the Potomac under General McClellan, an army which had at that time admirably demonstrated that it was improving daily in every quality of the soldier. There had been a very unpleasant experience on the part of the Army of Northern Virginia. Unfortunately, it was often confused in front of Yorktown. The rearguard action at Williamsburg had been anything but satisfactory; the army had been compelled to leave its wounded in the field and retire in bad weather over rough roads to protect the wagon train. On the thirty-first of May and the first of June had been fought that ghastly and inconclusive action at Seven Pines (Fair Oaks), a wretchedly mismanaged battle from the standpoint of the Confederacy. The result, I say, was not an impairment of morale but a destruction of that high confidence, perhaps that overconfidence, which had prevailed at First Manassas.

What, in these circumstances, was done by an officer who still in the eyes of most of the generals of brigades and divisions was an engineer? His record had not been brilliant in the field. He was still, in the eyes of combat officers, a staff officer, and I have heard that even in the army today, staff doesn't always look on the line with the utmost admiration, nor does the line regard the staff as the embodiment of infallibility. What did General Lee do? He had not fought with this army at any period of its career. With its favored and esteemed commander disabled, how was he to take the field, to organize these forces, when the enemy was, at that time, but seven miles from their major objective? About as difficult a task he had as faced Meade when he succeeded Hooker on the march into Pennsylvania. Indeed, you would have the precise parallel if, instead of maneuvering into Pennsylvania, General Lee had moved up to the Washington defenses and Meade had taken command in Washington when the city was virtually under siege.

Now, the steps General Lee took at this time, gentlemen, are those that above all others I would like for you to remember. You may face, some of these days in your nation's battles, exactly that problem. What did he do? He did the simple, commonsense things. If you look for any great administrative or grand strategy, so to say, you will be disappointed. He followed the law of common sense, the law of the mind of the soldier. The first step he took was to reorganize the service of supply. The soldiers' rations had been coming irregularly and were wretchedly cooked. The bakers of the army were the offscourings of Company K, the worst men in the army. The first step toward the creation of morale was directed to making the men comfortable. Those words, "making the men comfortable," occur again and again and again in General Lee's orders to his subordinates. Hardships there were, inescapable; dangers that none could avoid; long marches through mud; sultry days under summer suns; wounds, disease, death. That was a part of the lot of the soldier. Under no circumstances, said Lee, are these hardships to be exaggerated by incompetence in the service of supply; whatever can be done to make the men comfortable is a part of the code of *noblesse oblige* of the officer. I believe that stands as true today as it was then.

Secondly, General Lee proceeded to learn his officers and to know their qualities. He had, of course, a small army, a smaller army than some of you gentlemen are destined to command; when he went into action, he had less that seventy-five thousand men. His organization was not of a sort that permitted him to go to his division commanders and sit down and ask them about the qualifications of their brigadiers. He could not go to the brigadiers and ask them about the qualifications of their colonels. There is something in the spirit of a volunteer army that makes that very natural process unpleasant and distasteful. He had to find out for himself. He did it by going from camp to camp. He had no infallible rule, but I will say to you gentlemen who will be in command of troops, that the nearest approach he had to a rule of thumb for judging the competence of an officer was the condition in which he found that officer's camp. Other things being even, he assumed that a good army administrator is going to be a good combat officer. He reasoned in this wise: If a man is not careful in camp, how can we assume that that man will be careful on the field of battle? He denied promotion on one occasion to one of the best of his division commanders because while that division commander, as he said, "was careful in the field," he was negligent in the camp.

Going from camp to camp, meeting these men on terms of simple courtesy, he gradually, though not speedily, acquired a knowledge of the general officers. As the months passed by, he expanded that knowledge to include his colonels. In an army as small as his, it might often happen that an important mission—offensive or defensive—had to be entrusted to a colonel. It was exceedingly desirable that he know his colonels, and he did.

I never come to the war college and speak to you gentlemen, who soon ought to be in regimental commands, but that I cite that upset of the battle of Mine Run. There was a doubtful and difficult maneuver around the flank; it might mean a whole turning operation that would roll up the flank elements of the army. Report of it was brought to General Lee. The first question he asked, knowing there was but one regiment in position to strike, was, "Whose regiment is on that flank?" Many a time in that great and delicate task of judging offensive and defensive power, in which he was a past master, General Lee was guided by the fact that he knew not merely his corps commanders, his divisional leaders,and his brigade chiefs, but he knew his regimental commanders.

The third step he took was equally obvious. During the preliminaries of the Seven Days, he had to lay out a difficult plan of action. He had a small force that was going to undertake a very elaborate turning movement. He needed good logistics, he needed good combat, and he needed better artillery service than he had. Not knowing, by that time, all his officers, he worked on the simple, commonsense, sound rule of entrusting the most difficult or delicate missions to those men who had the best military records. It was common sense, and perfectly simple, and yet again and again in the Federal and in the Confederate armies during the War between the States, a rule utterly disdained.

If you will take Lee's order of battle for the Seven Days, you will find that in every instance, though he sometimes had to make long movements to place the troops where he wanted them, he put the heavy burdens on those men whose records indicated they could be trusted: professional soldiers, tried soldiers, and in the main, Mexican War veterans. Though it still involved shifts of men, he trusted the defensive function to those men of whose offensive ability he was the most doubtful. To whom was entrusted the defensive south of the Chickahominy when he tried to roll up McClellan's right flank north of that river? To Huger, who at that time must have been suffering from arteriosclerosis; to Magruder, who though a good general and soldier, had that fault of excessive excitability on the field of combat. To whom did he entrust combat? To Longstreet, who had fought the rearguard action at Williamsburg, and to D.H. Hill, who had admirably fought the battle of Big Bethel; to A.P. Hill, who was coming up, who had been the best colonel in the army, the best brigadier, and who was then given divisional command. The great test was the flank column. On that flank column depended the success of the whole command, the whole operation. To whom did he entrust it? To whom else than to that magnificent and mysterious man who had swept the valley of Virginia. I don't say that Stonewall Jackson was the greatest strategist of his generation. I think Sherman was a greater strategist. I think Lee was a greater strategist. I think that in cavalry, Forrest was.[3] But I say, as General Lee said when Jackson was dying, "There was the greatest executive officer that the war produced." To him (though this time he failed) General Lee entrusted the turning movement.[4]

Now, you see just three steps in that situation of disordered, if not impaired, morale: Make the men comfortable, reorganize the service of supply, have good administration of the army; learn your men, even down to your colonels; and meantime, if operations must be undertaken, pick the men whose records indicate they can best be trusted.

Now comes in that factor which above all others served most to raise the morale of the Army of Northern Virginia. On the twenty-sixth of June, the army struck at Mechanicsville; the next day the battle was at Gaines' Mill; the third day McClellan had sealed his line most amazingly; the fourth day saw the rearguard action at Savage Station; the fifth day, at Frayser's Farm; the last day, at Malvern Hill. Butternut coats were mingled with blue on every field from Mechanicsville to Malvern Hill, but the army had that greatest of all stimulants: victory. The enemy who had set his watches by the chiming of the Richmond clocks was now huddled under his gunboats at Harrison's Landing. The great tonic of victory had come. All that Lee had done to raise morale was accentuated, accelerated, and glorified, aye, sublimated, by victory!

He always worked on the theory—a sound and valid principle, gentlemen, which sometimes it may test to the utmost your character to apply—that after a campaign or a battle, the removal of the incompetent is just as essential as the promotion of the capable. We talk of what he did to promote the men who shone on these bloody fields: of how he praised Hood, how he put his eye on Pickett, how he remembered even in the shadows of Second Manassas that Longstreet then had not been slow. Aye, he remembered all these things; but let us not forget that in precisely the same way, he removed from the army within one week after the end of these first operations those two division commanders whom he regarded as incompetent. He pursued that all the way through the war.

But, gentlemen, he always removed the incompetents in a manner not to disgrace them publicly. I think he did that because it was his nature. I think he did it because it was his policy. I think he did it because he didn't want to put into the mind of any soldier the fear that error meant disgrace. In the case of some men, if they feel that error in offensive action means disgrace, what is the result on them? It paralyzes them. If I understand aright the mind of General Lee, he said, "I must remove this man, yes. Disgrace him I will not, lest in so doing I paralyze the initiative of another man." A sound rule. He applied it valiantly.

Promotion came, and came quickly. Regrouping came when he took all these brigades and put them under the two men whom he considered the best: Longstreet and Jackson. The morale created at that time carried the army through the Second Manassas campaign, that brilliant operation.

Following Second Manassas came a new test of morale in two ways. I wish to dwell on them only momentarily because they are tests that may come to you. The Confederate army told itself that it fought for the preservation of its homes against invasion. It did not believe in offensive war against the North. The invasion of the North, in the eyes of many Southern soldiers in the ranks (not knowing our modern theories of offensive-defensive), was too like an invasion of the South. Therefore, when the Army of Northern Virginia went into Maryland, a sudden change came over its morale. Never—except of course for Stuart's cavalry, McNeill's partisans, Mosby,[5] and a few others—never was the Army of Northern Virginia as high in morale north of the Potomac as it was south of the Potomac. That was not merely a matter of lesser intelligence, not a matter of more difficult espionage, not a matter of any impairment of the intelligence service; it was a matter that the army itself settled regardless of commanders. It was not at home, and it did not fight north of the river as it had fought on its own soil. That presented a difficult problem, more difficult I think than has been recognized.

In the second place, the morale of the Army of Northern Virginia was impaired in a singular fashion by the Maryland operation. The army had been fighting in the main in a country of soft dirt roads. It was called on to make long marches over the hard stone roads of Maryland. Those marches quickly destroyed the shoes of the men. The men became footsore, and straggling increased tremendously. You wouldn't think, in the abstract, that such a matter as shoes has any direct relationship to morale; but I believe, after such study as I have been able to give it, that if any man were to ask me what did most to hamper Lee's operations in Maryland, I would say first that the army was beyond the Potomac, and second that the army's shoes were worn out. You may face exactly that condition some of these days.

Lee fought that battle of Sharpsburg, and I hope that all of you gentlemen go over that field carefully. The trouble with all of us is that we do not study terrain carefully. As many times as I have been over First Manassas, I have never yet learned all of First Manassas. Every time I go there, I learn something else. Study Sharpsburg carefully. You will find it an example of a segmented battlefield, which raises tremendous problems for any staff.

After the battle of Sharpsburg, Lee came back across the Potomac. The morale of his army was perceptibly impaired. Straggling had been monstrous. For the first time under his command, the army had sustained what the enemy called a definite defeat. The army itself would never admit it; the Army of Northern Virginia never admitted it sustained but one defeat, and that was at a place called Appomattox. At a little place called Appomattox, they admitted there was some reverse that led to a reorientation of their military problem. But that is the first and only time it ever happened.

Lee knew the morale of the army was impaired. What did he do? He at once laid down the good old sound rule. What does a tired man need? Rest. Give it to him. What does a hungry man need? Food. Give it to him. Naked men need clothes and shoes; give them to them. The restoration of the morale of the Army of Northern Virginia after Sharpsburg was fundamentally a question of refitting, rest, and rationing. Now, note this, it may be useful to you sometime: The ration of the Army of Northern Virginia at no time was much better than sufficed to keep a man moving—that was about all that could ever be said of it. Whenever the morale of the army was in any way impaired and the army had been through a difficult operation, what did General Lee do? Regardless of what he had, he increased the ration.

He had no end of quarrels with Colonel L.B. Northrop, the commissary general. One of the most interesting and enigmatical figures in the military of the Confederacy was Colonel L.B. Northrop. General Lee had, in effect, to violate orders and military regulations; but he knew that if in the hearts of those boys there was a feeling that they had been somewhat roughly handled, nothing would restore their self-respect quicker than to line well the inside of their stomachs and the outside of their bodies.

General Lee applied this simple rule for improving the morale of that army; and as a result, after all the straggling at Sharpsburg, that great winter operation to Fredericksburg was undertaken with no straggling. Again, promotion for the worthy, removal of the incompetent; again, a regrouping, this time into two corps; and again—something that he regarded as very important—the removal of the pessimists.

In high command, caution is necessary up to a certain point. When caution becomes confirmed pessimism, it breeds despair, and that ruins morale. General Lee would never keep a confirmed pessimist in command in the Army of Northern Virginia. One of the ablest, technically, of all the division commanders, probably one of the best of all the engineers of the Army of Northern Virginia, was removed because he was too much of a pessimist.

Finally, as we approach the peak of morale, gentlemen, we come to Fredericksburg. Fredericksburg brought the final factor in the army's appreciation of its commander and in the army's development of morale. It was a very precious and a very important thing. Every soldier in the ranks of the Army of Northern Virginia who was not feebleminded was himself a strategist. Every campaign was discussed at every camp fire. The men saw more of battle than is seen now on a front of a hundred miles. They saw Fredericksburg. They noticed that Lee put up his fortifications, his field works. The first field works he directed. They noticed that he exposed his men no more than was necessary. They heard, and heard rightly, that Lee had virtually vetoed Jackson's plan for a night attack because he thought the losses would not be compensated by the gains. Then there dawned on the army this conviction, the final factor in the creation of that army's morale: said the men, in effect, "Marse Robert makes us fight when we must, but he doesn't make us take unnecessary risks and he saves us as much as he can." That became a part of the code of the Army of Northern Virginia. Its effect on morale was incalculable. The men said, when they were called on—even on that July day to storm Cemetery Ridge—"If he asks it of us, if he demands it of us, it is necessary; he wouldn't ask us to do that which was unnecessary or that which was murderous."

There is the final secret of the morale of that great army. It sustained that army in that retreat from Gettysburg, when the very heavens seemed to weep for defeated valor. It carried that army through the shivering, stormy winter of 1863-64, when rations barely sufficed for life. It sustained that army during that terrific strain which began with the crossing of the Rapidan on the fourth of May and swept on and on until the fourteenth of June, with the enemy in sight and in action every day save one. It enabled that army in the operations between the fourth of May and the twenty-first of June to put *hors de combat* a force as large as its own. It carried that army through the killing strife in front of Petersburg. It sustained every junior officer in the ranks.

I noticed Colonel McCabe in the audience as I came in. I will never forget how his father gave us one of the secrets of the morale of the Army of Northern Virginia. His father, captain and adjutant of one of the best artillery battalions in the Army of Northern Virginia, W.J. Pegram's battalion of the Third Corps, went one day to General Lee with a dispatch from General A.P. Hill. A first lieutenant he was then, a boy and no more. He went into the presence of the old man wearied, tired. The old man had no food to offer him, no shelter to give him, but with a spirit that marked him always, with that grave and gallant courtesy, he said to this young lieutenant, "Lieutenant, may I not get you a glass of water?" What a small thing! And yet, old Colonel McCabe, though he became a great savant and a great scholar and bore the honors of many American universities, never to his end could describe that little incident without tears.

Lee, by that spirit of his, kept that army alive; and the greatest tribute to him was not when the battleflags were planted there at Fairview,[6] not when riotous men plunging through the Wilderness like so many devils gathered them at Chancellorsville, not in that supreme hour of the first day at Gettysburg, not even in the Wilderness when always the army was between Richmond and Grant. No, the supreme vindication of the spirit in which that morale was created and maintained came at Appomattox.

My father used to tell me that though they had no rations from the second until they met the trains in Farmville,[7] though they were naked and the artillery was gone, though men fell from exhaustion all around them, they never believed that the Army of Northern Virginia under Lee could be defeated until that night when, with the oaks just tasseling to the spring in the forests of Appomattox, they bivouacked in the road. And then, to the south of them, where the body of the Army of the Potomac was spread, lights against the sky; to the east of them, where that magnificent Second Corps of Humphreys was pursuing, lights against the sky; in front, where Sheridan set his camp fires, lights against the sky. Ringed around on three sides, and only to the north, darkness and the open way. Then, but not until then, did the great work that had been done in the establishment of morale fall to the earth in the face of greater odds. And the supreme word? It was when, with the woe of the army on his heart and the burden of the South in his mind, he rode back through those weeping ranks. And what was the supreme tribute to him? "General, General!" they cried, their voices hoarse from hunger. "General, are we surrendered? General, say the word. Say the word, General, and we'll go after them again!"

Discussion Period

Q. I would like to hear you discuss briefly your understanding of the term *loyalty* as a soldier understands it, as we use it in the military service, and as it might be considered from the viewpoint of morale, and particularly as applied to the attitude of the senior toward the subordinate. We frequently think of it as a force that operates in one direction: from the junior to the superior, where there is also a certain element of compulsion that enters the picture. I would like to hear your discussion briefly of that factor where the element of compulsion does not exist, in other words, the relation between the senior and the subordinate.

A. A very important subject. I am glad you qualified it with the word *briefly* because it falls exactly in line with that famous dictum of General Charles Stern, the adjutant general of Virginia, in dealing with one of the greatest bores in Christendom. A man came one day into the Westmoreland Club, and the general knew that if the man got a hold of him, he was good for an hour. The general was without his watch and he wanted to know the time and he said, "Merriweather, will you tell me briefly the time of day?"

We have a great many examples in the War between the States to illustrate the principle that loyalty is bilateral. Quite often we are, in war, disposed to think, as the officer stated, that it is a unilateral quality, in short, that loyalty and subordination are synonymous. Just as much loyalty is due on the part of the commanding officer to his subordinates as is due from his subordinates to him. In fact, there is a different and a higher, if not a more delicate, moral obligation involved. In the one instance there is the army law; in the other instance is the higher law of *noblesse oblige*. I believe it can be said that with very few exceptions, those officers who have been most mindful of their obligations of loyalty to their subordinates are those men who have received from their subordinates something more than that loyalty which conforms to army regulations.

I could cite two examples in the War between the States that very admirably illustrate that very point. One is given by General Lee himself. General Lee was, in all things, loyal to his subordinates. He was very slow to believe anything unfair, unjust, unkind concerning them. He was so much that way that in this study I am making now, I am having the greatest difficulty in unearthing essential facts concerning some courts-martial, requests for courts-martial, and courts of inquiry. The reason is that when General Lee had settled the issue, he deliberately violated army regulations by destroying papers that needlessly reflected on his lieutenants. All the papers in the great controversy of 1862-63 between Stonewall Jackson and A.P. Hill have been destroyed.[8] I think they were destroyed by General Lee because he did not wish to leave to posterity memorials of a controversy which he thought had been settled, the details of which should not be displayed to the injury of the reputations of those officers.

There were some things that loyalty to his subordinates required of General Lee. One of them was, on all occasions, the relationship of man to man. He never high-hatted anybody. His relations to the humblest courier who came to his quarters were, in courtesy, on a par with his relations to his senior corps commanders. Another thing that he considered imposed upon him by loyalty to his subordinates was to give his subordinates the opportunity of advancement when they deserved it. There is not a single case in the Army of Northern Virginia when General Lee ever denied promotion to any man when that man deserved it and the army law permitted it.

He went to the other extreme. If there were little courtesies that could be shown an officer, General Lee regarded these as part of the code of the general no less than of the officer. Quite often during the winter, it was customary for staff officers and line officers to bring their wives as near the winter quarters as was permitted by regulations. Never did that happen to an officer that General Lee knew that he did not make a call of courtesy on that officer's wife. A beautiful little custom. It involved some hardship on his part, but it gave him the support of the Southern women even more aggressive than the support of the Southern soldiers. Suppose an officer after such a visit would begin to beef that General Lee had not done this or that or the other for him. What would his wife say?

Many other things he considered his loyalty to his subordinates demanded of him.

Some things he considered that if countenanced would be tantamount to disloyalty. One of them was drinking whiskey, which he never regarded other than with suspicion of any officer who drank. If we were engaged in muckraking this morning, I could give you the names of dozens of brilliant officers who lost all their hope because they drank. General Lee said, "How can I trust a man to command others who cannot command himself?" Another thing that he never countenanced, and which he never considered that loyalty, personal friendship or favor should cover, was laziness.

General Lee was not popular with his own staff. That is one instance in which I have not told the whole truth about General Lee in what I have written about him. The heirs of one of his staff officers possess letters in which General Lee is several times condemned vigorously by the staff officer. The staff officer says, "I could love Mrs. Lee, but I'll be damned if I could ever love General Lee." What was the reason? He was a little disposed to be indolent, and laziness General Lee would never countenance. He demanded more of his staff officers than he did of his line officers. He demanded that his staff officers give themselves as fully to the service as he gave himself.

In opposition to that, I can cite the case of General Jubal Early, lieutenant general of the Second Corps in succession to R.S. Ewell, in command of the Second Corps from the thirty-first of May, 1864, until the practical dissolution of the Second Corps following the operations at Cedar Creek and Fisher's Hill. Early had his defects as a soldier. He was one of those men who, in spite of all his training, never acquired a sense of direction. If there was any way by which Early could get lost in moving anything, from a company to a corps, he would get it lost. If there were two roads by which to go, he always would find the longer. He had defects in combat because he was too much disposed to save his reserves too long. He was entirely too much inclined to fight a battle of divisions instead of a battle of corps.

On the other hand, Early had some admirable qualities as a soldier. He had something more than presence on the field of battle. He had the cold courage of the battlefield, that type of courage which somehow gives a man a sharper rather than a duller mind in a day of danger. As a strategist, he was essentially sound. Many strategical combinations proposed by Early at different times would appeal to you as reasonable, that is to say, in a sense they were at once novel but practicable.

The great fault of the strategy of the War between the States, on the part of all save three or four outstanding leaders, was that they never distinguished what was practicable from what was desirable. A soldier who cannot make that distinction will never get anywhere. Beauregard will be wiped completely off the list of great commanders for that reason. He never knew his logistics. If anything looked as though it could be done in the Napoleonic pattern, it would be done.

Early was not that way, however, Early had about him a carping, singularly bitter manner that alienated nearly every man who was under him. Lee, if there was a doubt whether a fault was his or a subordinate's, would always assume it; Early, never. Sometimes his wit was good. You may not be familiar with his great exchange with John C. Breckinridge. Breckinridge had been, as you remember, a candidate for the presidency in 1860. Before that time he had been a great political leader, standing on the principle of the right of slavery in the territories. He fought with Early through a part of the Valley campaign of 1864. Early never forgot that he was a politician, though Breckinridge was a very good soldier. In a very desperate hour—I think it was at Winchester—when Rodes had been killed and the situation was very desperate, Breckinridge was in full retreat. Early met him in the road and said, "Well, General Breckinridge, what do you think about slavery in the territories now?" Always that was his fault: always critical, always cynical, always disposed to demand the utmost and to give the least.

Quite apart from its effect on the army, may I say this to you, that the spirit of loyalty concerning which the officer inquires is something more than loyalty. It is a matter of attitude toward youth; it is a matter of the absence of jealousy; it is freedom from what Ibsen describes in one of his dramas where the man speaks of himself when the younger generation is pushing him to the wall.[9] No man, be he soldier or statesman, is ever master of himself or ever purely happy in his relations with other men until he is willing always to give the other man the benefit of the doubt. Cast out jealousy, and one of the worst shadows disappears from life. That is true of every man.

Q. You say that after each battle or important campaign, General Lee systematically got rid of the inefficient. I happen to be assigned for study the subject of reclassification, which is the job of getting rid of the incompetents after battle. I would like to have you tell how he did it. It appears that outside of General Lee and the Confederacy, we haven't been very successful in doing that in such a way as not to hurt the feelings of the people we get rid of.

A. I can answer that as respects any number of men. The process was virtually the same in every instance. The first example might be Huger; the second, Magruder; the third, Blanchard after the operations at Sharpsburg; and one of the most interesting was that of General Anderson after the battle of Gettysburg. Later in the war you have the instance where he was compelled to rid himself of Early, and you have in the very last phase of the war the case where he rid himself of General Pickett and of General R.H. Anderson. Those two cases, I believe, ought to be ruled out, because at that time the army was in its *extremis*, and General Lee did not apply the technique he ordinarily would have applied.

A good example is Magruder. Magruder had one of the most interesting careers of any man in the army and was one of the most amazing figures. He had some good qualities as a soldier, but he had, in combat, tremendous excitability. That was largely due to Magruder's failure to take adequate rest during a period of strain. He seemed to think it was the duty of a soldier to be always available to superiors or staff officers or anybody else during a period of active operations. He never appreciated what I made bold to call, in one of my lectures at the war college, "fifth-day strain." The result was that during the operations of the Seven Days in front of Richmond, Magruder, I think, had no sleep, save one hour, between the morning of the twenty-ninth of June and the morning of the second of July. It was a terrible period of strain. He became so erratic that a good many people thought he had been drinking. I think the evidence that he was drunk can be disregarded. I don't believe he was drunk. He, however, terribly handled his troops. Left in charge of the rearguard action at Savage Station, he let himself be bluffed off his feet. At Malvern Hill, his misunderstanding of the route was complete, his errors regarding the strategical plan were terrible, and his tactics were frightful—just let his men be slaughtered by brigades.

General Lee had to get rid of him. To do it, General Lee did what, if possible, he always did, that is to say, he kicked him upstairs. He picked out a quiet command in Texas which had about it the glamor of being a departmental command. There had been some talk before the Magruder fiasco that he would be sent to Texas. So when it was over, General Lee said (I am not quoting his exact words, only giving the spirit of them), "General Magruder, I am deeply appreciative of what you have done in this campaign; and I know that if anything went astray, it was not through any fault or lack of effort on your own part; and now, General Magruder, I think that as you have done all you could for the army in the finest spirit, I ought not any longer to deny you that position of great influence and power that the president has deigned to assign you in Texas." He always, if possible, kicked the man upstairs.

He had one fault in that respect that ought frankly to be noted. He was too much disposed to put his incompetents off on other people. That is a common practice, I understand. He didn't, as a rule, pick out a combat command in another army and send the incompetent brigadier there. But if the commander of that army for any reason asked for somebody whom General Lee didn't want, Lee was very quick to let him have the man. There were two or three instances where men whom he had assigned to quiet sectors and commands in the rear were called on suddenly, in the case of raids or unsupported operations, to exercise command. That was true in the case of General Colston, whom Lee relieved after Chancellorsville, relieved him I think unjustly.

But merely kick a man upstairs if you can. Don't kick him too close to any explosives. Don't put him where he may set the house on fire.

Notes

The stenographic transcript of this lecture is filed in the archives of the U.S. Army Military History Institute, located adjacent to the Army War College at Carlisle Barracks, Pennsylvania. The lecture was originally entitled "Methods Employed by General Lee to Maintain Morale in the Army of Northern Virginia."

1. John B. Hood commanded the Texas Brigade from March 1862 to October 1862, when he was promoted to major general and assigned command of a division in Longstreet's First Corps. In the foreword to *Lee's Lieutenants,* Freeman noted that this letter to Hood provided him with the key to the organization of his book: "As this approach was examined, it was apparent that the high command of the Army of Northern Virginia was subject to a constant and heavy attrition—by death, by disabling wounds, by intemperance and by incompetence. The Army always was being built up and torn down. Aside from man power, no aspect of the whole tragedy meant more than "proper commanders"—where can they be obtained? The connecting thread of this book well might be that of the effort to create and to maintain competent senior officers. As they emerged in battle or in administration of the Army, the various leaders could be introduced. If they rose, the scene of their new successes would be the proper

setting for their reappearance. In the event they fell, they could be appraised and committed to posterity. All the while, the Army would be marching and fighting under such leaders as it had at a given moment. Where familiar battles again were described, the viewpoint would not be that of Lee but that of the men executing his orders or making decisions for themselves."

2. The Conscription Act, signed by President Davis on 16 April 1862, provided for the conscription of all white males between eighteen and thirty-five years of age.

3. Nathan Bedford Forrest was a renowned commander of cavalry in the Confederate Army of Tennessee.

4. Jackson was uncharacteristically slow and passive in the battle of the Seven Days: on 26 June he did not turn Beaver Dam Creek as planned, and the army ended up making the attack at Mechanicsville without him; on 27 June he was late in arriving at Old Cold Harbor; on 29 June he failed to support Magruder in an attack on the Union rear guard north of White Oak Swamp; and on 30 June he failed to cross White Oak Swamp in pursuit of the retreating Union army. In the first volume of *Lee's Lieutenants,* Freeman noted that "physical exhaustion and the resulting benumbment of a mind that depended much on sleep probably are the basic explanation of Jackson's inability to meet the demands of the campaign." (It is important to remember that Jackson's army had been ordered to the Richmond front just one week after the last battle of the arduous Valley campaign.)

5. John H. McNeill was one of several Confederate partisan leaders operating in and around Virginia during the war. The most famous of these leaders was John S. Mosby, whose "rangers" frequently attacked Union posts in northern Virginia and Maryland to cut communications and disrupt supply lines. So successful were they in this endeavor that the four counties of northern Virginia nearest Washington became known as "Mosby's Confederacy."

6. Fairview, a ridge overlooking Chancellorsville, was evacuated by the Union artillery in connection with Lee's victory there.

7. Lee's army began its retreat from Petersburg on the "second" of April, 1865. On 7 April the army reached Farmville, and two days later, on 9 April, Lee surrendered to Grant at the village of Appomattox Court House (about 20 miles to the west of Farmville).

8. On 4 September 1862, as Lee's army was marching north into Maryland, Jackson put Hill under arrest for "neglect of duty" in supervising the march of his men. Several days later Jackson released Hill from arrest to permit his participation in the Sharpsburg campaign, in which Hill performed brilliantly. After this campaign Jackson was content to let the matter drop, but Hill requested a court martial. Lee ignored the first request and denied the second (made in January 1863). Hill then provoked a new quarrel with Jackson by insisting that (contrary to common practice) all orders to his staff officers be transmitted through him. Before this issue was resolved, Jackson was mortally wounded at Chancellorsville and Hill was assigned command of the newly established Third Corps.

9. See *The Master Builder* (1892), by Henrik Ibsen.

8

Morale in the Army of Northern Virginia

Lecture of October 27, 1938

Freeman divides this lecture into two general questions. First, why study Lee's methods of promoting morale, and second, what were these methods?

In answer to the first question, Freeman states that Lee's methods are worthy of study for three reasons: first, because Lee faced conditions similar to those that might be faced in future wars; second, because Lee was able to establish, reestablish, and maintain morale; and third, because the nature of the morale established by Lee enabled the South to win the peace.

In discussing Lee's methods of promoting morale, Freeman summarizes these methods in four maxims:

1. *Know your resources, both human and physical.*
2. *Get good officers.*
3. *Be absolutely just.*
4. *Look after your men.*

Following the lecture, Freeman discusses Lee's system of discipline, particularly with respect to courts-martial, and Lee's methods of recognizing superior performance.

My assignment, gentlemen—and I am happy that it is an annual assignment to talk to you on General Lee's methods of inculcating morale—is so vast, so vital, and at least potentially so illuminating to practical soldiers that I try, from year to year, to vary these lectures. During the past year, my experience has been chiefly with General Lee's subordinates. I have tried in one work to look at the army from GHQ. In my next work I shall try to look at the army from corps, division, and brigade headquarters. This latter study has given me some new conceptions of General Lee's methods of promoting morale.

I divide my lecture into two general questions. First, why study General Lee's methods in particular rather than those of some other American commanders? Second, what were General Lee's methods of promoting and sustaining morale?

To the first of these questions I shall try to give a brief answer. First, we want to study General Lee because of three conditions in his career not unlike those we may face in a future war. These three conditions are, first, the fact that he commanded a citizen army that had no basis whatever of professional soldiers. Of course, the United States Army very soon engulfed the few regiments of infantry and cavalry that it had. Nonetheless, as the retreat from First Manassas and as the stand of the Federal right at Gaines' Mill plainly show, the very existence of a nucleus of professional soldiers means a great deal to the morale of an army. Lee didn't have it. Many of you, in case of future war, will have no professional units in your command whatever; you will, in essence, have a citizen army, and that citizen army you will need to discipline and to train by methods somewhat different from those employed with the regular army.

May I stop at this point to say that, if the breed of military historians (of whom I am an unworthy, amateur representative) should pass away before your time of testing comes, do your utmost never to let the United States rely in the slightest on any system of volunteering. In a major war, volunteering will soon have to be supplanted by conscription. The latter method is infinitely the better by every count, if one may read or write the lessons of military history.

Nothing, for example, better explains the bewilderment, indeed, the consternation of British diplomacy today than the fact that the men who should be at the head of the British government are now buried in France. Any system of volunteering takes your best materiel, and if the war is great, it destroys too large a part of that intelligent 50 percent of our civilization on which we must rely for the continuance of our institutions, for the development of our inventions. Germany, France, and Italy did not suffer so greatly in leadership because the casualties in their commands were a cross section of the nation. The casualties in British command, until virtual conscription came into effect, were excessive in the upper classes. If you have a citizen army, do your utmost not to destroy the seed corn of the nation by a system of volunteering.

General Lee's problem would be similar to yours because, in the second respect, he had always an inadequate staff.[1] I think experience in war shows that it is more difficult to train a competent staff officer than it is to train a man for adequate company or regimental command. The most costly mistakes in the War between the States were the mistakes that resulted from defective staff work rather than from tactical error on the part of brigade or division commanders, or even from strategical error on the part of the high command. We may not be able in a great war to build up an adequately trained staff quickly. In that case, we shall need to turn back and study again the methods by which General Lee was able to maintain morale and operate and administer his army in spite of the inadequacy of his staff.

Still again, General Lee's third condition was one that you may meet, because there was the greatest disparity in the efficiency of the three arms of the service during the early period of his command. The cavalry was rancid; the artillery, so far as massed fire went, was almost nonexistent. Think of General Lee having to launch the great offensive of the Seven Days when the artillery of his army was so undeveloped that at no previous time had more than twenty guns ever been used simultaneously in combat on the Confederate side! Think of what that meant. You will find, perhaps, that when you have to command armies, there will be disparity in the arms. For that third reason, it is very necessary, it seems to me, that we look at General Lee and ascertain by what methods he brought up the morale of the artillery and the cavalry to the established and sustained level of the morale of the infantry.

The second general reason why we ought to study General Lee's methods of promoting morale is because he was able to establish, reestablish, and to maintain morale. If you will take his operations from the first of June, 1862, when he assumed command of the Army of Northern Virginia, and pursue them through to the end, you will find that virtually every problem of mass morale that involves an army was exhibited in his career. There was the period of the upbuilding of morale through the operations in Maryland in the fall of 1862. Then came a period of reestablishment of morale after the discovery that the Army of Northern Virginia didn't fight as well north of the Potomac as south of it. That period went through Chancellorsville. Then came a vast and difficult question involved in the second invasion of the North. The whole Gettysburg period might worthily be studied by anyone interested in morale. The next period begins with Bristoe Station and ends with the operations in May 1864. From that time on, there is what I hope will never be paralleled in American history, namely, the maintenance of morale on the part of an army which has lost offensive power. In the winter of 1864-65 you see a final period in morale worthy of study, namely, how can the morale of an army be maintained when its service of supply has broken down and replacements can no longer be had? I think these are considerations worthy of your study.

The third reason of a general character I will reserve for my very last remarks, because this is the most transcendent consideration of them all at this time.

If we should study the methods of General Lee because of the three conditions which you may face and because he was able to establish, reestablish and maintain morale, then what were General Lee's methods? If one, after some study of his career, were compelled to state General Lee's methods of maintaining morale in the Army of Northern Virginia, I think they can be compressed into four general maxims. I may be wrong, but if I am right, I beg you through the whole of your military careers to remember these maxims. First, morale postulates adequate knowledge of all your materiel, human and physical. That is a perfectly commonplace thing to say, but it is a fact that is often overlooked in military operations. Again and again you will find men in divisional command, in corps command, even in army command who do not know their materiel. There is nothing more important, I think, in the whole realm of morale than that the man at the head of a force shall know his personnel as far down the line as he can possibly reach.

The Army of Northern Virginia was not a large army by modern standards. It was an army which in normal operations was about sixty thousand to seventy thousand; it never exceeded eighty thousand men, and in the end it was down to forty thousand effectives. General Lee did not assume command of the army until the greater part of it had been in being for one year. Yet, so diligent was he in this respect, so conscious was he of the importance of knowing his human material, that I believe it is an absolute fact that General Lee knew every colonel in his army. Of course he knew his division commanders, knew them intimately, certainly as respected their qualities of mind; he knew his brigade commanders and he knew his colonels as well. I believe that statement will stand that he knew them, for of all the colonels whom I ever knew who had been in Confederate service, there never was one who did not, in answer to that question, say, "Of course General Lee knew me."

His method in this respect was epitomized by an incident which I always like to call to the attention of soldiers. In the Mine Run operations of November-December 1863, General Lee, having waited three days for General Meade to attack and having found that General Meade considered his defenses too strong, began to plan a turning movement of his own against Meade's entrenched left. With that object in view, he put out his cavalry as far as he could. Very soon word came in that the Federals seemed to be on the move against Lee's extreme right. The first question that he asked was, "Who commands the regiment there?" It was a cavalry regiment, but the first thing he wanted to know in planning the method by which he might meet that turning movement was, who was the colonel of that particular regiment that had discovered this movement? He knew that the outcome of this operation would be postulated on the qualities of that colonel. He wanted to know who the colonel was because, knowing the colonel, he could judge whether he could rely on that man for adequate intelligence and proper dispositions.

In exactly the same way, General Lee studied the offensive and defensive power of his different units. I do not exaggerate and hope I am not guilty of any hero worship when I say that by the fall of 1862, General Lee could gauge, with measurable accuracy, the rifle power of every brigade of his whole army. Many of General Lee's dispositions that confuse students, many of his changes in the order of march, and not a few of his changes in the order of battle may be attributed primarily to his knowledge of the individual units. Nothing, for example, is more illuminating than Lee's careful and constant study of the Texas Brigade. They were his best shock unit, and one may judge the seriousness of the situation, one may judge General Lee's decision concerning where the most effective blow should be delivered or countered, by his disposition of that brigade. Hood's men had to march often and hard, because as that was the crack brigade of the whole army, Lee used it with the greatest care and skill. His one criticism of himself was that he called on the Texans too often to bear the burden of the day.

General Lee's second maxim, never expressed in words but displayed in a thousand instances, could be put in these words: The morale of an army is never better than the average competence of its command; to create morale in an army, start with your officers. In the basic tests of morale, competent officers, of course, are necessary. The labor that General Lee spent to get competent officers in order that he might have vigorous morale passes all man's power of estimation.

In the winter of 1862, General Hood wrote him a letter in which, having recovered from his difficulties at Fredericksburg,[2] he was indulging in grand strategy. He wrote Lee of a plan—and obviously he thought it difficult of execution because he defended it on the ground that the army was "capable of this performance"—and Lee answered, in effect, "I quite agree with you in all that you say concerning the army. There never was such an army; it could go anywhere and do anything if properly commanded." "But," he added, "proper commanders is our great consideration. How are they to be procured?" I repeat that he never assumed that the army's morale could be any better than the average competence of his corps of officers. To that end he labored assiduously.

Every soldier ought to turn to Part 3, Volume 11 of the *Official Records*[3] and to the correspondence that appears in *Lee's Dispatches*, and should study what Lee thought, wrote, and said about promotions in June 1862. He had just then come to command of the Army of Northern Virginia, an army that was very much divided because the old elements of the Army of the Potomac—Johnston's army—thought themselves superior to Magruder's army and to Huger's division.

Lee had three armies, so to say, in one. There had been some casualties, and the increase in the army called for the appointment of new commanders. He had several brigadiers to promote, and there were one or two who, unfortunately, had to be broken. Nothing can be more illuminating than the correspondence between General Lee and President Davis concerning the qualifications of these men. Lee knew he was about to assume an exceedingly difficult offensive which could only be made successful by high morale. He had to have the best men at the head of his army. He was a stiff disciplinarian dealing with his lieutenants—the closer they were to him, the harder he was on them. He was much more insistent in his dealings with Jackson—a thoroughgoing soldier—than he was with men who had come from civil life. He was frightfully hard on his staff. He demanded from them the same standard of performance that he gave to the army himself, and all the way through, busy as he was, he tried to emphasize this fact: Command is never competent unless command is physically and morally fit.

His great difficulty, so far as the physical and to some extent the moral fitness of the high command was concerned, was liquor. He had to deal with one brigadier general, a man who had distinguished himself at First Manassas, who, when he rode about, always had his orderly with him, and strapped conspicuously behind the orderly's saddle was a little barrel of liquor, a small keg, always ready on call of the brigadier. More than one of Lee's ablest men failed because of liquor. He frowned on it, as always he should. In one notable case, when he was urged to promote to divisional command a brigadier general of high competence, he said, "No. No, I cannot trust a man to command others who cannot command himself."

He set, of course, the example of moral and physical fitness, no less in the realm of moral than of physical, and vice versa. He believed, for example, that an officer needed to divert his mind, needed exercise during the period of hard labor at headquarters. The result was that every afternoon, unless his army was actively engaged, he went out and rode; and when he went out, he deliberately disciplined his mind to exclude military problems. He thought he would come back fresh to his task if, when he was out, he thought of anything but command of the army. All of which, gentlemen, is a justification for your golf.

In exactly the same way, General Lee discovered the interesting fact that one hour's sleep before midnight was worth two hours' sleep after midnight, and for that reason, he always went to bed as early as he could. He never minded at what hour he had to arise provided he could go to bed early. By this and other methods, he sought to emphasize the truth that I have stated as his second maxim, namely, that morale is never better than the average competence of command. To create morale, start with your officers.

General Lee's third maxim in the creation of morale could be stated thus: Be absolutely just but respect every individual; promote the competent, remove or render innocuous the incompetent; never seek a scapegoat for error.

Lee, early in his military career, made the great discovery that no matter how well they are trained, no matter how courageous they are physically and morally, some men have a nervous instability which renders them incompetent for high command. Nothing is more illuminating in the study of any military campaign about which we have adequate material than that somber truth. Some men will crack. General Joseph E. Johnston, from the fall of 1861 through the operations at Seven Pines, relied very heavily on a division commander who, by one of the strange quirks of military training, had never been under fire. The man was physically courageous, but when responsibility was placed on him, he cracked. Lee had to deal with men of that type.

He discovered this great truth, and I think one of the most illuminating results of my investigation of his lieutenants, a result I hope to set forth in my new book on them, is this: You have no assurance that a good captain is going to make a good general, but of this you can be absolutely sure, that if he is a good general, he was a good captain. You may take the men who rose in the Army of Northern Virginia and in that magnificent army, that rival body, the Army of the Potomac, and you will find that true. Some men are corking good captains, but their mental limitations stop there. There is no assurance because a man is a good captain that he will make a good brigadier general. But if you take the real soldier, you will find that from the first he is a good officer, whatever the rank he holds. There will never be a great American soldier who, when one looks back over his record, will not be found to have been competent in every rank he held.

Lee had to face that consideration. With the utmost care and interest he watched the competent colonels rise. Take such men as General W.D. (Dorsey) Pender, General John B. Gordon. Those men, when General Lee first had contact with them, were colonels. He promptly promoted both of them to brigadiers and watched them with the greatest care. Despite the difficulties under which he labored, the restrictions imposed upon him regarding the promotion of men, there was no concern he considered more sacred to himself than to see that the competent men rose promptly.

The incompetent men had to be replaced or, as I stated before, had to be rendered innocuous. If a man was not qualified for a combat post, General Lee saw to it as far as possible that that man was not humiliated, that other officers, who might or might not succeed in other posts, were not demoralized by any abrupt demotion. Study, if you will, how General Lee handled Huger, Magruder, Blanchard, Colston, Iverson, O'Neal, McLaws, and others who didn't fulfill his expectations. You will find that he followed this sound rule: I will not keep this man in command if he is not competent, but if I remove him from a post that he is not qualified to fill, I will not needlessly humiliate him, his command, or his people. The diplomacy, the consideration, the suavity with which an incompetent man was removed from brigade or even from divisional command reflected more than General Lee's kindness of heart. He believed that if a man were broken ostentatiously, the effect on the morale of his command might be serious; he wished to protect not only the feelings of the officer but the morale of the men.

I often say to you who may have to deal as brigade, division, corps, or army commanders with men of varying ability, that there is no episode in General Lee's experience much more commendatory than his little colloquy with General Hill when Hill was swearing violently that he intended to break the attack at Snell's Bridge. I shall not go into the episode, but if you are interested in seeing how a wise and great soldier dealt with the human material he had, read that little account that appears in the third volume of *R.E. Lee* about Lee's interview with Hill in May 1864 concerning the operation of Wright's brigade at Snell's Bridge. There is an example for every man to study.[4]

Another, and equally informative, is General Lee's attitude toward General Early during the Valley campaign of 1864. A British officer, Colonel Burne, is just about to issue a new study on Grant, Sherman, and Lee designed, I think, to be an answer to a somewhat familiar book issued not long ago by General Fuller.[5] He makes a very thorough study of Early's Valley campaign and comes to the conclusion that Early did much better than had been supposed. I am glad he said that, because the test to which Early was put at that time was one to which you may be put. Early had a difficult diversion to undertake with a minimum force, and he was man enough to use the means he had and not to be harassing and badgering headquarters with demands for replacements that could not be supplied. I am glad Early at last is vindicated.

Early, however, as you know, gradually lost the confidence of his troops. You will find perhaps in your experience some other general officer who has had that same fate. Read General Lee's correspondence to General Early. He did not attempt, from GHQ, to run Early's Valley campaign. That was impossible. No man can do that. The man who thinks that from GHQ he can handle a detached column with which he is not familiar, over terrain and under circumstances that he does not know, is kidding himself; it can't be done. Lee gave Early the maximum of discretion that he could and admonished him only in those respects that were obviously of importance, for example, not to attempt to fight battles by divisions but to use his whole offensive or defensive power. Early, as commander of an army, in Lee's judgment, still remained at heart a division commander. Study what Lee did. Study how, at the end, when Lee had to replace General Early, he did so with the utmost consideration and in a manner that did not break Early's morale or destroy his position in the eyes of his associates.

Right well did Early requite him. I remember the old general well. I can see him in my mind's eye now, wandering around the streets of Lynchburg with his stiff, long beard, chawing, chawing all the time. His greatest expression of excitement in battle was when he shifted his quid from the right side of his jaw to the left. When that happened, he was probably getting ready to change the flank of his attack. I know that to his last hour, Early's great pride, his chief satisfaction, was not what he had done at First Manassas, not what he had done when it looked as though Sedgwick was going to break him at Fredericksburg—what he was proudest of was the letter in which General Lee removed him from command.[6] A man who could do that is a man whose method of dealing with incompetents is worth studying (not that I would place Early among the incompetents).

On what basis was promotion or demotion determined? What was the rule of it all? I have stated it, perhaps with not sufficient emphasis, in the very first phrase of this third maxim: Be absolutely just. Promotion of the deserving and demotion of the incompetent are both expressions of the same ideal of justice. The method of expression may display all the difference between consideration and the lack of it, between the destruction and the maintenance of the morale of a brigade, perhaps even of a division.

The fourth of General Lee's maxims for the maintenance of morale I cannot state in terms of any single phrase that came from his calm pen. I prefer to state it in terms of his soldiers' own estimate of him. Born, as I was, twenty-one years after Appomattox, I had the privilege, through my father, of knowing literally thousands of Confederate soldiers. I began the study of their campaigns and operations in 1903, when I was seventeen, and I made it my business thereafter to see as many of them as I could. Nothing about them was more thrilling than their attitude toward General Lee. It was not merely because they felt that through him they had touched a great ideal and participated in world-stirring events. That played its part, but that was not the main consideration. When I asked them what, above all, did they observe in General Lee, what about him impressed them most, the answer came back with a uniformity that stirred my heart, as I know it may guide your future conduct. Nearly always the answer was the same: "Ah, General Lee looked after his men."

If I were to epitomize the fourth of his maxims, I would say it was just that: Look after your men. Look after them in respect to their discipline; maintain discipline according to the nature of your human material; discipline is protective, not repressive. Men who go forth without discipline, as you have heard from the time you were freshmen at West Point, are men who never can achieve their utmost either offensively or defensively. There are circumstances under which the best regiment in the world may be slaughtered by an unseen machine gun, but other things being equal, discipline is essentially protective.

General Lee had to inculcate a particular type of discipline because he dealt with a singular army. The Army of Northern Virginia was not, of course, an army of regulars; it never had the spirit of an army that had been called up for universal service. I think the key to the spirit of the Army of Northern Virginia was given me by my old friend Captain John Lamb, who belonged to the Charles City Troop of the Fourth Virginia Cavalry. Captain Lamb, in Congress for many years, had occasionally to go out and exhort the Confederate veterans who were at that time a considerable element of his constituency, and always he would take the occasion to defend the Army of Northern Virginia. "It was," said the captain, "a voluntary association of gentlemen organized and sustained to drive out the Yankees!" That was the whole story; that was his statement. That was the type of discipline with which General Lee had to deal; that, the type of man; and his discipline was shaped to his material.

He looked after his men in the second place by seeing to it that they had the best rations they could get, particularly after hardships. One of the oldest jokes among the Confederates was that the difference between themselves and the Union army was that one was fed and the other was corn-fed. The ration of that army, for a long time, was a pint of unbolted cornmeal and one-third of a pound of Nassau bacon—a horrible ration. As it was often said in the Confederate army, it is perfectly explicable why the Confederates fought as they did: Any man who had that ration would be so mad and so mean that he would fight naturally and without orders from his officers!

General Lee knew the rations were limited. The South never produced enough bacon to supply its population even before the war. He had to keep them on short rations. His logistics were based on rapid movement, which meant he could not have a heavy train. As General Ewell, the greatest marcher of all history, once put it, the road to glory is not covered with much baggage. That is well worth remembering.

When, however, those men had fought and had gone through hardships, no matter what the depletion of his reserve, General Lee saw to it that they were well fed. The best rations the Army of Northern Virginia ever had, subsequent to the first year of the war, were the rations issued after Gettysburg and after the fighting at Spotsylvania. He knew that men who had endured hardships still regarded their stomachs, and he saw to it that when he could, he would feed them as well as possible.

Look after your men with respect to their food!

As you know, the greatest uprising in the Confederate army at any time, the maximum of hate against the Federal army, was evoked at that period, early in 1864, after Grant had assumed command and abolished the system of sutlers. The Confederates were outraged when they heard that Grant had driven out the sutlers. They said it was a violation of all the honors and laws of war, because their chief objective when they attacked was not the Federal army, but it was the sutlers' stores. It is even noted that in the Bristoe campaign, which was conducted with great difficulty, the hopes of the Confederate soldier redoubled when he reached that point on the road to Bristoe where he found the Federals, in their retreat, were beginning to throw away their canteens, blanket rolls, knapsacks, et cetera. He scented plunder and that carried him on.

Look after your men, General Lee said, in respect to reclothing them after defeat. He never said that in words, but he exemplified it time and time again. His heaviest demands on the Confederate quartermaster corps came after Gettysburg. I believe his psychology there was perfectly simple and sound. He knew that after a victory men did not mind rags, but after defeat they were very mindful of them. Reclothe a defeated command and you improve its morale tremendously. If you doubt that, follow the exploits of Hoke's division after it was reclothed, at a time when the Confederate forces around Petersburg were well-nigh naked.

Look after your men, said General Lee, in respect to never marching them unnecessarily. General Lee's logistics, I always think, are worthy of the study of any soldier. No man knows American history who has not studied Lee's logistics at the time of Pope's advance in August 1862. There is a classic example of American logistics. Lee had a system of marching, very definite and very positive. From it he seldom deviated. If a choice comes between marching your men before a battle and marching men after action, always march them before action. Lee never hesitated to march an army all night and fight them all the next day. Why? Because he knew his men. He knew the excitement of battle would sustain them on the day of action even after one night of marching; but once the battle was fought and those men were weary and were suffering a nervous reaction, he never marched them any more than he should.

Some of you interested in military history might like to know that I have recently unearthed the real story of the difference between A.P. Hill and Jackson which arose out of Hill's marching orders in August 1862. We recently acquired the Jackson manuscripts which were preserved by Mrs. Jackson because they were a little too intimate to be made public, and in them are Jackson's detailed charges regarding Hill. All I said about Jackson's allegations that Hill did not live up to the letter of his marching orders is there fulfilled.

Never march your men unnecessarily. That is the voice of Lee, as he speaks to you from the past. Rest your men often.

As some of you may know, I have been making a study for a number of years, incidental to other labors, to develop my theory of the fifth-day fatigue. The basis of that theory is that almost without exception, if soldiers are given even five hours' sleep in twenty-four, they are good for active combat until the fifth day. On the fifth day, so far as my study shows, with almost uncanny certainty they will crack. I had my key to that very largely from General Lee's own marching policy, from his own rest orders. General Lee never, so far as I can recall, marched his men on the fifth day. There may have been one or two exceptions. If there were, they were necessary. But he knew the limitations of the human material, and there, as in everything else, he exhibited that maxim, Look after your men.

Finally, General Lee had this corollary to that particular theory: Look after your men; look after their discipline; give them the best rations that you can, especially after hardship; reclothe them after defeat; never march them unnecessarily; rest them often; and perhaps most important of all, remember that they are individuals, remember that they vary, as human beings must and will.

One of the most charming pictures of all that we have of General Lee, given in that admirable book of Worsham's,[7] a book that ought to be read by every soldier who wishes to study what can be done with the average man in the army, relates to General Lee's march from

Spotsylvania. General Lee was by the roadside. Worsham's regiment happened to pass. Out of the regiment, one man broke ranks. An old and perhaps a feebleminded man, a dull-witted man, went out of the line of march, went over to General Lee, and, putting his musket in one hand, he leaned over Traveller's neck[8] with the other and engaged General Lee in close and intimate conversation. I wish someone would paint that scene and hang it here in the war college, because it is a constant warning to brass hats. Remember that after all, he is a human being, and that he is the better soldier if you recognize his individuality.

That dated back a long way with General Lee. It was exemplified in one of the big rows he had at West Point when he was superintendent. He said, "I have always regarded the cadets at West Point not as soldiers in the ranks but as individual gentlemen whose wishes and dislikes should be respected as far as is compatible with discipline." That is a sound rule.

Look after the men by remembering that they are men.

One day on the Rapidan, General Lee found a man snooping around his headquarters tent. Like almost all the soldiers at that time, he was unshorn and perhaps looking much older than he was. Lee happened to come up, dismount, and enter his headquarters tent, and found this man looking around, trying to look through the closed flap of the tent. General Lee said, "Walk in, Captain. I am glad to see you." "I ain't no captain, General Lee. I is just a private." "Walk in, sir. If you aren't a captain, you ought to be." Maybe he ought not to have been; maybe he was not qualified to be; but that respect for the individual was at once the foundation and the culmination of that great maxim, Look after your men.

When I opened, I said there were three reasons why we should study Lee's methods of inculcating morale. I beg that I might save the last of them for my closing word. My reason is this: We face today in this troubled world the most strict economic law of national discipline that we have seen since Roman times. Never was man subjected, since the days of the Roman legions, to the sort of discipline that he today must endure in Germany. The reason for it is, I believe, the belief of the National Socialist leaders that from iron discipline will come national morale, demonstrated in industrial achievement and in the end by military success. Whether that assumption is justified or not, who can say? We don't know. Unless human nature has changed, this much we do know: While that discipline, while that morale in wartime may in the initial stages of operations give the German army a superiority, the reaction after the war from that iron discipline is bound to be cataclysmic in its destruction. Germany may build up an army and conquer the world, but the National Socialists will never change human nature. The army may win a war, but an army so disciplined, so trained, will never remain at that high pitch during the period that always brings postbellum reaction. It may be a great army in the field, but it will explode in case of another German defeat. I believe it will explode in case of another German victory.

Be that as it may, that is not the discipline that we can call the discipline we should maintain in America.

The great lesson of Lee's efforts to create and sustain morale, gentlemen, is shown not only in what the Army of Northern Virginia did in the field but in what the Army of Northern Virginia did after the war. Lee's methods of obtaining morale did not and could not succeed in winning the war. They could and they did succeed in winning the peace.

It was my privilege as a lad, in 1896, to see the great muster of the Army of Northern Virginia as it came back to Richmond. The army then was about the age of the average lieutenant colonel in the United States Army—no longer boys. There was Longstreet, there Gordon, there Hampton, there Fitz Lee,[9] Stephen D. Lee,[10] division commanders, not a few brigade commanders; almost a third of the army; but above all, there were the men who had fought. Were they proud of their association with the Army of Northern Virginia? Aye, they were! Did they lift their heads and did their eyes shine again when they said, "Yes, I followed Lee"? But what was the great fruit of their victory? What they did at Chancellorsville? How far they went at Gettysburg? How long they sustained Grant's overwhelming offensive after May 1864? No. Lee's methods of obtaining morale are vindicated because Lee's methods enabled the South to keep its self-respect, to win back its rights, and to turn a wilderness into a place of pleasantness.

Discussion Period

Q. The question of the use of courts-martial in maintaining discipline might have something to do with the subject of morale. I would be glad if you would comment on General Lee's application of courts-martial or the question of discipline as it affects morale.

A. That is very important. I am glad that you mentioned it, because so far as I know I have never written anything about it, and it is a subject of large potentialities.

In the first place, General Lee went into command of the Army of Northern Virginia with an utter distaste for courts-martial. The reason was that he had served on so many himself. For three years of his life, after he became a lieutenant colonel with the Second Cavalry, he had to spend at least half of his time as a member of courts-martial. He didn't like them and didn't believe they had very good results. He may have felt also that there was something wrong with the American system. I expect he was guided to some extent by the proceedings in the case of Robert S. Garnett.

Major Robert S. Garnett, of the Eleventh Infantry, I think it was, was in Texas, and he was ordered by General W.S. Harney to go up the river and disarm certain American citizens who were suspected of slipping over the line and joining a group of Mexican rebels. Major Garnett flatly refused to obey the orders on the ground that it was not the duty of the army to interfere with the affairs of individuals when martial law had not been declared. He was brought before a court-martial in Ringgold Barracks in 1852, and a very notorious court-martial proceeding followed. The army reeked with it. The result was the acquittal of Major Garnett, who at his own expense, for his further vindication, had the proceedings published. The government realized the court-martial in that case had been so unjust and unreasonable that Garnett received a little honor in compensation: he was made commandant of cadets at West Point at once, rather a step up.

That shook the faith of the army a lot; that court-martial brought the whole question of courts-martial into the arguments of men.

Lee had an utter distaste for them. When he came to command of the army, he realized that delinquents had to be handled someway; but he didn't believe that it was the policy of wisdom to take the time of officers when they were at leisure and hold courts-martial weeks or months after the event took place. He felt that if you are fighting a campaign, you cannot stop and take the number of officers required by army regulations and hold courts-martial—fighting is a more important duty. General Lee found that the delay of courts-martial was a very serious matter and that the employment of active officers on courts-martial duty disorganized their commands. He said that it was not fair to a man to cite him under charges and then wait months for those charges to be acted upon, and that a better system must be found.

Therefore, at his insistence, the Confederate Congress finally organized what were known as military courts; that is to say, a tribunal was set up for each corps, and invalid officers were assigned to those military courts. Those officers travelled with the army and held court just as precisely as three judges would hold court. Army regulations were taken care of and judge advocates were present in the usual form, but that military court was substituted for the old court-martial. Lee said the results were very satisfactory. It gave men a quick trial and did not disorganize their command for any length of time, and it didn't take the time of officers who were needed with the troops.

As for courts-martial themselves, Lee cared little for them and didn't have them unless he had to. Never, in his whole career, did he order an officer to a court-martial or court of inquiry. That was his rule.

Jackson, of course, had somebody under court-martial all the time. He didn't feel happy unless he had one court-martial going.

Q. A few years ago, General Summerall, then chief of staff, gave a lecture at the war college on leadership during which he made the statement that the greatest reward for a soldier is recognition by his leaders. Of course, we know many great leaders have followed that maxim, notably Napoleon, who gave recognition by promotion on the field of battle, citations in orders, and so on. Would you tell us how General Lee followed that maxim?

A. He did it under the greatest difficulties. The system of promotion in the Confederate army was, on the whole, the worst in the world, bar absolutely none. It was worse, if possible, than the system now prevailing in the United States Army.

Soldiers were regarded by the Confederate government as militia of their state brought into the field, that although they might be Confederate volunteers they were, after all, militiamen, and if the laws of the state provided that the officers of militia should be elected by their men, President Davis insisted that that should apply in the Confederate service. Just think of that! The Confederate army was reorganized and elections were held during the whole of the preliminaries of the siege of Yorktown, during the retreat, and almost all through the Seven Days. In 1861, a North Carolina regiment became so interested in the election of a colonel that it held a poll for seven days and only elected the colonel at the end of the seven days. That was a terrible system.

Once a colonel of that sort entered the army and commanded a regiment, he was entitled to seniority in the choice of brigade commander. That went so far down the line that Confederate army regulations actually required that in case of a vacancy in junior second lieutenant grade, he had to be chosen by an election held in his own company.

General Lee was unable to promote men on the field for gallant conduct. He had absolutely no power to interfere with the system or to promote for valor. There was a regulation put out in 1864 that did permit it, but it came too late.

What did General Lee do about it? He made the best of the law that he had and in the end found it worked very well. If a man deserved command of a brigade and was not in line for command of his own brigade, Lee frequently would avail himself of the law under which he could make temporary appointments and name that man to command some other brigade. In the Confederate service, there were always a number of vacancies. As a brigadier, you might have been wounded at Fredericksburg or taken prisoner; so long as you were wounded and not declared disabled, anyone who took command of your brigade would be only an acting brigadier. When you came back, it was still your brigade. It was a bad system. Lee had the vacancies and would always fill them, if possible, with meritorious officers who deserved promotion. He would get around army regulations by saying that it was a temporary appointment.

Again, as late as 1865, if he had a man who deserved command of a brigade and he could not get it for him any other way, Lee would shift his regiments around so as to create a brigade for him. He did that in 1864 in the case of a division. General Gordon had distinguished himself in the Wilderness, and Lee wanted to make him a division commander. To do it he shifted half a dozen brigades.

If he could not give them the rewards of promotion, he gave them other rewards that were dear to their hearts. For example, he was very chary with compliments in official reports and very slow to speak in loud praise of any man unless it was a man who could only be kept in high morale by praising. Jeb Stuart was such a man. Lee kept him steamed up by giving him an amount of praise he would never think of giving to Jackson.

With others, he had the subtlest little attentions that were regarded in the army as recognition as much to be cherished as promotion. Colonel McCabe's father well illustrated that. He was a great scholar of high distinction after the war. There is the picture of the man, asked which of all the honors in his life that he cherished was the greatest. "I went," said he, "to General Lee's headquarters—it was during the Spotsylvania campaign—and I was very dusty and very thirsty. I rode to headquarters with a dispatch from my brigade commander. I went to General Lee's headquarters; he admitted me. He said, 'Lieutenant, sit down, sir.' I sat down while he read the dispatch. Afterward he looked up at me and said, 'Lieutenant, I see you are weary. Will you permit me, sir, to get you a drink of water?' With that he got up, went to his bucket, took his dipper, and brought me a drink of water which I received from his own hands. If he had made me a colonel that day he could not have pleased me more."

There was a big fight on the north side of the James in which General Butler distinguished himself. General Butler was on Lee's left, and Lee had to throw him quickly to the right and ordered him to come by headquarters. He couldn't do anything to promote Butler for his fine conduct in the field, but when Butler came to the headquarters, General Lee had just received from a friend in Richmond a nice pan of fresh rolls. As Lee received Butler and thanked him for his action, he said, "General, as you go on your journey today, it would honor me greatly, sir, if you took this pan of rolls with you to refresh yourself on your journey." If he had made Butler a major general then and there, he would not have been any more pleased.

There were hundreds of other ways by which he met that system of promotion. He promoted competent men as fast as he could and sought, within the regulations, to recognize merit when the law did not permit. When that could not be done, he tried by personal kindnesses and expressions of gratitude and courtesy to show men that he appreciated their service.

Notes

The stenographic transcript of this lecture is filed in the archives of the U.S. Army Military History Institute, located adjacent to the Army War College at Carlisle Barracks, Pennsylvania. The lecture was originally entitled "Methods Employed by General Lee to Maintain Morale in the Army of Northern Virginia."

1. For a discussion of Lee's staff, see Appendix I-4 in the first volume of *R.E. Lee.*

2. During the battle of Fredericksburg (13 December 1862), Hood misjudged the strength of the Union assault on Jackson's corps and consequently failed to deliver an effective attack on the Union flank (as Longstreet had ordered him to do).

3. *The War of the Rebellion: A Compilation of the Official Records of the Union and Confederate Armies* was prepared under the direction of the secretary of war and published by the Government Printing Office in 69 volumes during the period 1880-1900. In the introduction to *Lee's Dispatches,* Freeman noted "the high standard of accuracy set by this monumental publication." "The Records," he continued, "have, of course, been condemned by many writers as the embodiment of everything unscholarly and unscientific in historical documents and they undoubtedly suffer from a rigid arrangement that separates, sometimes by volumes, related papers of interest and importance. The Records also suffer from an index which is the despair of beginners. But with all these faults, and others that might be named, the Records are surprisingly accurate and surpassingly complete."

4. Freeman also discusses this episode in detail in his lecture to the Army War College of 26 October 1939 (see chapter 9 of this collection).

5. Alfred H. Burne was the author of *Lee, Grant and Sherman: A Study in Leadership in the 1864-65 Campaign* (New York: Charles Scribner's Sons, 1939). Freeman wrote the introduction for this book. J.F.C. Fuller was the author of *Grant and Lee* (New York, 1933). In the bibliography of *R.E. Lee,* Freeman describes this book as written "by one of Grant's admirers."

6. This is the letter, dated 30 March 1865 and taken from Early's *Autobiographical Sketch and Narrative of the War Between the States* (Philadelphia, 1912):

General,—My telegram will have informed you that I deem a change of commanders in your Department necessary; but it is due to your zealous and patriotic services that I should explain the reasons that prompted my action. The situation of affairs is such that we can neglect no means calculated to develop the resources we possess to the greatest extent, and make them as efficient as possible. To this end, it is essential that we should have the cheerful and hearty support of the people, and the full confidence of the soldiers, without which our efforts would be embarrassed and our means of resistance weakened. I have reluctantly arrived at the conclusion that you cannot command the united and willing co-operation which is so essential to success. Your reverses in the Valley, of which the public and the army judge chiefly by the results, have, I fear, impaired your influence both with the people and the soldiers, and would add greatly to the difficulties which will, under any circumstances, attend our military operations in S. W. Virginia. While my own confidence in your ability, zeal, and devotion to the cause is unimpaired, I have nevertheless felt that I could not oppose what seems to be the current of opinion, without injustice to your reputation and injury to the service. I therefore felt constrained to endeavor to find a commander who would be more likely to develop the strength and resources of the country, and inspire the soldiers with confidence; and to accomplish this purpose, I thought it proper to yield my own opinion, and to defer to that of those to whom alone we can look for support.

I am sure that you will understand and appreciate my motives, and no one will be more ready than yourself to acquiesce in any measures which the interests of the country may seem to require, regardless of all personal considerations.

Thanking you for the fidelity and energy with which you have always supported my efforts, and for the courage and devotion you have ever manifested in the service of the country,

I am, very respectfully and truly
Your ob't servant,
R. E. Lee,
Gen'l.

7. John H. Worsham was the author of *One of Jackson's Foot Cavalry* (New York, 1912). In the bibliography of *Lee's Lieutenants,* Freeman describes this book as "among the best of personal narratives; written with much care and a sound memory."

8. Traveller was Lee's primary mount throughout the war. In his book entitled *Recollections and Letters of General Robert E. Lee* (New York, 1904), Lee's son Robert remembers Traveller as he appeared in the autumn of 1862: "He was a handsome iron-gray with black points—mane and tail very dark—sixteen hands high, and five years old. . . . He was never known to tire, and though quiet and sensible in general and afraid of nothing, yet if not regularly exercised, he fretted a good deal. . . ." For a charming story of Lee and the war as told through the eyes of Traveller, see Richard Adams' novel *Traveller* (New York: Alfred A. Knopf, 1988).

9. Fitzhugh Lee, a nephew of Robert E. Lee, was a general of cavalry in the Army of Northern Virginia.

10. Stephen D. Lee was a colonel of artillery in the Army of Northern Virginia and later commanded a division in the Confederate Army of Tennessee.

9

Morale in the Army of Northern Virginia

Lecture of October 26, 1939

This lecture is similar in structure and content to the one given a year earlier. Freeman begins by citing four reasons for studying Lee's methods of promoting morale: first, the numerical inferiority of Lee's forces; second, the fact that these forces consisted of both conscripts and volunteers; third, the inadequacy of Lee's staff; and fourth, the disparity in efficiency between the infantry, the artillery, and the cavalry.

Freeman then proceeds to discuss Lee's methods of promoting morale in terms of the same four maxims set forth in the earlier lecture:

1. *Know your resources.*
2. *Get good officers.*
3. *Be absolutely just.*
4. *Look after your men.*

In concluding this lecture, Freeman adds a fifth maxim: Put your trust in God. As an expression of this maxim, Freeman recalls Lee's favorite psalm, which begins with these words: "Blessed be the Lord my strength: who teacheth my hands to war, and my fingers to fight."

It is always a great pleasure to come back to the successive classes at the war college. My acquaintance with the American army is of sufficient duration to make it possible, I think, for me through the years to judge something of the general level of the army command. It is gratifying and reassuring beyond words to see that an army which always had outstanding men now, it seems to me, attains to its highest intellectual level ever; and that is no small element of American security.

The greatest intellectual asset of this army of ours is, I think, its broad intellectual curiosity. The army today does not accept—it questions. Curiosity has taken the place of what might, in an earlier day, have been described (not unjustly) as complacency. Research has superseded reminiscence. The army looks forward, not backward; yet the army does not neglect the historical approach.

Those of us whose field is that of military history are, I hope, reasonable in our judgment of what we have to offer. Any student of military history who pretends at the same time to be a tactician is, of course, a charlatan. We consider the fundamental truth of the great Napoleonic maxim that strategy never changes, but tactics change every ten years. We do not pretend that either a constant historical approach or the endless study of the same problem is in itself desirable. I think the Ecole de Guerre, at one time, went too far in studying the doctrine of the Napoleonic offensive. There were other things that should have been studied, and I think the campaign of 1914 was, in some sense, a price that had to be paid for the theory of the offensive from the beginning. Certainly the voice of old experience, the counsel of old leaders, is a part of the historical approach that no soldier can neglect; and nothing in all the realm of military experience can, I believe, mean more to the American army at this time than the studies which at this stage of your year's work here you are making of morale.

Your commandant has selected, among others whose methods of promoting morale are to be studied, General Robert E. Lee. In so doing he has been wise, I think, and for reasons that are quite obvious. General Lee had an army numerically inferior throughout the whole four years of his operations. Never did he face his adversary in equal strength.

General Lee had, likewise, the great and singular disadvantage of trying to combine conscripted with volunteer forces. Conscription in the South did not become effective until the beginning of the operations of the Seven Days. The law was passed in March 1862, but it did not begin to bring men into the ranks until June of that year. General Lee had, therefore, a diminishing force of first-line volunteers who had as their replacements conscripts more or less willing—less willing, I should say, than the average man who would be called now under a national draft. How to sustain the original high morale of the volunteers when he was filling the ranks with conscripted replacements was, of course, in itself a very important difficulty that had to be overcome.

In the same way, I think, your commandant has decided that General Lee should be given you as the example of the efficacy of high morale because General Lee, throughout the war, had to deal with an inadequate staff. On that point, gentlemen, might the voice of historical study be allowed to say this: You can never tell who is going to be an efficient officer until the test comes; some will always crack, some will always disappoint. But, with the exception of those officers who have to deal with weapons of a highly technical character, this certainly does seem to have been the experience of the United States: that the training of competent staff officers is a more difficult task than the training of competent combat officers. Whether that is universally true I do not know, but the old story of our past wars shows again and again far more casualties the result of inefficient staff work than the result of incompetent leaders in action. I believe I can justify that statement by a hundred examples in the War between the States.

When General Lee, therefore, had, with an improvised staff, to infuse a high spirit into this dual army of his, you can see the magnitude of the task that faced him.

He had, furthermore, great disparity in the efficiency of the three arms of the service. His infantry has been described by Swinton—and I think not unjustly—as the "incomparable infantry of the Army of Northern Virginia." His artillery was never as good. His cavalry, though spectacular in its performance, had steadily to deal with a decline in the horse supply, which little by little reduced the mobility of that arm. General Lee was never able to view the problems of morale in terms of an equal efficiency of all arms. Infantry? Yes, magnificent! It showed that quality through the Seven Days; it showed that quality on that long, dusty, stifling march through Thoroughfare Gap; it showed it again in Jackson's movement to the left at Chancellorsville; and above all, it showed it in that great charge on the third day at Gettysburg. General Lee himself said that if he made a mistake at Gettysburg in ordering the charge against the Federal center on the third of July, it was a mistake due primarily to his belief that his infantry could do anything. His artillery never had ammunition, never had fuses, and seldom had ordnance equal to that of the opponent.

These are some of the reasons, I think, why General Lee's methods of inculcating and restoring morale are worthy of your study. There are dozens of other reasons that might be given if our time sufficed.

Lee's methods of promoting morale can best be approached by dividing them, roughly, into two periods. These could be divided again so that they would make five, but I think two will illustrate the point. He assumed command of this army on the first of June, 1862, at a time when its ranks were primarily those of volunteers. He steadily raised the morale of that army, despite the fact that his replacements were, in many instances, unwilling conscripts, until he had passed through the Gettysburg campaign. From the time of the Gettysburg campaign, the morale of the army called for special treatment. The disparity in numbers had become so great that General Lee could not rely as much as he had on the offensive. He had steadily to sustain the morale of his army at a time when little by little it was revealed, even to the men in the ranks, that the fight was hopeless.

So you may assume him as having these two specific periods. First, that of raising the morale of the army for the great offensive he undertook, having started in the conditions I have described.

Thereafter, as the offensive power of the army waned, the necessity became greater of maintaining the morale through the long and difficult period of trench warfare in front of Petersburg, and at a time when the soldiers were subjected to many pleading letters from home and to all the demoralizing influences of proximity to great cities.

How did he do it? There is no mystery about it, gentlemen. You don't have to search through long and complicated reports, nor do you have to examine the specific performances of individual commands in crucial positions in critical actions. The principles of morale are fundamentally simple, are sound, and I am happy to think they are applicable by every commander, regardless of the size of his force. Those of General Lee I usually have put in the form of four maxims. This morning I want to add a fifth, which is, in some sense, a summary and an epitome of all the others.

See, as I progress, the simplicity of these maxims, the soundness of his principles of morale. There is no more mystery to this than there is to the man who exemplified it. His, fundamentally, was a simple soul, and in all his operations where human material was involved, his approach was simple. There is nothing Freudian about the approach of Lee to the great psychological questions of morale.

His first maxim was this: Morale postulates adequate knowledge of your human material. That is fundamental. Know your men. Here we have a singular contrast between General Jackson and General Lee. This morning, coming up on the train, I was carrying on my studies of the campaign of 1862 and was reading over once again the reports of the battle of Cedar Mountain, August 9, 1862. Jackson went into that action with one of his brigades under a colonel and with none of the regiments of that brigade under a colonel. One or two were commanded by majors, the others by lieutenant colonels—casualties were responsible—and it never concerned Jackson in the slightest. His theory was, Do what I tell you. Lee was not content to have the supreme realm dominate the army. That was necessary for the strategic plan, but when it came to the field of action, there, in his judgement, the human equation entered. Then, it was necessary that he know his men. And he knew them. He knew his colonels. Of course, he knew every peculiarity of the temperaments of Jackson, Longstreet, A.P. Hill, Dick Anderson, and Early. He knew the division commanders, the brigadiers, but he knew the colonels as well; and on the basis of his knowledge of human material, he based his appeal.

One of the most revealing passages of all came at the end of November 1863, when General Meade launched on the Rapidan that singular campaign that we call Mine Run. He had maneuvered his left and was facing west. Far southward, up Mine Run, the Confederate cavalry was screening the Confederate right and was conducting reconnaissances in force behind the left of the Federals. There suddenly developed a rather complicated situation on the extreme Federal left. The question then came up, What shall we do? The first question General Lee asked was, "Who commands that regiment?" He was speaking of the flank element. Small as the force was, he wanted to know which of his colonels was there, because in the belief that he knew his men, he then could judge pretty well what he needed to do.

In exactly the same way, it was on his knowledge of his human material that General Lee based his remarkable confidence in judging the firepower of his different combat units. Quite often, when Lee is moving into position, bringing up his forces, you will see that he might hold a division, certainly a brigade. In so doing, he might lose an hour or two hours in order to bring a certain unit to a certain point. It might be no more numerous than the others, but he wanted that unit there because he knew its offensive and defensive strength. He could not have known that had he not known fundamentally his human material.

If you will study the campaigns of the Army of Northern Virginia, you will find that when General Lee had time in which to arrange his order of battle as he desired it, he always had his strongest offensive units at the point of thrust. If he was on the defensive, he always placed those units he knew to have high defensive power at the point where he expected the thrust of the enemy. I don't know of more than three or four deviations from that. One of the most notorious, of course, is that of Bloody Angle. At that time he had to place his offensive corps at a point where, by preference, he would have put his defensive corps. That is to say, he put Ewell in there because he (Ewell) took up that line as he sideslipped from the left; whereas in normal circumstances, General Lee would have preferred that position be held by the First Corps, which at that time was under the command of Richard H. Anderson.

If this particular thing interests you, if General Lee's knowledge of his men as a basis of morale intrigues you, follow the story of the Texas Brigade. Ah, those Texans! The Grenadier Guards of the Army of Northern Virginia, Hood's Texas Brigade! Just the day before yesterday a man came into my office with shining face and said, "I think we have it." I knew immediately of what he was speaking. He was speaking of the possibility of our buying and presenting to the United States government the field of the Widow Tapp, there in the Wilderness of Virginia. I have always wanted to buy that and, with the cooperation of other students of the war, to present it to the United States government, because it was in that field, on the morning of the sixth of May, 1864, that that magnificent blue line began to filter westward out of the woods. Hancock's splendid troops, well led and well handled, and up the little ravine to the north of the Widow Tapp's they began to steal their way in a most cunning fashion. The fire started. Presently, out of the woods came the veterans of Wilcox and of Heth, driven by that tremendous fire. In front, Poague's battalion of artillery, soon to be left isolated; the whole of the Confederate right in the air. Lee drew back. Heth and Wilcox passed through the oncoming line of the First Corps. (Never was there a finer example of the manner in which an advancing column opened its ranks to let retreating troops pass through.) And then, just at the moment when it seemed it was not possible for Poague to hold for another round, there began to come out on the field of the Widow Tapp the leading brigade of Longstreet's First Division. Lee, turning around, said to them, "Who are you boys?" They said, in their excited drawl, "We are Texas boys!" And that old man, who so seldom let his feelings get the better of him, took off his hat and, lifting himself in his saddle on old Traveller, cried, "Hurrah for Texas!" And in another half hour that brigade had gone into that line and had stabilized it with casualties of 50 percent. Why did he say, "Hurrah for Texas!" Because from the day at Gaines' Mill to that hour, he knew he had never called on the Texas Brigade that it had not conducted a glorious offensive. To Senator Wigfall[1] he wrote in distress, "Can't you recruit my Texans? I have to call on them too often."

General Lee's second maxim—although he never framed it in so many words—was this: The morale of a command is never better than the average competence of the command; to create morale, get good officers. You say, why that is an ABC. Of course it is. But to get them, to promote them, to replace them—ah, that is the problem of the high command!

In 1863, General John B. Hood, absent wounded, indulged himself in some strategic suggestions to the commanding general. He was a division commander and wrote directly to GHQ and to the commander in chief. He made various proposals for an advance. General Lee, in his own handwriting, sat down and wrote him what he felt of it, what he thought of Hood's plans, and then he said, "Yes, I agree with you that our army can do anything and go anywhere if we have competent officers. How to get them is the problem."

He watched them. He never let a campaign pass that he didn't review, certainly with the division commanders and in many instances with the brigadiers, the performance of the different officers in their commands. Although he had no authority to promote on the field for valor and had to confine himself and conform his action to the most unreasonable laws covering promotion, he never failed to look for the competent man; and having found the competent man, he sought as rapidly as he could to advance him.

How many instances of that come to mind! Nothing, gentlemen, more surprises the military historian than to follow the trail of competence. Take, for example, the first men who occur to mind: W.D. Pender and John B. Gordon. Pender was a captain in the United States Army in 1861. He resigned to become colonel of a North Carolina regiment. The first time he was ever in action was in the turning operation Franklin undertook on the sixth of May, 1862, at a place we call Alban's Landing.[2] Pender went in that day; the handling of his regiment was perfect. The next time you see him is at Seven Pines; the same splendid behavior; he was promoted to brigadier general. Then, at Seven Days, fighting like a tiger in the swamp in front of the White House, following fast down the Darbytown road, and, at Frayser's Farm, throwing his brigade so deep into the ranks of McCall's division that it could scarcely be extricated, even though it was far in advance of the main line of attack. Competence—shown from the first, observed everywhere, and watched by Lee with the utmost enthusiasm.

John B. Gordon, exactly the same way, started as a captain. Caught at Seven Pines with his right flank in the air, he changed his front, faced an attack from his flank, carried his regiment back, and followed in perfect discipline. He fought at Malvern Hill until his flag was shattered, and one could trace the line of his brigade at the very forefront by the West house. Again, at Sharpsburg, in the Bloody Lane—only one little brigade left there—Lee riding up and down the front, passing Gordon, and Gordon saying, "Yes, sir, we will stand," and stand he did.

Just on his left were the Twenty-seventh North Carolina and the Third Arkansas, who filled that gap. The English language, even in the glorious days of General Hunter Liggett,[3] never presented such superlatives of profanity as when General Longstreet came down and asked Colonel Cooke of the Twenty-seventh North Carolina if he could hold his position. He did. Another man who was watched from the first and followed through. Competence—competent officers mean competent armies.

I might cite a hundred instances. Incompetence, laziness, and plain stupidity never hurt the Army of Northern Virginia as much as did intemperance. Lee had to fight liquor just as hard as he ever had to fight Meade.

General Lee's third maxim was, Be absolutely just but respect every individual; promote the competent, remove or render innocuous the incompetent; and never seek a scapegoat for error. I am not sure but that the last of those points is as meaningful as any of the others. You can read through Lee's reports, from Mechanicsville to those last tragic words written under the dripping leaves of those oak trees at Appomattox, and you will not find that he blamed an individual. If there was failure, he stated the fact, but he never made a scapegoat. He was not a Pope, who blamed a Fitz-John Porter.[4] No! When he went out in the red backwash of that third day at Gettysburg and saw that magnificent division of Pickett's reduced by 70 percent, when Wilcox came up weeping and Pickett was bewildered and the men were falling back through Alexander's cordons, what did he say? "It is all my fault."

I have heard some of his officers say, "Yes, we took chances; a desperate case demanded desperate chances. But we knew he would sustain us, and if we failed and had a good reason, he would never make us the scapegoat."

One of the best stories of them all, told me in his dottering old age by the chief of staff of A.P. Hill, is that little incident at Snell's Bridge, about the fourteenth or sixteenth of May, 1864. A.P. Hill was operating on the right in front of Snell's Bridge, an exceedingly difficult position and one worthy of study. Something went amiss; a position that should have been held was lost. Hill had to retake it. That night he sent in General Wright. Wright went in and made a mess of it—his tactical dispositions were wrong, he didn't approach from the right direction—and Hill had to send in another brigade and, indeed, disorganize a whole division to get a little position behind a church straightened out; and when it was over, he was furious. He came to Lee, who had ridden to the right to see what was amiss, and said, full of fire, "I am going to court-martial Wright." General Lee said, "Now, General Hill, I would not do that. General Wright isn't a professional soldier; he is a lawyer. He has come out here, fighting for his country, and is doing the best he can. What good would it do you to humiliate him in the eyes of the Georgia people by court-martialing him, and besides, whom have you to put in his place? Nobody any better." He said, "When I find a situation like this"—his voice was rich and resonant and rather in the lower register—"I take the officer and carry him into my tent, and I talk to him there, and I try to see that at least he won't make the same mistake again."

That doesn't mean he kept incompetents in office always. No! He got rid of them. But he got rid of them with a gentleness, a suavity, a consideration, and a diplomacy that passed all praise. We have had a certain type in the army that has assumed that if a man fails, there is nothing to do but break him and do it publicly. Lee said in effect, "If a man fails he must not be trusted with command, but what is the use of humiliating the individual? Send him to some post where he can do no harm, retire him, give him leave of absence; get rid of him, but don't put caution in the heart of every soldier, don't paralyze his initiative by having him remember that if he too makes a mistake he too will be broken."

I don't pretend that all officers agree with it. Old Jackson didn't. Jackson, at one time, when he was a general of a brigade, is said to have had every one of his colonels under arrest simultaneously. I believe that is an exaggerated statement, but Jackson worked on the theory that you had to punish them. Lee did not. I believe in the end that Lee accomplished the better results.

If you want to know—you who one day will be in command of a division—how to deal with the men who fail you in a long offensive, take Lee after the Seven Days. He went into that action with Jackson in command of three divisions and responsible for them (his own, Whiting's, and Ewell's); A.P. Hill in command of his division of new troops; and Longstreet, Huger, Magruder, and Holmes—six separate columns, each of which acted as if it were quite independent of GHQ. Hill and Longstreet came through with flying colors. Jackson didn't. Whether Jackson sulked, as Mr. David Lloyd George insisted he had done in exactly the same spirit as Haig sulked on him, or whether Jackson simply had obstacles he could not overcome, it is not for me to say. But Jackson did not cross White Oak Swamp and did not turn Beaver Dam Creek. Jackson never threw his full force into that battle. Huger failed utterly. Magruder failed for lack of sleep. That idiot went through those operations and during the four critical days of the fighting he slept three hours. The result was that on the last day he didn't know where his troops were, and he failed. Holmes failed through no fault of his own. General Lee saw that he must get rid of Magruder and Holmes and Huger. He did it; and with the exception of Magruder—who was a somewhat theatrical old rooster—with that exception, he got rid of them all with perfect suavity and ease.

Within thirty days after he took command of that army, he found three of his division commanders were incompetent; and yet within ninety days after he had taken command of that army, he had fought Second Manassas and was getting ready to go into Maryland. Dealing with Jackson, see how careful he was. He said to General Hampton after the war, "I never did know why General Jackson did not cross White Oak Swamp, and I don't know now after having studied it for years." But Jackson had the Valley campaign behind him. He had done wonderful things, and Lee had made up his mind that he might not be at his best but his record justified more time. So, what did he do? Quietly and calmly, for a trial period, he shifted the general command. Under the law he could not organize corps at that time, but he could put a senior in command of a number of divisions. Longstreet had done splendidly in that campaign. Lee gave him, I think, twenty-one brigades. Jackson had failed, but Jackson still was worth trial, and Jackson got seven brigades. Within three months Lee realized that Jackson could be trusted in subordinate positions, and Jackson then, of course, was given command equal to that of Longstreet.

What did it all mean? May I reiterate: Be absolutely just, but respect every individual; promote the competent, remove or render innocuous the incompetent; but never seek a scapegoat for error.

General Lee's fourth maxim was voiced not by himself, not by any of his corps commanders, but voiced ten thousand times by his old soldiers. It was my privilege to know thousands of them. I remember General Early, General Longstreet, General Stephen D. Lee, a great multitude of them; but most of all, of course, I knew the men in the ranks, and they were the men whose judgment counted most in the end. Oftentimes I would lead up to him in conversation with them; and with a singular uniformity, not based on any reading (not a tradition in the army perhaps) but formulated by every man for himself, I would always get the same answer: "Yes, he looked after his men."

He saw to it that discipline was protective, not repressive. I think he agreed thoroughly with my old friend Captain Lamb, who always described the Army of Northern Virginia as "a voluntary association of gentlemen organized to drive out the Yankees." Discipline was protective, not repressive. That was his theory, and whatever could be done for the men, he did it. He gave them the best ration he could find; and no matter what the quarrel with Colonel Northrop, the commissary general of the army, always, if the men had fought hard, he found an extra ration for them. He realized the importance of reclothing in relation to morale, and never did he come out of a campaign but that you find him besieging Richmond with requests for new shoes, new uniforms, new socks, new underwear. He knew what that meant to a ragged soldier. Of course, he would defend the contrary view when he had to.

One of the most charming of all the stories is that of the time when Lieutenant Colonel Woolsey, later Viscount Lord Woolsey and commander in chief of the British army, was over here as a young officer, and he happened to be present when Lee was going to review a division. The men marched by, and they were exceedingly ragged, particularly in their rear. Colonel Woolsey remarked quite casually (perhaps not very diplomatically), "They march very well; they look like fighting men; but my, how ragged they are in the breeches." To which General Lee replied, "Well, Colonel Woolsey, that doesn't matter very greatly because the enemy never sees their rear."

You would be surprised how he emphasized the matter of reclothing in its relationship to morale. You know it in your own experience. Sometimes even those brave, courageous, exuberant wives of army officers get down in the mouth. How they ever keep up is a mystery to me. But when they get down, what is the remedy? Well, a doctor, if she is seriously sick; if she is just casually down, a visit to the hairdresser; if she is in between those extremes, a new dress will restore any woman that ever was. Lee appreciated that and reclothed his men.

In looking after his men, he never marched them unnecessarily. He rested them often. He gave them the great morale of victory, and he convinced them—and probably this means more than anything else—that he never would expose them unless the strategy of the army demanded it. He taught those men to believe that he would not exact one drop of blood that he could save. What was the result? It is said over and over again in the personal narratives of those men: "Yes, we went out, we looked out over that hill at Cemetery Ridge. They told us not to go out, but we did, and we looked over it, and we measured with our eyes the distance to that little clump of trees atop Cemetery Ridge. And when we came back, we wondered." I have heard them say it a hundred times: "But we knew General Lee never would have commanded us to storm that position if he didn't think it was necessary." There, perhaps, is the whole essence of the thing. Keep them under cover when you can; don't expose them, don't march them unnecessarily; use your head. Instead of making every battlefield a slaughter pen, show your men that you seek to conserve their lives; and then, when you tell them that such and such an objective must be taken, they will take it. Respect the individual in looking after your men.

Just yesterday, with muffled drum and the dead march from Saul, we laid away in Richmond the last member of the Confederate Camp. He had a good record. In 1862, as a boy of fifteen, he had entered Parker's battery, which belonged to Stephen D. Lee's battalion of artillery at Sharpsburg; and you know what Stephen D. Lee did that day.[5] He fought through the war, surrendered, entered the National Guard, was a good colonel, was retired as a brigadier general, and received many honors at the hands of the veterans; and at the end he breathed his last. I had talked with him many times. He knew more about artillery and ordnance than almost any of the older veterans. Ninety-one years he lived; eighty-five years of memory he had. What cheered him most? It was to tell how one day Stephen D. Lee stopped under an apple tree of singularly fine fruitage and told him, his courier, to take some of those apples down to General Lee. He rode over to General Lee's headquarters, having ripped out the bottom of his pocket so that the whole side of his coat would carry apples. He went over to GHQ, took out the apples, and presented them to the commanding general with the compliments of Colonel Lee. The old man thanked him and then said, "Now, sir, won't you sit down and eat one of these apples with me?" The boy of sixteen did it, and if he had received an accolade he never could have been prouder.

Worsham, in that fine book on Jackson's foot cavalry, tells of the manner in which, on one of those desperate marches from the Rapidan to the Totopotomoy, his brigade, part of the old Stonewall Brigade, passed down a dusty road. Lee was standing out in the field; and there, leaning over the neck of Traveller with his gun by his side, was an old private, talking with General Lee just as familiarly as if he had been talking to a comrade in the ranks.

Every one of them regarded that point of personal contact as the supreme hour of their lives. I hear my own father's voice now as he described that dreadful day after Sayler's Creek, when, as they were forming in Farmville to get their food—the only rations they had received since they left Petersburg—the Federals came over, and his command went out to meet them opposite High Bridge. Until the day of his death, that old soldier's shoulders would straighten and his eyes would brighten as he said how Lee rode out and told them, "Men, you must hold this bridge until I get the army out of Farmville." He looked after his men.

Last of all, the fifth maxim, which I have never cited here before, but which, with the threat of war in Europe now looking our way, I must mention. It comes from that book he loved so well. I have seen his field Testament. It isn't so well thumbed as some think, but there is one little strip of paper in there at one psalm you can scarcely read because his thumbs so often were on that page. It isn't what men thought he might say. It was that psalm, "Blessed be the Lord, my God, who taught my hands to fight." That was his psalm.[6] But with it, in all that related to the morale of his army, I believe he embodied this: "It is the spirit that quickeneth, not by might nor by power, but by my spirit."[7]

Behind the great record of the Army of Northern Virginia in 1863 lay the great revival of religion in the army in the winter of 1862-63. Through it all, in it all, and at the end of it all was the spiritual influence of that man. He didn't win the war. No! In that last day there at Appomattox, when he surrendered that army— how magnanimous Grant was—he came back through the ranks. The men were weeping and demanding of him, "General, are we surrendered?" And then they said, "General, say the word, and we will go after them again!" That, when the night before they had seen the ring of fire all around them save to the north. "General, say the word, and we will go after them again!" He didn't say it, but he offered, in the years that followed, the proof of his methods of promoting morale.

If the *Reichswehr* stands, we will have a long and dreadful war, but one thing is certain: The compulsion that lies behind the *Reichswehr* now means chaos after the war. The spirit of looking after the individual displayed by Lee in the Army of Northern Virginia meant exactly the reverse. They lost the war, but under God they won the peace.

Notes

The stenographic transcript of this lecture is filed in the archives of the U.S. Army Military History Institute, located adjacent to the Army War College at Carlisle Barracks, Pennsylvania. The lecture was originally entitled "Morale in the Confederate Army."

1. Louis T. Wigfall commanded the Texas Brigade from October 1861 to February 1862, when he resigned his commission to take a seat in the Confederate Senate.

2. This action occurred in connection with the Confederate retreat from Yorktown to Richmond. Franklin was the Union commander involved in this engagement.

3. Hunter Liggett commanded the First American Corps and then the First American Army during World War I.

4. On the first day of the second battle of Manassas, John Pope (the Union commander) ordered Fitz-John Porter (then commanding a corps) to attack Jackson's right flank. Before Porter's corps could be brought into position for the attack, Longstreet arrived and reinforced Jackson's flank. Porter then decided not to attack, for which he was court-martialed and dismissed from the service. Many years later this court-martial was overturned and Porter restored to his rank.

5. In the second volume of *Lee's Lieutenants,* Freeman noted that "the artillery of the Army had won at Sharpsburg honors that equalled those of any of these infantry commands. . . . On the center . . . the most shining figure was Col. Stephen D. Lee, who commanded a battalion of six batteries that were stationed near the Dunker Church during much of the heaviest fighting."

6. The "field Testament" cited was Lee's copy of the Book of Common Prayer of the Episcopal Church. The psalm is Psalm 144, which begins with these words: "Blessed be the Lord my strength: who teacheth my hands to war, and my fingers to fight."

7. "It is the spirit that quickeneth; the flesh profiteth nothing: the words that I speak unto you, *they* are spirit, and *they* are life" (Jesus to his disciples in The Gospel According to St. John (6:63)).

10

Lee as a Leader

Lecture of February 11, 1937

Freeman begins this lecture by stating that in order to judge a general's leadership, one must take into account the circumscribing conditions under which he fought. In the case of Lee, Freeman cites four such conditions: first, Lee had to operate the army within the political context of a revolutionary government firmly committed to states' rights; second, Lee was fighting a numerically superior force that controlled the sea; third, Lee was always outclassed by that force in every type of equipment and supply; and fourth, the strategy imposed on Lee was the defense of a fixed point, namely, Richmond, Virginia, capital of the Confederacy.

To meet these conditions, says Freeman, Lee had to develop a superior strategy based upon two principles: surprise and economy of force. Freeman then proceeds to analyze how Lee applied these principles by emphasizing the following factors:

1. *Intelligence.*
2. *Field fortifications.*
3. *The accurate gauging of the offensive and defensive power of his units.*
4. *Morale.*
5. *Logistics.*

I am to lecture to you this morning on General Lee as a leader. I lectured on this same subject to last year's class. Happily, perhaps, for me, no record of what I said at that time was preserved. I am, however, this morning materially to change my lecture, and I hope if I am privileged to speak to the class of 1937-38, I shall again change my lecture. I do so not because there is any material change, of course, in the events of the War between the States. I do so rather because as study continues, the problems change in their aspect, and we get new light. It seems to me that in the study of war, as in the matter of religious experience, there is a constant evolution. Save, of course, for those battles of classical times concerning which our source material is complete, we have no full history of any fight. For example, I suppose the most comprehensive study we have of any American battle is Colonel Bigelow's *Chancellorsville.*[1] I had occasion this winter to review *Chancellorsville,* and while I have the greatest admiration for the splendid work done by Colonel Bigelow, I confess I was surprised at the amount of new information that has come to light.

Since last I addressed the war college, my own researches have been largely in the matter of the attrition of the high command in the Army of Northern Virginia. I may state that I have a book which will appear in the autumn of 1938 to be called *Lee's Lieutenants.* The study of Lee's lieutenants has disclosed to me some facts about him that I did not know before. It is for that reason, among others, that I am changing my lecture this morning.

Let us approach the study of Lee as a military leader by recognizing at the outset the four conditions under which he had to fight. Circumstances, I have had occasion to remark elsewhere, are incommensurable.[2] Nothing is more unprofitable or more unscientific than to compare one soldier, in the abstract, with another soldier who may have fought under circumstances altogether different. No two wars ever are alike; few campaigns are ever identical. When you view the whole career of any man, if you are to judge his generalship, his leadership in its larger aspects, you must take into account the circumscribing conditions under which he fought.

In the case of General Lee, these were four. The first was the fact that he represented a revolutionary government that was determined to pursue constitutional methods. That had a far larger part in determining both the method and the outcome than some of our historians have ever, I think, realized. So far as our purposes this morning go, this is of importance to us in this respect: General Lee had to take the military material that was available; he could not altogether overlook that bane of every American war—the politician general. That vast difference between the armies of the Union and the armies of the South is in nothing better illustrated than in the fact that if a Federal general failed, there was no question about breaking him; if a Southern commander failed, the effect of his retirement upon his state, upon the fortunes of the Confederacy, and upon the loyalty of the people had always to be taken into account. General Lee solved this problem as best he could by putting into high command the professional soldiers. He selected them with the utmost care. In many instances he had seen them rise from regimental command, and he watched their careers with great interest. As far as he could, he placed the divisions and the brigades under professional soldiers. Where circumstances, politics, the orders of the administration, or the existence of states' rights required that he give brigade command to a politician, it is interesting to see the pains he took, where such a man failed, to retire him as quickly as he could.

I think it is greatly to the credit of Lee's generalship that politics played less part by far in the high command of the Confederacy, despite states' rights, than it played in the high command of the Union armies. Nonetheless, the facts were there: a revolutionary government that insisted upon adhering to the strictest constitutional procedure; the president, himself a former secretary of war, accused at one period of hostilities of selecting mediocre secretaries of war in order that he might dominate them; politics prevailed in Southern councils; the army had to be operated in spite of politics.

I may pause to say that you gentlemen who went through the World War have no idea how little part politics played, material though it was in some instances, compared with the part it played in the War between the States. Mr. Baker[3] told me on one occasion that in all the period of the war, Mr. Wilson had never given him an order, that the most he ever did was to ask him, "Have you ever thought of doing thus and so?" How different was the fate of Stanton! How wretched was the fate of other Federal commanders, Halleck[4] among them, in respect to orders from politicians, orders that in many instances were prompted by politics!

The second circumscribing fact that General Lee had always to take into account was this: With inferior force and the advantage of inner lines, he had to combat a superior force that commanded the sea. That, of course, is a consideration so large in its implications that I can do no more than to remind you of it. I think the Union navy won the war. Despite all the magnificent achievements of the Army of the Potomac and of the Army of the Tennessee, it was essentially the fact that the Federal navy made it possible at all times to put large forces within striking distance of the line of communications, the line of supply of the Army of Northern Virginia that weakened that army at critical junctures. Take your map of the Atlantic; mark the battlefields in Virginia; trace the railroads on which Lee was dependent for the subsistence of his army. Note that in almost every instance it was possible by the use of sea power to land a force within striking distance of his communications at any point between the Savannah River and the James. That was a tremendous factor in causing that dispersion of force which is, of course, one of the fatal errors of war. The Confederates kept an exceedingly small army in Richmond, compared with the force that President Lincoln kept to garrison Washington. At times Wilmington was defended by about one thousand heavy artillerists and one regiment of infantry, and there were times when even that regiment of infantry was needed on the fighting front.

The third circumscribing fact that should be taken into account is one familiar to you but not always familiar to some of the British critics of the American campaigns. It is that in every type of equipment and supply, General Lee was outclassed by his opponent. This applied not only to his ordnance and his ammunition, but to his ammunition fuses, to his wagon train, to his commissary, to his uniforms, to his tentage. It applied to every item, and above all, it applied to his horses. I had occasion the other day to study the replacement of horses in the Army of the Potomac after the battle of Sharpsburg. That campaign, following so closely on Second Manassas, greatly depleted the Federal horses. I was startled to find that through the magnificent work of Quartermaster General Meigs, supported by the fine activity of Colonel Ingles, chief quartermaster of the Army of the Potomac, the Army of the Potomac in three weeks received more replacements of horses than the Army of Northern Virginia received in any one year after the campaign of 1862. Think of that!

The artillery was never equal to the Federal artillery. As you know, the Confederacy bought a great many guns abroad. Most of those guns were disappointments. The only successful ordnance they ever procured from abroad was the Whitworth gun. Unfortunately, the ammunition for that gun was never manufactured successfully in the South; all of it had to be imported. The Whitworth gun was a superb weapon for its time. I did not know until quite recently that there had been successful artillery practice with it at 3¼ miles in 1862—a surprising range. But that was the exception. The Army of Northern Virginia never had more than four Whitworth guns at any time, and I suppose never boasted more than two hundred rounds of ammunition for them at any one time.

As you know, the need for small arms ammunition was so great that beginning in 1863, every battlefield that remained in the hands of the Confederates was scoured for the recovery of stray balls. Hundreds of pounds of lead were picked up by men who went over the field and raked it. The Confederacy needed that lead if it was to supply ammunition. But even then, the supply of ammunition was exceedingly scanty. The Confederate army during the Gettysburg campaign fired an average of only fifty rounds of small arms ammunition per man. Chancellorsville, which in our minds we regard as a battle of resounding volleys that echoed through the Wilderness, saw the expenditure of thirty rounds of small arms ammunition per man in the Confederate army. They didn't have it.

Finally, as a circumscribing factor, we have to take into account that the strategy imposed on General Lee was the defense of a fixed point—always, according to Napoleon, a dangerous thing. He had to defend

Richmond, and all other considerations, until the late winter of 1864-65, had to be subordinated thereto.

Such were the circumscribing conditions. How did he meet them? I think the answer can be put in one word, though it might be elaborated in more volumes than I have written about General Lee. It was this: He had to develop a superior *strategy* on the basis of surprise and economy of force. Whether we will ever be compelled in America to fight another war of the type General Lee had to fight, I don't know. The probabilities are against it unless, of course, which God forbid, we should have more civil strife in America. But if we ever are compelled on our own shores to approach and fight a campaign with inferior forces, circumscribed in any degree as Lee was, then those great old canons of surprise and economy of force, the canons that Lee exemplified above all others, should be remembered by you gentlemen who have to conduct and to plan those operations. When all is said and done, the more I study General Lee the more I become convinced that he had to rely upon superior strategy, and that when it is analyzed, his strategy rests upon two things: surprise and economy of force.

The application of those two basic principles was in four directions, which I now wish to analyze. Remember, he fought, in the main, in a tangled country. You may have to do the same thing if ever the eastern seaboard is invaded again. If you think the field of maneuver is certain to be open, take a plane any day from Washington and go south, say, no farther than Fort Bragg; you will be over woods more often than you will be over open fields. I have often thought that one of the finest tributes ever paid to the American soldier was paid by General Gouverneur Warren when he was chief topographical engineer of the Army of the Potomac, before he took command of the Fifth Corps. He was a very able engineer. In one of his reports on the operations of 1862-63, he dwelt at great length on the fact that the campaigns of that year in the East had been fought, as he said, "in vast forest, the openings of which were so narrow that a sharpshooter standing on the edge of a clearing usually could fire across to his opponent on the other side." He went on to say, "It is this condition which has led European soldiers to speak so lightly of the American armies on both sides. They do not realize the conditions under which we have to fight." I thought it was remarkable that he took pains to defend Confederate generalship, as well as the Union, on the ground of the terrain of action.

General Lee had to fight in this tangled country. It involved tremendous problems of maneuver, problems that despite the airplane might be duplicated very largely in our own day in eastern Virginia and eastern North Carolina. He didn't have the men, he didn't have the equipment, he had to defend Richmond with the troops and the generals he had—relying on surprise and economy of force.

His first application, the beginning of all his strategic combinations, is summed up in one word: intelligence. If you never remember, gentlemen, but one lesson of General Lee's career, I think I would ask you to pick a phrase from a letter of General Lee to General Longstreet in the winter of 1864-65, when the Army of Northern Virginia was so reduced that it was unable to put its men closer than five paces apart on the whole sector of forty miles in front of Richmond. General Lee was speaking to General Longstreet about the probability of an early attack. He was not certain whether the attack would be delivered north or south of the James. General Longstreet thought it would be north of the James; General Lee thought the probability greater that it would be south. He said, "In any event, we must rely upon early and accurate information of the movements of the enemy." A familiar enough principle, but the linking of the two together is the secret of the intelligence service of the Army of Northern Virginia. Early and accurate. It may be early but inaccurate; it may be accurate but late. The two of them go together.

If you are interested in that aspect of General Lee's career, the very starting point, I repeat, of his strategic combinations, I can suggest to you no better studies than two. Study, for example, how he met the transfer of the Eleventh and Twelfth Corps of the Army of the Potomac to reinforce Rosecrans on September 25, 1863. Chickamauga had been fought; the army of the West needed assistance. It was decided hurriedly to transfer the Eleventh and Twelfth Corps. That transfer was one of the greatest feats of American transportation. The first intimation given the B. & O. Railroad, which was entrusted with the transfer, was on the night of the twenty-fourth of September; they were told that these two corps, twelve thousand men with their horses and their guns, had to be moved. By the night of the twenty-eighth of September, the railroad had these troops moving and the vanguard was then in Ohio—an exceedingly good movement for those days. It was a matter of great importance to General Lee to know it because when he ascertained it, it would, of course, give him an opportunity for the initiative. He assumed the initiative the next month in the Bristoe Station campaign, which was thwarted for him by very adverse weather.

There was, judged by modern standards, a very rudimentary system of intelligence. Here are the facts. The first troops moved on the afternoon of the twenty-fifth. On the afternoon of the twenty-fifth, a Confederate scout reported to General Lee that a large Federal encampment had disappeared. On the twenty-sixth, the first of those troops came through Washington, bound west. On the twenty-sixth, a Confederate spy in Washington got the information which corps were moving and where they were moving, and he struck out at once through the lines, on foot. It took him two days to get to headquarters. On the twenty-eighth, Lee had this spy's report. He was not quite certain of it; but on the twenty-eighth, information came from the line of the railroad, which he constantly watched, that heavy troop trains were moving westward. By the thirtieth, he knew the troops had moved and where they had gone, and he was making his plans to take the offensive. Early and accurate information.

I invite you in the second place, if you are interested in that aspect of his career, to take the classic example of the buildup of intelligence reports, namely, Lee's study on May 7, 1864, of the movements in his front. They were among the most critical movements of the entire war. General Grant had fought on the fifth and sixth until he was heartsick. Two of his corps had been thoroughly whipped, though they had put up the best fight that the Army of the Potomac had ever made, up to that time, south of Gettysburg. He decided the only thing to do was to move to Spotsylvania Court House, beginning that wonderful slide, always sliding to the left. I haven't time to go into the details of the buildup of General Lee's intelligence reports that day. There was no one thing that led him to believe that the Army of the Potomac was moving up its left flank toward Spotsylvania Court House. He didn't see any movement of troops, but from early morning there was this bit of information, that bit of information, some of it contradictory, but little by little he built it up. That afternoon, as you know, he sent two of his staff officers at breakneck speed with instructions to the cavalry to hold Spotsylvania Court House. As they went, one said to the other, "How in God's name does the old man know General Grant is moving to Spotsylvania Court House?" He knew because of the gradual, detailed, critical study of his intelligence reports, built up step by step. Early and accurate information, I repeat.

The accuracy of that information had to be tested by the very factor that operated against its value of immediacy. He needed it to be early, but he had to wait until it was accurate. I have often said to myself, though I don't think I have printed it, that General Lee had essentially a scientific mind. He never accepted anything without reservations until he was sure of it. There were exceedingly few assumptions other than those based on absolute necessity. Sometimes, of course, he had to throw his troops blindly forward, but he never did it unless the necessity was appalling. Always those two factors: early and accurate information. That, of course, lent itself to surprise.

The second application of those principles of surprise and economy of force came, above everything else, in General Lee's use and development from the outset of field fortifications. I have said in print that General Lee began field fortifications at Fredericksburg. In my next edition I am going to revise that statement, because I believe the evidence indicates that from the time Lee took command of the Army of Northern Virginia on the first of June, 1862, he constructed field fortifications wherever the opportunity was offered. In front of Richmond he did it not merely to protect Richmond against the long range of the artillery of the Federals, but he put up that screen, that curtain between his redoubts, in order that he might hold them with a very small part of his army and then concentrate north of the Chickahominy River. I believe the idea of field fortifications was in his mind then. He did not fortify, to be sure, at Second Manassas, because he didn't have time; he didn't fortify at Sharpsburg, primarily because he didn't have time, because his force was too small. But when we take into consideration the fact that he did fortify in June for economy of force in attack, that he did fortify in December, and that thereafter it was a matter of routine, I think I may revise my statement and say he began on the theory that economy of force and concentration of movement demanded field fortifications from the outset.

And could they fortify! They had at that time no pioneer troops, no organization of engineer troops. The best they could do was to get some axes and, if possible, some shovels, and dig. The first regiment of engineers was organized in 1863; pioneer corps had been organized a little before that time. They were very good, but they were not always available. Through the war, Lee's men had to do the greater part of their field fortifications themselves. There are hundreds of miles of field fortifications in Virginia today that were dug with tin cups and bayonets. That was all they had.

You remember that in that great movement when General Grant was shifting from the Totopotomoy, the situation was exceedingly critical. Lee threw Hoke's division in, threw Fitzhugh Lee's cavalry in, and then had to slide his line by its right flank. When his troops came in, there were some of those old veterans of the First Corps, and when they came into position, the Federals were in sight on the other side of the woods. The Confederates had moved down a little farm road, which afterward disappeared, and the men stopped in line. They did not wait for orders. As soon as they saw that magnificent blue host (which was then at its very best) across the field, they began to dig; and the chief engineer said that when he came down the line a few hours afterward, there were exceedingly few points on that line that he had to rectify. Every man was his own field engineer, but that line of fortifications withstood General Grant's attack on the third of June, 1864.

Field fortifications for economy of force. If you doubt what it meant, study what Lee did on the first and second of May, 1863, at Chancellorsville, when he was holding the right with sixteen thousand men, when Jackson had taken twenty-eight thousand to go around the flank of the Eleventh Corps. I think General Maurice was right when he said General Lee was probably the father of modern field fortifications.[5]

The third application by General Lee of these basic principles, that is, surprise and economy of force, was in respect to the accurate gauging of the offensive and defensive power of a given number of men. I think it is an astounding thing, if you will study carefully the campaigns of the War between the States, to see how vastly our generals differed in their judgment of the offensive and defensive power of a given number of troops. Take for example the action at Savage Station on the twenty-eighth of June, 1862, when General McClellan was changing base from White House to the James. That was intended to be a rearguard action. General McClellan thought his rear was sufficiently covered. His army was moving down to White Oak Swamp to cross. At that time he had four crossings—no great difficulty in getting his men across. One of his corps commanders in his report says that when he went on the field at the head of his corps and saw the number of troops in position and in reserve, he concluded there was no need for his corps and resumed his march across White Oak Swamp. As a matter of fact, he was right—there was no need for his corps—but if there had been coordination of attack as General Lee had hoped there would be, there would have been good use for that corps.

Time and time again you see in the battles of the War between the States an excessive concentration of troops on a front where only a few thousand men could operate. General Lee could never indulge in that luxury. He never had the reserves needed for his lines, much less a number of men that he could waste in ostentatious demonstrations. He had always to find exactly what the rifle power of a given division was. He had to know exactly how long a particular brigade would stand. I have always thought that one of the most significant remarks he ever made was in that operation at Mine Run at the end of November and beginning of December 1863—a wretched campaign, under the most adverse weather imaginable, both sides marching to Mine Run in the midst of an autumnal storm and spending three days seeing who could build the higher parapets on either side of Mine Run. At an early stage, word came to General Lee that there had been a dangerous demonstration on his right and that a regiment of cavalry was in action there. The first question he asked was, "Who commands that regiment?" He wanted to know whose regiment it was, because it had been his duty so to learn his troops that he could tell when, from his scanty reserve, it was necessary to reinforce heartsick men, or when the valor of those men was so well established that they could stand repeated onslaughts.

You would be surprised if you knew how even veteran brigades differed both in their offensive and their defensive strength. Apparently they were under commanders of equal capacity; they might even be in the same division, certainly in the same corps. Yet this one would be twice as strong in attack as the other; this one could resist four hours, the other would need reinforcements in two hours. General Lee studied every brigade and every brigade commander in the Army of Northern Virginia. Nothing is more humorous, and in a sense more pathetic, than to see the manner in which the old man, once he found that good troops were being demoralized by an incompetent commander, would work to get rid of that commander. He had one cavalry brigade commander who had affronted Stuart very early in the preliminaries of Second Manassas by not having placed his outposts as he should. This officer was sent for a while into North Carolina but came back into Virginia. He caused a great deal of trouble for reasons that have never been quite plain. He was a highborn gentleman, a good patriotic soldier, but he simply could not get the fight from his men. I suppose it took General Lee six months and a succession of the most diplomatic letters before he could get the administration to transfer this general to conduct, as General Lee said, "a camp of instruction for cavalrymen, a duty which I believe no man could discharge better than General ________ ." That happened with half a dozen men, and it had to happen, despite the difficulties he faced in removing men. It had to happen because he had to get the maximum from his troops.

And what results did he get? You can go on some of the battlefields of Virginia now, study the ground, and can see where he threw perhaps a thousand or at most fifteen hundred men in to perform a task that seems to one's mind to be impossible—but they did it. He knew his men. I never cease to marvel at the story of what was done by the Texas Brigade on the morning of the sixth of May, 1864, in front of the Widow Tapp's house. Eight hundred men went in and stopped a division—an incredible performance. Unfortunately, two-thirds of the eight hundred stayed there—dead.

He not only put in good men when he could, he relieved weak men when compelled to do so, and he wished many times that he could have done it when it was not possible. It was necessary for economy of force. Sometimes, you know, it is said in a war that incompetents are broken too soon, before they are given their chance. I want to go on record here, gentlemen, before you of a war college, and say that in my judgment, however humble it is, 20 percent of the casualties of the War between the States were attributable to the incompetence of commanders; and that is a terrible bill to have to pay.

In order to get the maximum of fighting power out of his men, General Lee had to develop the morale of those men. As I have already spoken to the war college this year on that subject, I shall not elaborate on it now, but I must remind you that morale was a tremendous factor in economy of force.

Finally, in the application of these two basic principles of surprise and economy of force, General Lee had to develop maximum mobility and had to develop it with the poorest wagon trains and the weakest horses used in an American campaign since 1780. The weakness of that wagon train passed all belief. The feebleness of the Confederate railways has never been given its proper weight as an element of disadvantage on the part of the Confederate high command. Think of taking twenty-four hours to carry one division fifteen miles! It happened. It was late in the war, but it happened. General Lee, for these reasons, was compelled to perfect his logistics. I have always believed and have many times asserted that with the possible exception of his incredible buildup of his intelligence service, his greatest single quality as a commander was in his uncanny logistics. You can check that in nearly every campaign of the war.

You will find it in that remarkable transfer of the Army of Northern Virginia from in front of Richmond to the line of the Rapidan to meet General Pope in the summer of 1862. You will find it again in many aspects of the Maryland expedition. You will find it superbly illustrated in Second Manassas.

Despite the ultimate failure, what could have been finer than the logistics of the first day of Gettysburg? A.P. Hill comes up from the west, finds a heavy force there. A magnificent Federal commander, Reynolds, is killed by almost the first salvo but has enough troops to put up a stiff resistance that almost threatened Heth's division (not very well led that day). Just at the moment when it seems as if it isn't going to be possible for Hill to throw them back, click, as if it had been a time clock, into action comes Rodes, marching down from the northwest. After Rodes had that very unhappy episode with Iverson's and O'Neal's brigades, when Rodes' flank is in the air and there is no certainty of his success, again the click of the time clock, and Early comes in straight from the north, straight on Rodes' left. Magnificent logistics!

Think of the logistics of the Wilderness, Spotsylvania, North Anna, Totopotomoy. I don't believe there was a time in that whole operation when General Lee had more than a margin of three hours of safety;

and yet, with the exception of the situation on the morning of the sixth when Longstreet was slow in reaching the Plank Road, there was not one time in that campaign when General Lee did not have troops in position when the enemy struck.

I know of only two serious mistakes he ever made in logistics. I haven't time to dwell on either of those. The most injurious was in his estimate of the time that would be taken for the march to Harpers Ferry at the time of the Maryland expedition in 1862.

Remember this: logistics depended in large part on his knowledge of his men. He knew what could be done by the Second Corps; he knew the marching of the First Corps. He knew, other things being even, if he put a division of the Second Corps on the road and a division of the First Corps on another road, that the division of the Second Corps would outmarch the division of the First Corps. Just day before yesterday, I was reading a reproach that had been sent from GHQ of the Army of Tennessee to General Longstreet for slowness in starting his operations against Knoxville, to which General Longstreet replied indignantly, "I have never lost any time anywhere in this war" (or words to that effect).[6] I think that is a claim that no soldier perhaps ever could make before. Whether Longstreet justified it is for you gentlemen to say.

Now, I have given you a very elementary lecture. May I recapitulate? I said General Lee had four circumscribing factors, which I need not repeat. This made it necessary for him to rely on superior strategy, the essential elements of which were surprise and economy of force. In order to develop these qualities, he tried to perfect his intelligence service. In order that he might have men to concentrate in superior number at the weak point of the enemy's line, he used field fortifications for defensive purposes as far and as often as he could; I repeat that I believe he did that from the very beginning of his command in eastern Virginia. Having so few men, he had to get the maximum from them in rifle power, in offense and defense. To that end he studied every single unit of his army, and he strove to put their morale at top pitch.

Didn't he do it? Didn't he have some wonderful men to help him? I never follow Jackson's march from Jeffersonton up through Thoroughfare Gap, an arid but a beautiful country, that I don't hear the tramp of those pounding troops on those limestone roads and Old Jack crouched there on his horse with that insistent order: "Push on, men, push on, push on."

General Lee needed, in the application of these two principles, sound logistics, and he developed them. I commend to you the study of those logistics. They were based on nothing profound, but on a knowledge of men, on a knowledge of material, and on a knowledge of what full devotion to a cause could accomplish.

I have said that Jackson was epitomized in the words "Push on, men, push on." Although General Lee had to fight an offensive-defensive for two years and then a defensive for two years more, although he had these hampering circumstances from the outset, although he never could be lavish with men or ammunition or even with food, I would not like to leave you the picture that he was primarily a defensive general. He believed that the surest economy of force was in taking the initiative and in concentrating quickly, on the basis of accurate information, at the determined weak point of the enemy. That, after all, is one of the great objectives of all military operations. He believed it and he did it.

What words epitomized him? I think they are the words he spoke that morning in that pine forest of Chancellorsville, the morning of the third of May. He had fourteen thousand men facing two corps. He sent orders to Anderson and to McLaws to demonstrate up to the very front of the enemy but not to make a major attack—orders obeyed with so much zeal that a regiment of the Twelfth Virginia went into the Federal works and brought out the flag of an Ohio regiment and laid it at the foot of the general. That terrible afternoon—the suspense; twilight—the sound of the horrible wails that never sounded so loudly to a homesick Federal anywhere in the world as the wounded that night in the Wilderness; and then, as the shots fell, that rumble from the west; and then, a little later, that rising red cloud of the bursting shells of battle as Jackson swept on. Eleven o'clock—a silence had fallen; and then, weary from the day's struggle, he laid himself down in his bivouac. An aide, a horseman, an excited voice, and the worst news that could have come to him: "Jackson wounded." News so bitter that he would not let Jackson's signal officer, who brought him the news, elaborate on it. Yet just as soon as the military situation was plain to him, he sprang up with the words that I believe epitomize his career: "I must strike them today."

Notes

The stenographic transcript of this lecture is filed in the archives of the U.S. Army Military History Institute, located adjacent to the Army War College at Carlisle Barracks, Pennsylvania.

1. John Bigelow, Jr., *The Campaign of Chancellorsville* (New Haven, 1910). In the bibliography of *R.E. Lee,* Freeman describes this book as "a model in the comprehensive treatment of a battle."

2. This well-known Freeman phrase is taken from the final volume of *R.E. Lee.* At the end of the chapter entitled "The Sword of Robert E. Lee" (which reviews Lee's achievements as a soldier), Freeman wrote: "When the story of a soldier is completed, and the biographer is about to leave the last camp-fire of a man he has learned to respect and to love, he is tempted to a last word of admiring estimate. . . . May he not claim for him a place in the company of the mighty captains of the past? Yet who that reverences historical verities can presume to say of any soldier who rises above the low shoulders of mediocrity, 'In this he outshone or in that he rivalled another who fought under dissimilar conditions for a different cause in another age?' Circumstance is incommensurable; let none essay to measure men who are its creatures. Lee's record is written in positive terms; why invoke comparatives? The reader who can appraise the conditions under which he fought can appraise the man."

3. Newton D. Baker was Woodrow Wilson's secretary of war from 1916 to 1921.

4. Henry W. Halleck was the general in chief of the U.S. Army from July 1862 until March 1864, when Grant was appointed to that position. Halleck thereupon became the army's chief of staff.

5. Sir Frederick Maurice was the author of *Robert E. Lee the Soldier* (Boston, 1925). In the bibliography of *R.E. Lee,* Freeman describes this book as "the best brief study of Lee's strategy."

6. Longstreet and most of his First Corps were detached from Lee's army in September 1863 to reinforce the Confederate Army of Tennessee. They returned to Lee's army in April 1864 in anticipation of Grant's offensive in Virginia.

11

Lee as a Leader

Lecture of February 10, 1938

In this lecture, Freeman examines four qualities of Lee's leadership: first, Lee's rare combination of extraordinary intellectual ability and physical endurance; second, his belief in offensive action despite serious limitations in men, equipment, and supplies; third, his reliance on superior strategy to overcome all obstacles; and fourth, his moral leadership.

In discussing Lee's emphasis on strategy, Freeman sets forth seven of Lee's basic rules:

1. Never underestimate your adversary.

2. Try to know what your adversary is going to do before he knows what you are going to do.

3. The offensive calls for surprise by inferior forces and for superior concentration at the critical point by equal forces.

4. Every movement must be measured in terms of an early start, accurate staff work, the endurance of the troops, and the marching capacity of their leaders.

5. The commander must have a good eye for ground.

6. Always interpret strategy in terms of available position and lines of march.

7. Know your subordinates.

During the discussion period, Freeman discusses Lee's work habits in the field and Lee's emphasis on the individual personality in dealing with others.

It is, I assure you, a real privilege to be with you again and to talk with you concerning General Lee as a leader. You will recognize, of course, that it is a somewhat large order to try to condense in one brief morning's lecture the observations of thirty years. I have, moreover, so often burdened the faculty of the war college with this same lecture that I, from year to year, change its contents. I shall not, therefore, this morning attempt any general consideration of the whole field of General Lee's leadership. To do so would be to repeat what

I have said before and secondly, it would be to prolong unduly your morning hour.

I wish, therefore, first to recall to your mind briefly four limitations under which General Lee labored as a leader. I wish then to outline four of the qualities of leadership that he exemplified. Note please my exact words: four of the qualities of leadership that he *exemplified.* I use that term rather than to speak of him directly as a leader, because the latter topic has larger implications than I am able this morning to cover.

In treating these four qualities of leadership exhibited by General Lee, I shall dwell at considerable length on the third of these, namely, the strategic principles that he illustrated, and I shall give you seven subheadings of his strategy.

I dislike at the outset to have to explain the limitations under which any man fights. Yet always these limitations exist. Military comparisons always seem to me to be futile as among men because, as I often have said, circumstances are never the same, circumstances are incommensurable. If, however, we are to understand some of the qualities of leadership displayed by General Lee, we must remember at the very outset that he had no trained, adequate general staff behind him. One of the great advantages that the Union had during the War between the States was the fact that while many of the staff officers resigned, the staff remained in being. I think we have, incidentally, a very good illustration of that fundamental fact now, as one may draw a comparison between the situation in Russia after the death of Marshal Tukhachevsky[1] and the situation that may exist in Germany today. The old Russian general staff was destroyed by the revolution of 1917. Germany, on the other hand, might see some of her great leaders demoted, cashiered, even executed, and yet it would be a matter of exceeding difficulty to destroy the long background and all the studies and experience of the great general staff of Germany. General Lee had no general staff to start with. The staff he received was no more than a name. He had to build it up as best he could.

In the second place, he had very few trained personal staff officers. The line between the general staff and the personal staff of a commanding officer in the field was not so precisely drawn during the War between the States as it has since been drawn. In many instances during active operations, officers of the general staff served on the personal staff of the commander, and not infrequently, personal staff officers had to discharge duties that now would fall upon the broad shoulders of the general staff. You may judge for yourselves of the circumstances when I say that General Lee was never privileged, at any time during his command of the Army of Northern Virginia, to have on his staff more than one West Point officer; and that West Point officer, who incidentally had been a paymaster before the war, was not a man who gave himself with special cooperative spirit to his duties. He had one graduate of the Virginia Military Institute on his personal staff. He had one professor from a college, one lawyer, one man already turning to the ministry, and he had one engineer. These were the men from whom he had to build up a competent personal staff to carry out his orders in dealing with an army which at one time reached eighty-five thousand men.

Remember again that the leadership of this army was, prior to 1861, 50 percent untrained. I have just completed a rather difficult and quite tedious study of the division of the officers of the United States Army in 1861, and I have been surprised to see how few officers relatively were at the command of the Confederacy.[2] A much larger percentage of the professional officer corps of the United States remained with the Union than joined their respective states in secession. The Army of Northern Virginia, for example, insofar as it was organized on the basis of Virginia personnel, had only thirteen officers, staff and line, ranking major and above, and only sixty-four officers of junior grade who had been in the United States Army; about 75 percent of these were West Pointers. At least 50 percent of the regimental commanders of the Army of Northern Virginia at the beginning of its major operations during the Seven Days consisted of men who, prior to 1861, had received no military training. The Army of Northern Virginia, insofar as its regimental command was adequate, owed its existence primarily to the Virginia Military Institute and to the Citadel, the South Carolina military college. Nearly half of the regimental officers, field and above, of the Army of Northern Virginia in the campaigns of 1862 consisted of graduates of these institutions.

Finally, in surveying General Lee's limitations, you must remember that at no time during the war was his equipment in any sphere equal to that of the Union army. His service of supply was never comparable; his wagon trains barely could move; his horses, save those in the cavalry, were soon worn down and underfed; his ordnance was always inferior; he had few good rifles, save those that were captured. In every essential respect, his equipment was inferior to that of his adversary.

These factors I think, without any apology, must be taken into account in measuring his leadership.

What then were the particular qualities of leadership that he exhibited? I wish this morning to mention, as I have indicated, just four.

First, General Lee exemplified above everything else that essential quality of combined intellectual and physical leadership. Lee's mind was a singular one. He had what I have often termed "the engineer's imagination." He had very little imagination besides. He believed in looking at fact without illusion. No quality of his mind is more definite than its precision. First of all, Lee had high intelligence. With that was combined that indispensable quality of endurance, which has always to be distinguished from mere physical strength. Quite often, men who are physically powerful lack endurance. Lee was a man of normal physical strength, but he was a man of most abnormal physical endurance.

Quite recently I have been making a study of the two types of physique in the armies of the 1860s: the powerful man and the man who, while not so strong, had endurance. It is quite surprising to see how, sooner or later, those men who were merely strong cracked under the strain, whereas those men who had the higher quality of physical endurance were the men who held on to the end. Of course, occasionally you come across a man—A.P. Hill, for example—who was neither physically strong nor capable of very great endurance. Those men are sickly and have to pay the price, and oftentimes their troops do.

General Lee had that rare combination of intellectual power and physical endurance. If he hadn't possessed that power, if he hadn't been blessed with that endurance, then when the army leadership by circumstance and casualty was almost destroyed in May 1864, it would have been absolutely impossible for him to have conducted operations. Even as it was, when he reached the North Anna on the twenty-fourth of May, 1864, he had a bad attack of diarrhea which for virtually a week incapacitated him for command. Never forget that combination, however, of intellectual eminence and physical endurance. I believe nearly all the great captains will be found to have possessed that rare but indispensable combination.

Secondly, General Lee exemplified this essential quality of leadership, namely, to make the most of what he had in men, equipment and supplies, to recognize the limitations thus set and the duties thus imposed, but never to admit that these limitations or these duties ever rendered active operations impossible. We don't know what the future holds for us. There is such a thing as an army becoming so dependent upon complete and lavish equipment and supply that initiative is paralyzed when for any or many reasons these things may be lacking. If ever that becomes your lot in future operations, remember the example of Lee, who oftentimes had no harness for his guns save ropes, who rarely had at his advance base more than three days' subsistence, who often went into operations with only a hundred rounds of ammunition per gun, and yet who never admitted that these limitations should paralyze the initiative. How often and how wonderfully he exhibited those qualities!

Of course, there were limitations; there were duties. I would draw the line on Lee's operations offensively after the second battle of Manassas, the end of August 1862, and I would say that thereafter Lee's offensives were never military—they were commissary offensives. Both advances into Maryland, with all they entailed, were essentially movements to relieve the South of feeding the army, to avail the army of the lush valleys of Pennsylvania and of the full granaries of Maryland. Nonetheless, though the necessities of feeding his men sometimes shaped the direction of his offensives, Lee never admitted that any limitation could destroy the initiative of his army. He never admitted but one superior adversary; that one superior adversary was the weather. He didn't attempt the impossible in bad weather.

I may interject here to say that no general ever has gone into the field who didn't find some elements of staff work unsatisfactory, some factor in the service of supply inadequate. What is the general in command to do in those circumstances? If Lee points a moral in this respect to you who are to be the future commanders of the American army, it is, Look after the weak element of the general staff. He had a good chief of ordnance; very seldom did he ever have to act in respect to bringing up ammunition. He had, in the main, a fair quartermaster general; very rarely did he have to busy himself there. But though he had a good commissary of subsistence, that officer had to deal with a very difficult man in the person of the commissary general, General L.B. Northrop. There was constant difficulty and friction. Lee busied himself there. Above all, realizing after the operations of 1862 that the weak link in the Army of Northern Virginia was the horse supply, Lee assiduously and persistently, to the very end of operations, worked to procure horses and to save the horses that he had.

You will be interested to know that in later days when he was at Lexington, teaching boys, a new professor came and asked him if he had any particular instructions to give him.[3] Lee said, "I have only one thing to tell you, and that is the advice of the stagecoach driver: 'Look after your weak horses.'" He personally, despite all the burdens that he had, looked after the weak elements of general staff work. Lee was, and of necessity had to be, a great army administrator. Any man who, no matter what the size of the army, expects that he, at the head of a division, corps or an army, is going to be able to devote himself solely to the study of large strategic combinations in cooperation with his general staff is destined to be disappointed. I don't believe I have ever known a great general, as we judge him by his strategic achievements, who was not at the same time a first-class military administrator. No man can neglect administration, in the light of the lessons of the War between the States, and not risk his strategic results.

I come now to the third quality exemplified by General Lee. I believe it can be put in the form of a brief military epigram, certainly a maxim, to this effect: Strategy is the supreme function of GHQ; tactics, of the corps or divisional command; rely on strategy to overcome all unfavorable conditions of combat. That is a rather broad statement, but I believe that it can be justified by a study of Lee's campaigns. Lee never had an even chance tactically. He was outranged; he faced better artillery all the time. Very, very seldom was his volume of rifle fire equal to that of the enemy. In fact, when Captain Scheibert of the Prussian army[4] asked General Lee what he thought of the breech-loading repeating rifle which was just then coming into use, General Lee said it might be admirable but he could not use it in the Army of Northern Virginia because he never had sufficient ammunition for his men to throw any of it away. "The men," he said, "will rely more on the accuracy of their fire if they have to take all the trouble of muzzle-loading."

That illustrates one small matter that shows how, tactically, Lee was consistently disadvantaged. He knew it. He knew that all the odds were against him. He knew that his one hope, save that of arousing the continued and full activity of the Southern people, was in the wise employment of strategy. He fought very few battles himself, that is, actually conducted the combat. He did it on the second of May, 1863—and he did it most admirably—when with two divisions he engaged the whole left of Hooker's army at Chancellorsville. He had to do it again in part in the Spotsylvania and Wilderness operations. He did it as seldom as he could, because he felt his duties of military administrator plus his duties of directing the strategy of the army consumed all his time. He was better off, he said, if he left to Longstreet, Jackson, or to Hill or Ewell, as the case might be, the tactical dispositions of the field of battle.

Strategy is the function of GHQ. Rely on strategy to overcome all unfavorable conditions.

Now, I am going, this morning, for the first time in my lectures here, to attempt to epitomize seven of Lee's basic rules of strategy. In doing that I am going to surprise you by the simplicity of those statements. There is going to be very little in there that you have not been taught from your first studies of strategy at West Point. When all is said and done, the greatest principles of strategy are nothing more than successfully applied common sense. I doubt very much the adequacy—I almost said the utility—of studying those principles of strategy which are rationalized by a great leader in the light of his own campaigns after they are over. Napoleon's maxims are to be read with many reservations. Those principles of strategy that are most useful to the soldier are those which you will find exemplified in actual daily operations. Maxims announced from Saint Helena, in the light of all the after events, may be maxims superb to read, but after all they are maxims rationalized rather than maxims that can be applied in all the uncertainty and confusion of battle.

Lee's main qualities of strategy, I think, can be summarized in these seven maxims, not his own words but, as it were, an epitome of his great basic principles. First: Never underestimate your adversary. Lee put that in one of the few maxims that he wrote in the field. He was telling President Davis of his plans for meeting a Federal offensive, and he said, as he outlined his own plans, "It is always proper to assume that the enemy will do what he should do." You remember that when Lee was told that General Meade had been placed in command of the Army of the Potomac in succession to General Hooker, General Lee didn't like it. He knew Meade of old. He knew what these topographical engineers could do once they were brought into the field and given a little training in combat, and he said, "Meade will make very few mistakes, and if I make any mistake, he is very apt to find it out."

In contemplating a strategic problem, Lee always assumed that his adversary was going to make the best use of his position, his force, and his mobility. He believed that his function was to look for the adversary to make some mistake in what on the whole would be a good design, to make some mistake on which he himself could capitalize. That is to say, he worked on the strategic principle that your enemy's plan is going to be 90 percent sound. In conception it may be 100 percent perfect. The defect will be in the execution. Somewhere in the execution of a sound strategic plan, a mistake will be made. Your opportunity comes in finding that mistake and capitalizing on it immediately. It is well to write that down: No matter who your prospective adversary may be, never underestimate him.

I think now how often in the days before the war some of the German military men, high on the general staff, were disposed to underestimate their adversaries. After all, it is better to overestimate him than to underestimate him. If you prepare your defense based on the assumption that his offense will be 100 percent intelligent and his offense proves only 80 percent effective, you then, of course, have his extra mistakes on which you can hope to capitalize.

When it came to the outworking of a strategic proposition after this basic assumption, that his adversary was going to do what he ought to do, that was General Lee's first great military quality.

The second was his intelligence service. I think it was last year that I took as my text for my lecture on Lee's leadership Lee's letter to Longstreet in the winter of 1864-65 in which, reviewing the great odds against which the Army of Northern Virginia had to contend, he said, "Our success will depend upon early and accurate information of the movements of the enemy." I have elsewhere analyzed at considerable length Lee's method of procuring his intelligence and of integrating his intelligence reports. His intelligence reports as a rule are informative only as they are cumulative. Lee had a singular aptitude for developing in a cumulative manner the information that would come in in a given day. I have often said to young soldiers that you can make no better field study of intelligence than to read what happened in the Wilderness of Virginia on the seventh of May, 1864. There is a perfect textbook example of the wise employment of the cumulative method in the integration of intelligence reports.

If I were to summarize Lee's emphasis upon intelligence, his reliance upon it as a factor in strategy, I believe I would say this: Prior, accurate intelligence is the intelligence on which to base decisions. Now what is that but plain everyday common sense? He knew that in Virginia his intelligence service was superior to that of General Grant or General McClellan, as the case might be. He knew that in Pennsylvania his intelligence service was wholly inadequate in comparison with that of General Meade. When all is said and done, the people of the neighborhood are after all the best intelligence officers an army has. Lee had them on his side in Virginia; they were on the side of General Meade in Pennsylvania. Lee knew his adversary would get information; he knew his adversary was building up an intelligence service. His adversary did build up a very excellent intelligence service. I don't know, in the whole of military literature, a better intelligence report than the report of General Godfrey Witsell prepared for General Ord and General Butler in advance of the operations against Fort Harrison in 1864—a perfect report of amazing accuracy. Lee knew this would happen. Therefore he said that the intelligence on which to base action is prior intelligence, accurate intelligence.

To put it in the simplest form, Try to know what your adversary is going to do before your adversary knows what you are going to do. That, I think, epitomized Lee's intelligence service.

Again, Lee believed in the offensive. But I think you can put his rule regarding the offensive in the veriest ABCs of military experience: The offensive—usually though not universally desirable—calls for surprise by inferior forces and for superior concentration at the critical point by equal forces. The supreme test of the offensive is to find the critical point. That is ABC, isn't it? Isn't that just as simple as anything could be?

If you are on the offensive, which is usually desirable, and have inferior force, says Lee in one hundred illuminating instances, you must in those circumstances rely on surprise. Jackson must come down through the mists of Thoroughfare Gap. Those troops of the Eleventh Corps bivouacked there across the Plank Road must suddenly be astonished by bugle calls on the western horizon and then by the swift passage through their camps of the frightened creatures of the forest. Surprise, if your offensive must be undertaken by inferior forces. If there can be no surprise, if you have to make a concentration and can undertake the offensive at a time when you are practically on the same terms with your adversary, then, superior concentration.

That is the whole gospel of the offensive as taught by Lee, resolved down into those simple words. And if you will study his campaigns, I don't believe after the Seven Days you will find a single example of the offensive that cannot be tested by that simple elementary rule, which every second lieutenant ought to understand and indeed has been taught.

There is nothing mysterious in the strategy of great captains. There is no fathoming of the deep seas, no compassing the heavens. It is sound common sense, accurately applied at the right moment.

Feeling-out operations Lee always regarded as essential in the outworking of the offensive. Superior concentration at the critical point. Problem: Find the critical point. There were many ways by which he found it. Sometime I hope to have the pleasure of lecturing to you on that very point: the feeling-out operations of the Army of Northern Virginia; how Lee would test where his critical point was.

General Lee, I say, relied greatly on intelligence. He relied, generally speaking, on the offensive. He relied next on his logistics. In fact, if any man were to ask me what part of Lee's strategy I consider the most important in the instruction of professional soldiers, I believe I would say without hesitation—distinguishing this now from his work of administration—that it was his intelligence service and his logistics.

Lee's logistics can be put in another very simple maxim: Every movement must be measured in terms of early start, accurate staff work, the endurance of the troops, and the marching capacity of their leaders. I need not enlarge perhaps on any of these but the last named: the marching capacity of leaders. Conditions may be changed, now that we have the motor horse instead of shanks' mare. I am not so sure yet how far conditions are changed thereby, but all my studies, gentlemen—and they are small compared with those of superior authority here—have led me with surprised discovery to the fact that you can take two parallel roads with exactly the same mud or exactly the same dust, precisely the same obstacles, precisely the same number of breakdowns on the road, and you can put two divisions on those parallel roads, and one of those divisions is certain to reach its objective far ahead of the other. That is inevitably the case where there is any great difference in the marching capacity of the leaders. That difference is greater historically than you would believe that psychologically it could be. There are no better examples in history than the contrast between Jackson and Longstreet, or between the man who really was responsible for Jackson's marching and Longstreet: R.S. Ewell was, I believe, the greatest marcher in the Army of Northern Virginia. The basic principle of his marching was to carry nothing but his ordnance wagons and his ambulances. Leave all your other supply trains behind you; give the men three days' cooked rations (which would be sufficient in the Army of Northern Virginia for one good meal) and take your ordnance trains and ambulances; leave all your knapsacks and equipment behind, and start out. He was a great marcher. Longstreet never was such a marcher.

In every instance where you find Lee's logistics working out perfectly, as they almost always did with only two exceptions, you will find that he judged the march to be made by the men who were to make it, by the marching capacity of their leaders, by an early start, and by competent staff work. He was very hard on his personal staff. (I have heard that is characteristic of quite a number of American soldiers; I don't know whether it is true or not.) He expected them to hold up always to his own standards. His men were forever grumbling that General Lee would be up, on the march, and at the crossroads before the head of the leading division was even in sight. His men complained bitterly of that. It was not simply that General Lee was an early riser. No. He believed in an early start, and many of his marches are to be explained on the basis of an early start.

Jackson was one of the greatest marchers in American history. He had an absolute and inflexible system that he never varied. As you know, on one occasion he virtually sent to court-martial one of his division commanders for stopping five minutes on the half hour instead of ten minutes on the hour. The man said, "What difference does it make? It is ten minutes in the hour." "Ah," said Jackson, "it makes all the difference in the world. It makes two starts and two stops instead of one start and one stop." And Jackson under no circumstances would permit it. Ten minutes on the hour, no more and no less! And always, in marching—I think it is the secret of no small part of the logistics of the Army of Northern Virginia—always on the march, that ghost-like voice of Old Jack as he went up and down the lines at a gallop, up and down the column: "Close up, men. Close up." Sound logistics mean no straggling.

Again—and I now approach my conclusion—General Lee exemplified that fine quality of an eye for ground. Much of Lee's strategy was based on his eye for ground. I often say to soldiers who are interested in Lee's campaigns that if you want to learn whatever this American has to teach you about position, go some day by motor car to Spotsylvania Court House. Take your large-scale maps with you, stop your car at the Bloody Angle, or go over to Lee's left and follow his course around to the right, and then give yourself a little exercise to this effect: Here is his line, drawn in the face of the enemy; could I improve that line, and how? Having studied that, go on to the North Anna and study how Lee's quick eye caught the one position of strength there. Lee had that eye for ground, I believe, like von Moltke. As we remember, in von Moltke's voyage down the Danube a study of ground must have been one of the occupations of his idle hours.[5] It was amazing how quickly he could understand terrain and how carefully he studied it. He said, "I have to do my own reconnaissance. I am so stupid that I cannot rely on the eyes of others." And I think it is a wise general who doesn't rely too much on the eyes of others.

Lee's fine eye for ground led him to lay down another simple maxim to this effect: Always interpret strategy in terms of available position and lines of march. Now that is not quite the ABC that it seems, for this reason: We are more disposed to interpret position in terms of tactics, and vice versa, than we are to consider position in terms of and in relation to strategy. Lee is the master who says that the available positions in your front have more than tactical importance; they have a place in your broad strategic plan. That doesn't mean the Blue Ridge of Virginia. It doesn't mean the line of the Potomac or the line of the James. It means that in strategic combinations, simple little features of the landscape have an importance that the negligent eye will overlook.

One of the fascinations of my idle hours is to discover again the positions of the armies in the woods and fields of Virginia. As you go over the ground with your maps, with all the after knowledge of the events, you can approach the position and you can say, I'll bet there are earthworks there. And though you will have to dig through smilax and honeysuckle vines, nearly always, if the position was a good one, you will find the works there. They were considered not merely in the tactics of battle but in the strategy of campaigns. Quite often Lee relied on the strength of a little stream no larger than the Po, the Totopotomoy, Beaver Dam Creek or such to make sure that there he could hold with a small force while moving offensively in another direction. The essence of that in its use to you is this: The spirit of Lee says to the American soldier, Despise not the near position in shaping your strategy; do not believe that mountains or vast, defiled rivers are the only features of nature that will be useful to you in your strategic plans.

We have a few instances of Lee's mind, as it were, unveiled. When Lee was working on a strategic plan, almost always we have the same effect. Sitting there with his map unfolded and on his lap, his glasses on his nose, studying, studying—studying first of all the roads for his line of march and then secondly those small features of the terrain that in close combat often mean so much. Despise not the small barrier that nature has placed for your protection or for the disadvantage of your adversary.

Lastly, in the strategy of Lee, his dealings with all his commanders could be put into one single sentence: Know your subordinates. You cannot rely on close logistics unless you are sure that the leader of that column has marching capacity. You cannot strip a front and leave one brigade to defend half a mile unless you know the defensive rifle power of that brigade. The whole thing was epitomized by Lee that day on Mine Run when they brought him an excited report of a flanking operation around the head of the Run. He said, "Who commands the regiment there? Whose regiment is there?" There could not be but one regiment. He wished to know who commanded it. Knowing that, he could gauge its power of resistance.

I have tried to make plain to you these three qualities of leadership exemplified by General Lee: the combination of the high intellect and the great powers of endurance; the dauntless will that never accepts inevitable limitations as paralyzing action; the belief that strategy is the basis of victory. And lastly, in a few words, Lee represents moral leadership. His staff, I say, lived hard because he demanded that they set an example. What could be more tragic than what he demanded of them at Christmas in 1864, when admirers sent to that hungry staff, subsisting on sweet potatoes and corn bread, a whole barrel of turkeys. One of the staff officers took them out and said, "This one, of course, being a big gobbler, is for the general; this one, being next in size, must be for Colonel Taylor;[6] and then, other things being equal, I am entitled to the third in size." Just then the old man, the Great Tycoon as they called him, came in and said, "How splendid that these have been sent to us! Take them immediately, Colonel Taylor, and put them back in the barrel and carry them over to the hospital of Heth's division. The men over there have been on short rations for a long time, and I know they will enjoy these turkeys." He demanded that of his men: hard work, that they set the example. No less did he set the example of cooperation.

I have been engaged during the last year in a study of the operations from secession to the opening of the Seven Days, which will be the first part of the book I hope to get out next year called *Lee's Lieutenants*. That has been fundamentally a study of the command of the Army of Northern Virginia—then called the Army of the Potomac—by General Beauregard and General Joseph E. Johnston. I was never aware, until I made that intensive study of the documents, of the ceaseless friction between Beauregard and the administration and a little later between Johnston and the administration. It is so easy for the administration to blame the high command, so easy for the high command to find an alibi in the derelictions of the administration.

Lee is to every man an example and a challenge. You may not have a perfect president or an ideal secretary of war, and the chiefs of the general staff bureaus may seem to you incompetent. Be that as it may, moral leadership implies not only example but cooperation. How often Lee himself was denied that cooperation!

I read in the current issue of the journal *Military History* a long article by Major Hanson in which he explains Grant's splendid move across the James in 1864. Magnificent! But there is no explanation of the fact that Lee's intelligence broke down because the intelligence of the column across the river was inadequate. No cooperation. Yet that which he lacked, he gave, and that is the final test of the soldier. It is easy enough to be tolerant of those who are tolerant, but the test of tolerance is to be tolerant of those who are intolerant. It is easy enough to cooperate with a friendly spirit; the test of the true soldier is to cooperate with the arbitrary man.

Yes, moral leadership in example, moral leadership in cooperation, moral leadership last of all in self-denial. No nation's leaders are ever more correct or greater in generalship than they are in spirit. No man, entrusted with a desperate cause, can ever afford to withhold from himself that reserve strength that comes from daily self-denial. Lee epitomized it all.

Across the river, here in Alexandria (when, after a visit to Washington, he crossed for the last time that river of contention), in a house in Alexandria—I would I knew the place that I might put a tablet there—the widow of one of his officers brought him a little child for him to bless. The old man took the child and looked at it, and then I can imagine him saying to himself, "This is the next generation, that is to supply teachers and soldiers and leaders for a reunited America. What message?" I think in a quick flash it went through his mind, "What message have I for these boys? What message for this generation that I can summarize here in a word to this child?" He said then what I think every man who wishes to serve his generation must remember first of all, and no man more than a soldier. "Madam," looking up at the mother and stroking the head of the child, "Madam, teach him to deny himself."

Discussion Period

Q. I have been impressed by the items under which you discussed General Lee's leadership and how closely they approach those which we have on our efficiency reports on which officers are rated each year: cooperation, physical endurance, intelligence, common sense, and just one that you did not touch on, I think, and that is physical activity—the ability to accomplish work quickly. Will you discuss that point?

A. Very happily. It is a point that is very little emphasized. General Lee had a very definite regime of life in getting his work done quickly. He had the very unpopular habit of getting up very early. He believed in discharging his important duties the first thing in the morning. If he had an important dispatch to the administration to write, he would write it before breakfast. Of course, breakfast in the army was not enough to surfeit a man, but, such as it was, he didn't even take the chance of writing on a full stomach; whatever the contents of the stomach, he wrote his mail dispatches before breakfast.

He tried, as far as possible, to leave the afternoon free for physical exercise. In doing that he tried always to get a ride. If he could not ride he would take a walk, and he had a very sound rule, which was to relieve his mind by thinking during his exercise of subjects other than those of his daily duties. No matter what he was doing, if four o'clock in the afternoon found it possible for him to go out and get his exercise, he would spend half an hour in contemplating the beautiful landscape around him, in thinking pleasant thoughts; and he always said that when he came back, as the result of that recreation he found himself very much rested.

He went to bed early. He had the peculiar theory—I have never seen it enunciated anywhere else, but I believe it is true—that one hour's sleep before midnight is worth two hours' sleep after midnight. He didn't mind in the slightest arising at four o'clock in the morning. During the Wilderness campaign he was up usually by half-past three and directed the movements of the day. But if he could, he wanted to get to bed by nine or ten o'clock.

His activity in handling his daily duties was based on the principle that he would put into every task that energy that it called for and no more. His repose of manner was a deliberate conservation of energy. He believed that nervous exhaustion hastened physical decline. He tried never to let his body be wearied or his judgment be marred by excitability. Very rarely was he excited. To every task he gave that measure of energy that it required.

He disliked paperwork profoundly. He turned it over to his assistants as often as he could. He started out in a clumsy fashion by calling all his staff in and giving each of them certain parts of the correspondence of the day to handle. But he found it didn't work. He therefore availed himself of the unusual qualities of his assistant adjutant general, Colonel Taylor, a man of very swift memory.

I believe that is, in general, the answer to your question. Active, yes. Nervous, no. Energetic, as required. Excitable, no.

Q. Can you tell us the emphasis that General Lee placed on the personality of the individual in connection with leadership?

A. I think he best illustrated that at Lexington when, one day, one of his faculty members, at a faculty meeting, said that a certain course of action was not according to precedent. He said, "I always believe in adhering strictly to precedent." Lee said, "I never do. I always believe in taking the personality into account."

Now, that is the key to his treatment of the individuals in his army. He had some men as contrary-minded as ever were in the world. He treated every man as an individual problem, every man as a gentleman and a soldier whose wishes and temperament should be taken into account as far as possible. As early as 1853, when General Lee was superintendent at West Point, some question came up from the War Department about the uniform treatment of all cadets; and General Lee, writing as superintendent, in answer said, "With all deference to the department, I do not believe in treating the cadets of the military institute as though they were common soldiers, subject to stern discipline. I believe in treating them as gentlemen who are preparing for the profession of arms." Wasn't that nice?

Lee treated Jackson in a very different manner from that he displayed toward Stuart. His treatment of Longstreet, a difficult man who was a little deaf—that is not always remembered—and one reason why Longstreet sometimes seemed slow in conversation and slow to take orders was that Longstreet was distinctly deaf. Lee always took that into account. After all, he had a group of volunteers. As one old captain told me, "You know, the Army of Northern Virginia was an aggregation of Southern gentlemen voluntarily assembled to repel the invader." Lee knew that and tried always to remember the individual in that fashion.

One of the most charming stories was that one day he met a man with a full beard prying very curiously around his tent. He happened to be a cavalryman who seldom came to GHQ and wanted to see how the general lived. You can imagine him with his saber rattling and his boots loose and with his ungainly, uncomfortable walk—not that that is characteristic of cavalrymen—and General Lee saw him there and happened to alight from his horse and go into his tent. He said to him, "Walk in, Captain." The man said, "I ain't no captain. I is just a private in the Ninth Virginia Cavalry." Said General Lee, "Ah! You ought to be a captain, sir. Come in."

Notes

The stenographic transcript of this lecture is filed in the archives of the U.S. Army Military History Institute, located adjacent to the Army War College at Carlisle Barracks, Pennsylvania.

1. Mikhail Tukhachevsky served as chief of staff of the Russian army from 1925 to 1928 and was made a marshal of the Soviet Union in 1935. In 1937 he was arrested and executed during Stalin's purge of the army.

2. For the results of this study, see Appendix II of the first volume of *Lee's Lieutenants*.

3. In September 1865 Lee became president of Washington College (now Washington and Lee University) in Lexington, Virginia. He held that position until his death in October 1870.

4. Justus Scheibert was one of several foreign officers assigned by their governments to observe the operation of the American armies during the Civil War. After the war Scheibert set forth his observations in a book entitled *Der Burgerkrieg in dem Nordamerikanischen Staaten: Militarisch beleuchtet fur den deutschen Offizier* (Berlin, 1874) (translated into French and English). In the bibliography of *R.E. Lee,* Freeman noted that this book was "especially important for its statement of Lee's theory of the function of the high command."

5. Helmuth von Moltke was the chief of the Prussian general staff from 1858 to 1888. From September 1835 to March 1836, as a young army captain, von Moltke travelled to Vienna, Constantinople, Athens, and Naples on a six-month leave. The journey from Vienna to Constantinople included a trip by steamer down the Danube River. For von Moltke's account of this trip, see *Moltke: His Life and Character (Sketched in Journals, Letters, Memoirs, A Novel, and Autobiographical Notes),* translated by Mary Herms (New York: Harper & Brothers, 1892).

6. Walter H. Taylor joined Lee's staff in April 1861, when Lee was assigned command of Virginia's military forces, and remained with Lee for the rest of the war. In the spring of 1863, Taylor became the assistant adjutant general of Lee's army.

12

Lee as a Leader

Lecture of February 2, 1939

This lecture examines the question of why Lee was accepted as a leader. In answer to this question, Freeman states that Lee was accepted as a leader for the following reasons:

1. *He demonstrated that he knew best what to do.*
2. *He regarded offensive strategy as the key to victory.*
3. *He was always the master of himself; he never lost his head.*
4. *He was a good army administrator.*
5. *He convinced his men that he would never call them to needless sacrifice.*
6. *He was just and considerate.*
7. *He was a man of great spiritual force.*

In discussing Lee's belief in offensive strategy, Freeman breaks his strategy down into six components:

1. *Intelligence.*
2. *Thorough study of the terrain.*
3. *The value of surprise.*
4. *Daring (as distinguished from rashness).*
5. *The wise choice of offensive agents.*
6. *Logistics.*

I assure you, gentlemen, that in all my adventures as a tramp through the United States, none brings me more pleasure than my semiannual visits to the war college. I brag about these successive classes a great deal, and as I go from one college or university to another, I often tell the students that for attention and alertness, I believe the brag students of them all are the students of the war college.

I have been assigned this morning to present to you some aspects of General Robert E. Lee as a leader. I think I have delivered a lecture on this same subject every year at the war college for the last four or five years. Of course, the great facts remain essentially the same; they are not changed by any rearrangement of the material. I have, however, tried from year to year to vary the statement somewhat. The reason is that if you take a great leader of men, whether he is a soldier, a sailor, or a public man, you can approach him from different angles and will find him interesting whatever be the line of approach. It has been my great privilege to have known many of those who fought under General Lee, and my particular privilege to have known rather intimately three of his own staff officers and quite a number of the chiefs of staff of the Confederate corps of the Army of Northern Virginia. They give you, almost without exception, the same picture of the general, but they always approach him in the most fascinating manner from different angles.

I have always thought the most interesting picture was the one given by one of his own staff officers. I happened, among other things, to run across the file of letters written to his sweetheart during the war by one of General Lee's staff officers. I cannot say that they showed any great affection on his part for General Lee. At moments of irritation or amusement, he would call the general the Great Tycoon, which seemed to be his nickname; and again and again he would complain, after the manner of personal staff officers, of the burden of work that had been put on him by the general. Every staff officer of General Lee seemed to think the general picked him out to bear the burden of staff duty—a condition that I daresay was not singular to General Lee or to the period of the War between the States. We have, however, even in those letters, that bright light of the military leadership of the man. You will find a different point of view represented by the staff officers or their generals who came to his headquarters, and still another point of view represented by the corps commanders themselves.

So this morning, with your permission, I would like to approach General Lee's leadership, as it were, from below and from above. I should like to discuss why he was accepted as a leader and how he exercised his leadership. Logically, of course, the second of these comes before the first, but practically, for convenience of treatment, we may put the first before the second.

Why was General Lee accepted as a leader? No matter how good a man is potentially, dynamically his leadership postulates acceptance. You might be the best soldier ever turned out from West Point or polished off at the war college or Fort Leavenworth, but unless your leadership is accepted by your men, your qualities, nine times in ten, will never have adequate opportunity of display. Leadership postulates ability; it postulates no less acceptance of that ability, recognition of that ability by those whom one must lead. Why was General Lee accepted as a leader? It was, first of all, because victory against odds convinced all of his subordinates that he knew best what to do in a given situation. There is no single attribute of a commissioned officer in war, obviously, that has the same effect as victory.

General Lee came to the command of the Army of Northern Virginia immediately after the drawn battle of Seven Pines (the thirty-first of May to the first of June, 1862). The army at that time had been most wretchedly mishandled. A worse executed battle than that of Seven Pines seldom has been fought in America. Everything went awry that could go wrong. Losses had been heavy: three brigades had been practically wiped out; the commanding general had been wounded and incapacitated; the senior division commander, who was practically a corps commander, had cracked and had fallen victim to a nervous disorder which he, at the moment, mistook for paralysis. General Lee seemed to be the most available man. He was brought in. He had all the difficulties and handicaps that a staff officer encounters when he comes to deal with line officers, who have their own caste and their own organization. They regarded him above everything else as an engineer. His West Virginia campaign had not been successful; his operations in South Carolina had been primarily those of an engineer engaged in defensive operations against amphibious power. There was no loud vocal opposition to him, but there was certainly no welcome for him. The old element of the Army of Northern Virginia that had been at Manassas formed practically a clique, an inner circle, devoted to General Joseph E. Johnston. These men looked with a certain patronizing air upon this newcomer. You may find that same condition if you, from the outside, at some future crisis are called to command an organization that already is in being.

General Lee did not increase feeling in his behalf by his first step. He realized he had to protect the city of Richmond against an attack by superior force with much better artillery than he commanded; consequently, he put those soldiers to digging dirt. They called him the King of Spades. That was the first day of June. On the twenty-sixth of June, General Lee assumed the offensive. That operation of the Seven Days campaign culminated at Malvern Hill on the first of July. You might say, therefore, that from the hour he assumed command, with no previous connection with the Army of Northern Virginia, until the end of this offensive operation, precisely one month elapsed. During that single month he won the admiration and support of the army, and he did it primarily by winning a victory against odds. He won it by showing to these men of divided counsel that his was the wise course. He did it primarily by demonstrating capacities greater than those of his subordinates. Always in the case of Lee, as in the case of most other soldiers, the fundamental consideration was brainpower.

It is amazing how quickly all the opposition to Lee disappeared after that initial campaign. I believe it is safe to say that with the possible exception of D.H. Hill, there was not in the Army of Northern Virginia after Second Manassas a single officer who did not believe that General Lee was the supreme military mind of the Confederacy. Jackson, a very great soldier himself—the more I study his career the more I am convinced of that—said after the Seven Days that he was willing to follow Lee blindfolded, and that was not primarily because of Lee's handling of Jackson's corps—though it was called three divisions—during Seven Days. It was because, I think, Jackson knew to what extent Lee had been responsible for the strategy of the Valley campaign, which had immediately preceded the operations of Chickahominy. Perhaps the best tribute to that quality of mind, which won the allegiance of all his men, was the familiar one of the soldier who, in bivouac in 1862-63, used to participate in the debates on the theory of evolution. *The Origin of the Species* had then been three years in circulation, and it was the most continuous of all questions. Every camp fire of intelligent, educated volunteers was a forum for the discussion of the doctrine of evolution. In one such debate, one strong protagonist of the new Darwinian theory had amassed evidence which, as he thought, was irrefutable. Content with his argument, he stood at the end, he thought, the vindicated champion of the new theory of evolution. From the side of the crowd, a man who had been in the shadows arose to make one observation. "Well," said he, "you may be right. All of *us* may be descended from monkeys, but I will tell you it took God Almighty to make a man like Marse Robert." You could not get a finer tribute to the acceptance of leadership through victory, through the dominance of the mind of man, than in that brief and simple little tribute by that nameless and now forgotten soldier.

Why was General Lee's leadership accepted? It was, in the second place, because he had the correct, sound theory of leadership. That, I think, is a point that we must always remember. He regarded leadership in combat as essentially a question of offensive strategy. What made Lee a great soldier? His belief in offensive strategy. If you will go over all his campaigns, if you will survey everything he did, if you will study all those campaigns from the Seven Days on to Fort Stedman, it seems to me that through it all you will find that fiery thread of belief in offensive strategy. There were times when he had to take the offensive-defensive, but even to the last he never abandoned his belief—which personally I think to be a sound belief—that victory depended primarily on offensive strategy.

What were the elements of the offensive strategy to which he adhered? First, he believed that strategy must rest upon the accurate and early intelligence of the movements of the enemy. I think it was last year or the year before that I took this as the text for my whole analysis of General Lee as a leader. The extent to which his whole offensive strategy was based on his intelligence service has, I think, been appreciated by few. At the bottom of everything that related to offensive strategy was just that: accurate and early intelligence of the movements of the enemy. May I say on that score—for I haven't time to illustrate this great truth by citing specific examples—in modern war as it is featured from the standpoint of the military historian, the question is not one of the accumulation of intelligence. Facts, half-facts, rumors, falsehoods come in from many quarters and in many forms. We have good examples of manners in which intelligence services can be organized. Oftentimes difficulties are presented. In some instances, an impenetrable screen seems to be placed between you and the enemy. Believe me that I think I speak for all military historical writers when I say that procuring intelligence reports is by no means as difficult as their correct evaluation. If I had one suggestion to make about the development of the intelligence service of our own army during the difficult months that lie ahead of us, it would be that we lay more emphasis upon the evaluation of intelligence reports, that we check ceaselessly the methods we employ to evaluate the multitude of reports that come into us from all parts of the world. General Lee based the whole structure of his strategy on those two things: that the information be early and that it be accurate.

In the second place, his offensive strategy rested upon thorough study of the terrain. Some of you while you are here probably will go down into Virginia to examine some of the ground over which he fought. I suggest to you, if you are interested in the question of the study of terrain, that above everything else you examine the defensive position he occupied at Spotsylvania Court House from the eighth to the twenty-second of May, 1864. I suggest that you then go on to the North Anna River and study the remarkable position he took up there when he started from Spotsylvania Court House to resist the left flank movement of General Grant. I don't know in American history two better examples of the complete utilization of position than those. Remember, General Lee did not interpret terrain simply in terms of tactics. There is too much disposition to make terrain an aspect of tactics. With General Lee, terrain was primarily a question of strategy. We have many monuments to that great man. One of them lies between my home and my office; and whenever I pass him, there as he sits on Traveller, erect, his rein drawn in, I feel like saluting him, because generations of Southerners are passing in review before him. If to these we might add another monument to this great soldier, I would like to see him represented on his camp stool or on the stump of a tree or on a log. I would like to have him pictured for you in that pose, with a map spread out on his knees. There is the second element of his strategy, his offensive strategy. He knew his ground in terms of strategy and didn't wait to study his ground simply in terms of tactical combinations for combat.

General Lee's offensive strategy rested in the third place on his sense of the value of surprise. We have assumed too much from aerial observation. It is quite possible that campaigns may be fought in country where there will be no cover, where the advance and concentration of troops, even at night, will present great difficulties, where the element of surprise will be reduced. But if we ever have to fight a war in South America or the eastern United States or on the West Coast, where there is adequate cover, all the airplanes under heaven are not going to preclude the element of surprise. Any system of strategy that disdains the element of surprise is, in my judgment, fundamentally foolish. If you doubt that statement, get in a plane and go over that part of the United States which might conceivably be the zone of enemy occupation—that zone south of the Potomac River and north of Cape Fear. Believe it or not, more than half of that country today is covered so completely that you can hide an army there, in my judgment, against the best observation of which modern planes are capable. If you doubt that, go down there and see for yourself; it is amazing how much cover there is in that country. We must not forget that the great masters interpreted their strategic problems in no small measure in terms of surprise, and surprise, of course, postulated cover.

The offensive strategy of General Lee, in the next place, rested upon one consideration that is very easy to outbalance. It is this: He developed quite a daring, as distinguished from rashness. Nothing is easier than for a soldier to be rash and to tell himself he is original. Nothing is more difficult than for him to be daring and at the same time to avoid rashness. I can give you many examples of that in the work of both Lee and of General Jackson. I would suggest to you that if you have to make a study of this particular question, take the campaign from the Rapidan to the James in May-June 1864. Lee then was facing the first phase of the long period of defensive operations. He chafed against the restraints which reduced numbers imposed on him. He desired to maintain throughout the offensive, if he could. To study his correspondence and his reports day by day, to see him striving always to strike, to get General Grant in motion, and again and again to hold himself back because daring might easily become rashness—to do that, I say, is to get a very essential lesson in war. I often say to younger students that if they want to see the difference between the practical and the theoretical, between the daring and the hypothetically rash, study the proposed operations presented in the one instance by General Beauregard and in the other instance by General Lee for the defense of Richmond during the weeks from the thirty-first of May to the eighteenth of June, 1864, the period of Grant's crossing of the James. The plans of General Beauregard were grandiose, rash; the plans of General Lee, no less determined, were practical, full of daring but free of rashness. I am not sure but that that is one of the highest ideals that the soldier ever has to set before himself—to be daring but not to be rash.

General Lee's offensive strategy rested, in the next instance, on the wise choice of offensive agents, officers and men. We assume an equality of elements within a given force. Grant like training for a new national army, grant like equipment, like quality of men, and you will find you will be inclined to think that there is equality among those troops. I hope you are right, but if you are, it will be the first war in the history of the world that I have ever studied of which that was true. No matter what the circumstances, no matter how careful and equal the training, experience is going to demonstrate that for some combination of reasons, some troops will outmarch others, some troops have a larger rifle power than others, some troops have greater staying power on the defensive than others. Explain it as you will—probably it is a question of leadership primarily and of training—but the fact remains.

Knowing that to be a fact, General Lee always showed the greatest care in the selection of his offensive agents. To put it in its simplest form, he regarded the First Corps, Longstreet's, as primarily a defensive corps and the Second Corps, Jackson's, as fundamentally offensive. I was talking with your commandant this morning about one aspect of this. A good defensive soldier, a soldier who has a defensive state of mind, may occasionally render a fine service offensively; but at bottom, the mind of man is either offensive or defensive. Other things being even, for the offensive operation pick the man of the offensive type of mind. Lee relied on Jackson more than on any other single soldier he had for that reason. It was not that the Second Corps was better disciplined than the First or that its morale was higher or that its materiel was better. It had the offensive state of mind inculcated by Jackson, and that offensive state of mind made it possible for Lee to select his agents for offensive operations.

I shall not take time to dwell on the sixth quality of Lee's offensive leadership because on that, if I were to start, I would take all day. Namely, there was in his mind no effective offensive strategy apart from accurate logistics. I believe if anyone were to ask me to pick out two qualities of Lee's strategy that distinguished it from that of other American soldiers of distinction, my answer would be, without hesitation, intelligence and logistics. I have just had occasion recently, in the course of a current study, to investigate anew the logistics of Jackson in the Valley campaign of 1862. I may say that the discovery of recent material throws that campaign into a somewhat different light. Instead of being perfectly designed and conceived overnight by a master mind, Jackson's Valley campaign was wrought out carefully but clumsily, slowly, and experimentally, hour by hour. And maybe the most interesting aspect of it is the development of his logistics. The development of the logistics of the Second Corps, which was based on the Army of the Valley, made possible the logistics of the Army of Northern Virginia. The Second Corps set the pace for the army; Ewell's division set the pace for the Second Corps; Ewell himself set the pace for his division. He said, as you know, in one of the great phrases of American military history, one of the great maxims that have originated in this country, "The road to glory cannot be followed with much baggage." An absolutely sound principle. When he had some troops coming up in support, as he hoped, for the Valley campaign, he wrote their general and said, "This army can get on without anything but food and ammunition. Don't bring a wagon train except your subsistence train and your ammunition train." No effective offensive strategy without sound logistics.

I pass over the obvious consideration of concentration of force. That was not common to Lee any more than to any other man.

Now I pass on to other considerations. These are some of the basic reasons why Lee was accepted as a commander. Very simple. He knew better what he was doing than anybody else, in the judgment of his men. He had a sound and correct theory of offensive strategy. I turn now to other aspects. He became a leader in the eyes of his men because, among other reasons, he always was the master of himself. He never lost his head. There was only one time in his whole career during the War between the States when it could be said that he showed any definite excitement. That was on the sixth of May, 1864, in the Wilderness, when two of his divisions broke under surprise attack by Hancock and then rallied almost instantly. Somehow, it is psychologically explainable. The weak man seeks the inspiration of the strong man. In a time of doubt and difficulty, men with misgivings rally to the men who are the masters of their own mind. They never rally to the stolid fool; they never fail to rally to the strong leader.

The extent to which the morale of the Army of Northern Virginia rested upon the imperturbability of the mind of Lee is in itself a lesson for every soldier who would defend his country's honor. It is so easy to put up a bluff and pretend to coolness when there is turbulence within. I shall try to show, ere I close, that there is a deeper vindication for that strength to which men will rally in the day of misgiving.

General Lee was a leader in the mind of his men because, likewise, he was a good army administrator. The strategist can no more afford to neglect administration than the administrator can afford to neglect strategy. That principle should be obvious. The only aspect of it that the military historian would, in all humility of spirit, bring to the soldier is that quite often the line officer is disposed to look down on the army administrator. It certainly was so in the Federal army, despite the magnificent work done by Ingles and Meigs. It certainly was so in the Confederate army. No great leader can afford to neglect army administration. He cannot for one moment assume that because he is, in his judgment, a strategist, he can, on that account, disdain to be an administrator.

In the next place, General Lee was regarded by his men and was accepted by them as a leader because his lieutenants believed he never called his men to needless sacrifice. Oftentimes he would put them to the test, many an hour he would demand of them bloody sacrifice, but they never thought it was butchery. One of the most dramatic episodes of my childhood attended the publication of General Longstreet's *From Manassas to Appomattox*.[1] He was trying to defend himself from the charges of negligence and delay at Gettysburg,[2] and in so doing he said the third day at Gettysburg was fought because Lee's appetite for blood had not been satiated. Probably it was not meant seriously, but those two lines in *From Manassas to Appomattox* almost revived the War between the States; at least, they almost revived the war in the South. "What!" said those men, themselves aging. "Accuse General Lee of an appetite for blood!" General Longstreet went then into a moral discard from which to this day he has not recovered. It simply illustrates that attribute of Lee's leadership, that he had convinced his men he would not demand of them sacrifices too great for them.

In the last place, he was a leader and his men accepted his leadership because they believed he was just—and more than just, that he was considerate. Oftentimes it has been said that he was too considerate; for example, at Gettysburg. To that I always answer that perhaps he was in one or two instances too considerate, but it never cost him a victory or lessened the advantage he might have gained. On the other hand, it won for him a moral ascendancy over his men that otherwise he could never have had. Here is a man who, having done his best, has found that best not good enough. Is he cashiered? Is he demoted? On the contrary, unless the offense was flagrant, General Lee would call him to his quarters, explain to him the nature of his mistake, and tell him how to avoid it for the future. In a few instances he was imposed upon, but in a very few. Because he was just, men were not afraid to display initiative. They knew if they failed, he would take into account their purpose. They knew if they succeeded, he would give them full credit.

There was one other thing, more basic still than all of these, in the acceptance of his leadership. It was the spiritual quality of that leadership. Army men do not, as a rule, pass through that singular period of skepticism and cynicism that marks, let us say, the average medical student. I think the spiritual life of young soldiers is pretty sound. The moral tone of the officer corps of the United States is remarkably high. Nor is that altogether a matter of army regulation; it is a matter of selection, a matter of national character. At the same time, in this bloody business of war, the average man may conclude—and never was there a time when he was more apt to conclude it than now—that this is a materialistic world where the spiritual values have been eclipsed. Gentlemen, that was not true in the mind of General Lee. Lee had something more than a belief in the righteousness of his cause. Every soldier has that. Lee had a deeper spiritual belief in the justice of God. To him undoubtedly there came what Marshal Foch said was his on the Marne, at Ypres, and in September 1918: clear vision. Lee caught it. He caught it from no other source than what he believed to be Eternal Right. His imperturbability was not physical alone. He was something more than a perfect nervous mechanism. He was a spiritual being.

I am sure, gentlemen, that if the shadows of those great men who walked the streets of Washington ever go back to the Potomac, Lee finds his greatest satisfaction in that picture that you must always see at least once before you leave Washington. Go over to the Mount Vernon Boulevard, go down to the high ground beyond Alexandria, and then turn around and come back toward Washington. There is a point where on your left the purple hills of Blue Run die away in the haze; on your right the whispering river, with its ancestral story of strife; directly ahead, beyond the city, the Lincoln Memorial on your right, pillared Arlington on your left;[3] between them a Memorial Bridge that is a symbol of a reunited America. Sometimes I have seen both the Lincoln Memorial and Arlington bathed in mist or hidden in fog and even the majestic spans of that river bridge for a time obscured, but always above them the shining choir and unfinished transept of Mount Saint Alban.[4] Gentlemen, that is the picture that Lee would like to see of a reunited America, the ideal that I believe he would like to set before young American soldiers—that above every other consideration in the making of man is the Source of spiritual strength.

Notes

The stenographic transcript of this lecture is filed in the archives of the U.S. Army Military History Institute, located adjacent to the Army War College at Carlisle Barracks, Pennsylvania.

1. *From Manassas to Appomattox: Memoirs of the Civil War in America* (Philadelphia, 1896), by James Longstreet. In the bibliography of *Lee's Lieutenants,* Freeman describes this book as follows: "It was written, with literary assistance, late in life, and without consulting his earlier contributions to *Annals* and to *B.&L.* Because of inaccuracies, the book is even more unjust to the wartime Longstreet than to any of those he criticized." (*Annals* is the book *Annals of the War, Written by Leading Participants North and South,* Philadelphia, 1879; and *B.&L.* the book *Battles and Leaders of the Civil War,* New York, 1887-88, 4 vols.)

2. After the war, it was widely believed in the South that the defeat at Gettysburg was due to Longstreet's slowness in attacking Cemetery Ridge on the second day of the battle (thereby permitting the Union army to fortify the ridge heavily). Freeman's research for *R.E. Lee* served to confirm this view. However, following the publication of *R.E. Lee,* the protests of an amateur historian (Runyon Colie of Newark, N.J.) caused Freeman to reexamine the evidence; and in *Lee's Lieutenants* he renders this judgment: ". . . the traditional picture of an unoccupied ridge, waiting seizure while Longstreet loitered, is entirely false. Cemetery Ridge on the 2nd of July, all the way from Cemetery Hill to Little Round Top, was adequately defended from the earliest moment, 9 a.m., at which the Confederates could have launched a strong attack."

3. "Pillared Arlington" was the home of Lee's father-in-law, George Washington Parke Custis, the grandson of Martha Washington and the adopted son of her husband, George Washington. Lee was married in this house in 1831, and it was the principal residence of his family from 1834 until the beginning of the Civil War. Occupied by Union troops in May 1861, the estate was confiscated by the Federal government in 1863 and used as a national military cemetery beginning in 1864. Today the house is known as the Custis-Lee mansion and is maintained by the government as a memorial to Lee.

4. Mount Saint Alban is the site of the National Cathedral.

13

The Objectives of the Union and Confederate Armies

Lecture of February 8, 1940

In this lecture, the last of the Army War College series, Freeman addresses a new topic: the relationship between the commander in chief and the field command with regard to war aims and grand strategy during the War between the States.

In discussing this topic, Freeman examines this relationship for both North and South in terms of the two primary factors governing it: first, the organization of the military; and second, the personality of the commander in chief. It is significant that Freeman cites the relationship between Lincoln and Grant as close to ideal.

At the conclusion of this lecture, Freeman sets forth five statements summarizing the proper relationship between the commander in chief and the field command:

1. *The determination of war aims is the exclusive function of the commander in chief.*
2. *The war aims must be such as to maintain the morale of the nation and to provide sustained economic support for the duration of the war.*
3. *The war aims must not be shaped to placate politicians by giving them military appointments.*
4. *When war aims are thus determined, the strategy required to achieve them must be entrusted to the field command as soon as competent leaders can be found.*
5. *The commander in chief must make every effort to identify and promote these competent leaders.*

It is a great pleasure to see you again and to me, if not to you, a great pleasure, a special pleasure to be privileged to deliver a new lecture. Usually when I come to the war college, I speak once to each class on the methods by which the morale of the Army of Northern Virginia was maintained, and then I speak of the career of General Lee as a soldier. Every time I come, I am reminded by the members of the faculty that I am addressing a new class and that what I will say will be repetition only to the faculty. At the same time I cannot quite get away from the presence of these tin hats on the front seats, and from time to time I reshape those speeches.

This morning I am to have the pleasure of a new topic, one of great importance, I think: the relation between the commander in chief and the field command as respects war aims and grand strategy during the War between the States. This subject is one concerning which there may be in your minds a measure of confusion. That measure of confusion is due primarily to our lack of accurate definition concerning several military terms. I think we confuse the terms *objective* and *war aim*. Obviously, an objective may be set for a detailed operation of small magnitude for a particular campaign; there may indeed be an objective of grand strategy. That certainly is true if you construe the term *grand strategy* to mean that employment of larger strategic combinations for the attainment of a major objective of war, a major military objective of war. If, however, you apply the term *objective* to war aims, you get into a realm where you confuse military and political terminology. A war aim cannot properly be described as an objective; it cannot even be regarded as synonymous with grand strategy. A war aim, as I shall attempt to show you, is fundamentally political; an objective, as we apply that term even in its relation to grand strategy, is essentially military. This is a matter of very great importance to some of you gentlemen here.

There are probably two persons in the United States today to whom this may be a subject of supreme interest. One of those is the man who will be the commander in chief in the next war; the other is the man, perhaps here present, who is to be general in chief in the next war. Unless there is on the part of those two men a proper understanding of their relative functions, a true conception of the balance between war aims and grand strategy, then the results may be disastrous. If there is correct understanding, then we may hope to approach close to the ideal of cooperation between the commander in chief and the field command.

I think I can best approach this by quoting my old friend Newton Baker. Some years after the war I was talking with Mr. Baker about this general subject, and I said to him, "Mr. Baker, did the president, during the World War, give you many orders?" He said, "He never gave me one, and as far as I know he never gave an order to General Pershing. I believe if General Pershing were present he would bear that statement out. The most the president ever did was to say to me at cabinet meetings or when we met, 'Have you thought about thus and so?' I would tell him that I had or would, and there the matter was dropped."

The relationship between the president and the field command during the World War was, on this basis, I think, ideal. Why was it so? I think the answer will be found in the fact, among others, that Woodrow Wilson had been a fairly close student of the War between the States. In a little series of histories issued about 1899, he had written a volume on *Division and Reunion.*[1] In that, he set forth again and again the blunders into which President Lincoln and President Davis both had fallen by a confusion of grand strategy and war aims. I think Woodrow Wilson himself was, by reason of his historical knowledge of that period, able to avoid some of the great mistakes that had been made during the War between the States. Those mistakes were of different sorts on either side, but they were, I believe, equally informative and I think equally monitory to professional soldiers.

To understand the nature of those mistakes we must recall, first of all, the difference in the organization of the Union and the Confederate armies during the War between the States. That is a subject to which very little attention has been paid, even by men who study large campaigns. They fail to see, quite often, that the organizational differences explain many things that would, on any other score, be quite obscured. For example, I often quarrel with General Fuller of the British army because he doesn't take into account these military values, these ponderable differences in the organization of the two armies. His book on Grant and Lee is a classic example of a misunderstanding of factors which mean as much, in the end, as any tactical and probably most strategical combinations.

Please remember that the United States had, in 1861-65, very definite advantages in organization. In the first place, it had an army staff in being. The importance of that scarcely can be exaggerated. It was not, in all its parts, a wholly competent staff. Some of its divisions were—that of engineering, for example; others were quite inferior. But they already existed and that meant much, especially after the battle of First Manassas, when it became necessary for General McClellan to undertake at great speed a large expansion of the army.

Second, the Union had the great advantage of an assured continued existence. There never was any question on the part of the Union regarding the future of the United States. The Confederacy might win, conceivably. If it did, the Union would be weakened in area and in wealth; but never was there, in the mind of any Federal commander—least of all in the mind of President Lincoln—any idea that the outcome of the war would mean the destruction of the United States, whatever its boundaries might be. You say, Why labor about that? I labor about it because it is a consideration of utmost importance in comparison with the condition of the Confederacy. Lincoln could always say,

"Well, McDowell doesn't seem qualified for command; Buell isn't suited; Burnside manifestly was correct when he told us that he didn't feel capable of handling a large army; Hooker is better suited to corps than to army command." He could make and break as he saw fit, in the knowledge that he didn't thereby disrupt his organization. How different the situation was with President Davis, I shall explain in a moment.

In the third place, the Union had the great advantage of possessing a general in chief. Lieutenant General Scott was, on the outbreak of hostilities, the ranking general officer of the army. He held the rank of lieutenant general by brevet and always magnified his office. He called himself general in chief. Whether he ever had that title formally vested in him by law, I don't know; if he did not, he took it. But I am not depreciating him. On the contrary, if there was one man in the army of the United States above the others whose estimable service was disregarded, that man was General Scott. He was the great instructor of the men who fought the campaigns of 1861-65. He was very old and very feeble at the outbreak of hostilities. In November 1861 he retired, and his place was formally assigned to General McClellan. McClellan held it until the eleventh of March, 1862. On that date a presidential proclamation relieved him of his duties as general in chief because he had been assigned to command the Army of the Potomac. From that time until the eleventh of July, 1862, the army had no general in chief. Then Major General Halleck was appointed as general in chief. It was an anomalous position—the authority was vague, the duties confusing and oft-changing. Halleck, however—a man of remarkable capacity in many directions—held that position until the twelfth of March, 1864. On that date, General Grant became general in chief of the army, and Halleck became the first chief of staff of the United States Army.[2]

This meant much or little, this position of general in chief, according to the men who held that position. The general in chief, as that office was discharged by General McClellan, meant little, as I shall show you. Where General Grant was concerned, it meant a great deal.

Still again, the United States had, in the fourth place, the advantage of virtually the same secretary of war from the outbreak. Simon Cameron served for a short time, and thereafter Stanton took office and remained as secretary until after Appomattox. I don't say he was a great secretary. At the same time, I say there never has been anything more infamous in American history than the theory put out by Mr. Eisenschiml to the effect that Stanton was a party to the assassination of President Lincoln.[3] It meant a great deal to the Union to have a secretary of war who was continuously in office and who at least learned in time to know and mind the details of his office.

I need not dwell on the fifth factor of advantage to the Union, namely, that of sea power. No man can understand the land operations in the Confederacy without realizing the tremendous advantage the North enjoyed by being able to coordinate with land operations the navy of the United States. It was sometimes an exceedingly difficult task. It called more for the diplomacy of the secretary of state than for the activity of the commander in chief of the army. But it was done. There are a dozen operations in the war that show how advantageously it was done.

So much then for the advantages that the United States had in its approach to this problem of the coordination of war aims and grand strategy.

What was the situation of the Confederacy? It had one advantage, as pointed out a good many years ago by Mr. J.C. Ropes, the Massachusetts historian, and elaborated by General Spaulding.[4] I refer to the fact that as the Confederacy created a new army, it did not have its trained personnel tied down, as did the Union army, to the regular military establishment. To the student who approaches the campaigns from the Southern point of view and who assumes the army had to be built up, nothing is more astounding than the restrictions imposed by Federal army regulations on the employment of professional soldiers. Quite frequently you would find, especially in the artillery, numbers of highly skilled, professionally trained soldiers under a political major general. There often were regimental commanders who held that position and were under the direction of a Butler or a Banks or some other political appointee.

The South didn't suffer from the requirement that an artillery officer of the regular army remain in the artillery, that the regimental officer, although he may have twenty years of training, could not be promoted except under this condition or that. The Confederacy, organizing an army from nothing, could take its personnel and employ those personnel where and as it chose. The result was that the professional soldiers, few in number, were pretty well scattered through the army. It is interesting to see with what continued persistence General Lee or General Johnston, as the case may be, set out to bring forward the men who had the professional training. Don't for a moment deceive yourself that they were not men who deserved to be brought forward. Occasionally you will find a Forrest or a Gordon who comes from civil life and displays great military capacity. Let not the exception vitiate the rule.

If there is one fact that stands out above every other in the history of the War between the States, it is that command of troops by trained, professional soldiers is the surest means of keeping down casualties and obtaining military objectives. All that General Scott ever said about the value of West Point is absolutely true.[5] To military historians, the most gratifying aspect of the whole situation today, as we look forward to possible involvement in war, is the fact that we now have a corps of professionally trained soldiers adequate for high command. There will be no excuse to put politicians in office.

While the Confederacy had this great advantage, it had the disadvantage of a measure of dependence upon the support of powerful representatives of states. This is in sharp contrast to the condition I described as respects the United States. President Lincoln could make and break, as I say, without regard to the sensibilities of the individual. President Davis had always to face the jealousies within the states: that North Carolina took her part of the major generals, that Georgia could not be denied the distinction of at least one lieutenant general. Quite often political considerations in the Confederacy forbade the proper employment of the trained personnel, even though these personnel, as indicated, could be carried wherever the situation required.

The Confederacy had no general in chief until February 1865. Still again, the Confederacy had no real chief of staff. There were two men who acted as military adviser to the president: General Lee for a period in 1862 and General Bragg for a period in 1864. While General Bragg often has been assailed as an incompetent and impossible person, I think the concentration in front of Richmond in May 1864 shows that President Davis needed such a man. I think the escape of Richmond from capture in May 1864, when the Army of the James made its landing at Bermuda Hundred, was largely the result of the presence in Richmond of the military adviser to the president. Even so, there was no chief of staff. The president, unfortunately from the Southern point of view, was his own chief of staff.

Still again, there were five secretaries of war in the Confederacy and one *ad interim* for a short time. That speaks for itself.

In the same way, the Confederacy had no sea power except for a few super-raiders. If any naval men are present, they will find it interesting to compare the operations of the *Shenandoah, Florida,* and *Alabama* with the operations of the *Graf Spee,* and perhaps after the war is over, with the *Scheer* and the *Deutschland.*[6]

Such were the differences in organization, and these differences manifestly had much effect upon the relationship of the field command to the commander in chief.

No less influence was exerted because there was an equal difference in the personal attitude of the opposing presidents. In fact, if anyone were to ask the military historian to give an initial opinion on the probable relationship between the president and the field command,

I believe he would say that after organization itself, nothing is so important as the personality of the president. Woe to that nation whose chief executive thinks himself a competent soldier! Woe to that nation! The coordination of political and military power effectively is possible only under a Napoleon. We may see one aspect of that in this war—the extent to which the great general staff is dictating to Mr. Hitler, or Mr. Hitler to the great general staff, we cannot tell as yet. Other things being even, the historian will gamble that if Hitler is exercising anything like the measure of control he is assumed to be exercising, it is only a question of time before he makes a fatal blunder. It can't be done, this task of combining the grand strategy and war aims in one person, unless that one person be a Napoleon; and even he, in the end, came to Elba and then to Saint Helena.

The personality of the two chief executives is a factor of major importance. See the difference between Mr. Lincoln and Mr. Davis in this respect. Mr. Lincoln had practically no military experience. He had fought a bit in the Black Hawk War, that is to say, he wore a uniform; whether he was ever under fire, I don't know. He never was under fire during the War between the States, although he was almost within artillery range when General Early made his attack on Washington in 1864. Mr. Lincoln didn't pretend to be a soldier. Among the greatest of his qualities was his humility of mind in this respect. He had no military experience, but he had fundamental wisdom in the choice of his war aims and in the selection of the economic weapons to attain them. On that I shall elaborate in a moment because it is a matter of great importance.

Mr. Davis, on the other hand, seemed to have every advantage from the military point of view that could be desired for a successful revolutionary president. He had himself been a graduate of West Point (had barely escaped being fired from West Point for the not unknown practice of bringing liquor into the post). He had been a successful commander in the Mexican War. His operations at Buena Vista were excellent. No matter whether it was chance, good strategy, or good tactics, he fought well and came back with much praise. Thereafter, he had been chairman of the Military Affairs Committee of the Senate and had been secretary of war.

As secretary of war he was *the secretary*, too! He was the only man who tried to damn General Scott during the time General Scott was general in chief. There arose between the two of them a correspondence which for length and vehemence I don't believe is exceeded in the whole military history of the United States. I sometimes have thought that maybe the failure of the army to advance as much as might have been anticipated under the Act of 1855 was due to the fact that the general in chief and the secretary of war had their energies so much absorbed in this correspondence that they could not give the attention to the military reorganization that they might.[7] If you want to be amazed, read those letters between General Scott and the secretary of war. You will find each of them calling the other by names that you haven't heard for thirty years.

What ideal equipment for a president if there had been political wisdom in proportion! But there was not. Mr. Lincoln had not the experience, but he had the wisdom to see the war aims, to attain them, and to give economic support for their attainment. A very essential condition. Mr. Davis had the military training but lacked the political sagacity.

These differences in organization and in personality involved, of necessity, a different conception of the relation of the commander in chief to the field command and to grand strategy.

Mr. Lincoln's political sagacity was steady throughout the war in his proper sphere, namely, that of attaining his war aims. And the war aims were perfectly simple: to put down what he chose to call rebellion, to restore the Union. He could state his war aims in a single sentence—clear, definite throughout. War aims pursued with the greatest political sagacity. Very few mistakes did Mr. Lincoln ever make in politics.

Of course, he made some mistakes in other respects. I hate to say it, but he cost the lives of tens of thousands of Union boys by some of his political appointments to army command. The naiveté with which he would name a politician to command a division or a department and then entrust that politician with the direction of a campaign is enough to make a man shudder! Mr. Lincoln never seemed to realize, until 1863, the importance of professional training for army commanders. There he erred!

He erred, too, in 1862 by trying to shape the grand strategy of the campaign outlined by General McClellan. I doubt if I need take your time to dwell on that, because it is familiar. It is set forth in all histories of the campaign of 1862. General McClellan goes into it at exhaustive and exhausting length in his official report on the operations. I need do no more than say that while President Lincoln had his war aims clear from the first, General McClellan had a campaign of grand strategy. It was not a perfect campaign—I think you will see defects in it—but it was clear. It clashed with the war aims of the president to a very limited extent; but the political methods of the president, the appointments of the president, and the direct interventions of the president by his general presidential orders marred whatever probability of success there was in General McClellan's grand plan of operations.

What was it? His plan was first, the detachment of that part of the Confederacy west of the Mississippi. Sea power was to be used up and down the Mississippi. That done, the West was to be detached. As you will see, that great basic principle of grand strategy, involving the coordination of the army and navy, was the one concept of grand strategy to which all the Federal commanders throughout the war adhered. General Scott had seen it before the war; General McClellan saw it; Halleck and Grant saw it.

Second, General McClellan believed in the isolation of Virginia by way of West Virginia and East Tennessee. In this he was guided largely by the fact that he had himself fought in West Virginia and had what one might say was Hoffmann's own conception of the value of the Masurian Lakes.[8] He knew the strategic possibilities of that terrain and held to that theory. A right interesting conception! As to whether he was right in saying that he would accept Virginia as a battleground and would attempt to isolate Virginia primarily by operations through West Virginia and East Tennessee, there are arguments that will occur to you as to why this was both a good and a bad plan.

His great objective of grand strategy was perfectly clear: Virginia has been made the battleground; there we will fight it out!

That was General McClellan's plan of grand strategy stripped to its pure fundamentals. How it was defeated by President Lincoln's regard for the defense of Washington, how long General McClellan was denied the power of going down to the Peninsula and starting his operations there, all those are a familiar story to you.

Mr. Lincoln did not learn a great deal from that unhappy experience. On the failure of General McClellan's plan after the battles of Seven Days, Mr. Lincoln did not draw the proper line between war aims and grand strategy. For twenty months he coped with a lack of coordination on all matters except that of splitting the Confederacy in twain by dominating the Mississippi. During all that time, President Lincoln attempted to direct the war through the supervision of seventeen different military departments, in all of which there were more or less active operations. Think of trying to coordinate seventeen departments for the attainment of either grand strategy or war aims! An impossible task!

All the while, too, President Lincoln had heavily upon him the pressure of public opinion for the speedy prosecution of the war. All the while, too, he combated the unwillingness of these separate commanders to coordinate, to assume responsibility, and to act. You cannot blame them, but at the same time you do become disgusted with them. The secretary of war, General Halleck, or Mr. Lincoln decides this operation shall be undertaken. Immediately, word is sent to the commander of the department that this or that should be done, that it is for political reasons, or that it is part of the general war aim to undertake an offensive hither or yonder. Immediately there comes back to Washington the stereotyped answer: "I cannot count on the coordination and cooperation of the forces on my flank in the other adjoining department. I haven't the proper troops. I must have these reinforcements before I can do anything." Mr. Stanton, I imagine, could easily forecast the answer he would receive to every letter he sent out during that period in which he requested an offensive operation. That went on for twenty months. But after Vicksburg, General Grant stood out, and almost in the same measure stood out General Sherman.

The president began to see that he had found two men, and in March 1864, as you know, he brought General Grant to Washington, named him as general in chief, and held with him an interview that clarified many things. You will find the story of that interview told at considerable length in Nicolay and Hay's *Abraham Lincoln: A History*.[9] You will find it told with perhaps less military understanding in Carl Sandburg's *Abraham Lincoln: The War Years*.[10] You will find it condensed in one paragraph in the second volume of Grant's *Memoirs*, page 122.[11] Every soldier who looks to high command should learn that paragraph by heart. General Grant went to the president. Mr. Lincoln said he had brought him to the East and put him in general command because, said he, he always had with him the pressure of public opinion and had always under him officers who would not assume responsibility and act. Said Lincoln, "I have issued these presidential orders. Some of them were bad, some may not have been, but I had no alternative. Now, if you will act and assume responsibility, I will support you to the limit of my power." Remember, that was almost three years after the opening of hostilities. It took that time for the relations between the commander in chief and the field command properly to be clarified. But clarified then they were, and thereafter the story was entirely different.

General Grant had a plan of operations. He had devised it on his way east. He had talked it over in great detail with General Sherman, whose judgment he highly valued. The president said, "I don't want to know what your plan is; but here I have a plan of my own, and I would like to submit it to you. If it is good, accept it; if it isn't, just reject it." He thereupon presented a plan to General Grant in which he assumed that the base of operations would be the Potomac River and that the line of advance would be between two flanking rivers. I have never seen exactly which rivers he had in mind. Said he, "Now with our sea power we can use this river as a base of supplies, and these estuaries we can use as lines of advance, and that may be a good plan."

Of course, he failed to see at the outset that the two rivers which he supposed could give him penetrative power into enemy territory would be excellent flank covers for the army in opposition. General Grant said, "Thank you," and let it go at that. The president didn't ask him for his plan. "Nor," said General Grant, "did I tell him."[12]

There you come close to the ideal relationship. "General Grant," said the president in effect, "my aim is to end the war as soon as possible by an active general offensive that will destroy the Confederacy and restore the Union. I will give you the necessary resources therefor." An ideal statement of war aims. Said General Grant, "The war aims being clear, I will devise a plan accordingly."

He had the plan all ready. It was, of course, to retain command of the Mississippi, to put an end to the sideshows, to stop the Red River operation, and to withdraw all the troops from Texas save those necessary to hold the lower Rio Grande. I wonder if there may not be some importance in that today for those gentlemen in Europe who again are planning sideshows. Think it over.

He decided that for the first time there was to be what the Union never had: one front. Said he, "The Army of the Potomac on its advance will be the center. The left will extend down to Fort Monroe, where General Butler is to assume the offensive simultaneously with the Army of the Potomac. The right is to extend to Memphis. All forces beyond those points are to be considered as forces in rear of the enemy."

That was his bold plan, and he proceeded at once to elaborate it in its great essentials. He ceased to emphasize the strategy of fixed positions, and as all soldiers know, conceived wisely that position meant little compared to the destruction of the Army of Northern Virginia. Of course, his plan for the destruction of the Army of Northern Virginia was very elaborate; it called for combined operations similar to Lee's concentration of the thirtieth of June, 1862. Just as Lee attempted the simultaneous convergence of too many columns at Glendale (or Frayser's Farm), so General Grant was overelaborate in his assumption that he could launch and sustain four simultaneous offensives against the Army of Northern Virginia. Three of them broke down within a week after they had been started. The operations on the left, which should have been successful, were thwarted by the activity of Pemberton and Bragg and by the singular mistake of General Butler in going to the wrong side of the Appomattox River. If you are interested in the ifs of history, consider what might have been done under a competent military commander if Grant's orders to Butler had been obeyed and Butler gone to City Point instead of Bermuda Hundred—all the difference between potential success and absolute failure.

Here were the war aims; here the grand strategy. From that moment, the doom of the Confederacy was sealed. President Lincoln had two men he could trust: General Grant and General Sherman. General Sherman's plan, of course, was to cut the eastern half of the Confederacy in half again. The operations up and down the Mississippi meant dividing the Confederacy in twain. General Grant intended to use his right, based on Memphis, for the final drive that carried him on against Johnston's army at Dalton and then on into the Atlanta campaign.

Contrast that with Mr. Davis' mistakes. Mr. Davis didn't have definite war aims. Most of all, he failed, it seems to me, to appreciate the economic relationship of such war aims as he had. His economic policy was at fault. He relied entirely too much upon intervention. He overestimated the peace sentiment in the North. In other words, politically he was as incorrect as Mr. Lincoln was correct.

Note, too, how even Mr. Davis' knowledge of military affairs played him false. He knew his generals—at least he thought he did—and he stuck to those whom his military judgment told him were good soldiers, even when they failed. He was tied to his men by his technical knowledge of them. That accounted for Bragg, for Northrop. Fortunately, it accounted for Lee, but it accounted also for that tragic change of commanders in front of Atlanta. Mr. Davis did not believe, on the basis of 1862, that Joseph E. Johnston would fight, and following his hunch he relieved him of command.

So far as he had any definite plan of grand strategy, Mr. Davis sought the maintenance of communications with the trans-Mississippi, the severance of the east-west railroad (I need not dwell on the fact that the B.&O. was one of the immediate strategic objectives of the Confederacy), the simultaneous invasion of Ohio and Pennsylvania, and a decisive field victory. So, I should say, roughly speaking, the difference between the grand strategy of the North, as conceived by General Grant, and the grand strategy of the South, as conceived by President Davis, was in reality the difference between attrition and a decisive field victory.

Mr. Lincoln and General Grant agreed that the South had to be worn down. If we may go to a military comparison with the World War, March of 1864 corresponded in their mind to, say, June 1916, when the attrition was undertaken on the Somme. Mr. Lincoln and General Grant held to that view: attrition; worry them down. Mr. Davis still believed that it would be possible to end the war by a great decisive victory. His hope was that the Army of Northern Virginia would be able to enter Pennsylvania and to move on, having broken the B.&O. railroad to Harrisburg, and then get in rear of the large cities and take Washington, Baltimore and Philadelphia in reverse.

Simultaneously he hoped there would be a strong offensive from Kentucky into Ohio that would prevent the transfer of troops from west to east. He was wrong. He didn't have the sea power to coordinate, didn't have the manpower, and was unable to bring together all the necessary forces.

He was equally wrong in his war aims economically, and how important that is! He delayed preparation for the campaign of 1862, wore down the Southern railroads, forced General Lee to conduct subsistence campaigns (those of Sharpsburg and Gettysburg) when they were not justified by the condition of the army, and little by little a bad economic policy gradually wore down the morale of the Southern people. There is the contrast.

Now, may we summarize and restate, on the basis of this experience, the relationship that should exist between the commander in chief and the field command. I can put it, I think, in five small and simple statements.

First, the choice of war aims is the exclusive function of the commander in chief. I don't think that is disputable. It is not for the general in the field to say to what ends the war will be conducted; that is the political function of the president.

Second, those war aims must be such as to maintain the morale of the nation and to provide sustained economic support for the duration of the war. In short, I have put on the war aims of the president, who is the political choice of the nation, those two definite limitations. He may say that we must destroy the Southern Confederacy. Well and good. That is a permissible political aim. With it there must be, however, a correct conception of those war aims in terms that will involve two things: first, the war aims must be those that will sustain the morale of the nation; second, they must be war aims that will provide adequate economic support. Beware of the president who neglects those things! If he has those, his army will go marching on. Read Sandburg and see how Mr. Lincoln kept those war aims clearly before him. Read the life of Salmon P. Chase, and see how he fitted his whole fiscal and currency policy to capitalize on the support the nation was willing to give the war aims of the president.

Third, the war aims of the president must not be shaped to placate politicians by giving them military appointments. There the voices of thousands of Federal soldiers call out from their graves! They were sacrificed by politicians given military command.

Fourth, when war aims are determined within the limitations indicated, the strategical combinations necessary to effect them must be entrusted exclusively to the field command as soon as competent leaders are found.

Fifth, the utmost diligence must be displayed by the commander in chief in discovering and in promoting such men. How slim are the chances that, when the dice of appointment are thrown in the first hour of war, they will spell out the number of the man who possesses the qualities that make him the chosen agent for developing, for achieving this strategic combination! Only by a miracle will a president, no matter what the system of promotion, have in key positions the men who can do that. Joffre had to put 108 general officers into the discard before the Army of France was ready for the campaign of 1915. How many failed before President Lincoln found the men who would take responsibility and act? Due diligence must be exercised by the president in finding those men and in promoting them. One could wish there had been, so to say, a certain electric eye from Washington which, from the moment Grant and Sherman began to show their ability, had been able to follow them step by step. Two and a half years were required to clarify the scene, to weigh the men, to make it appear that these were the agents for this great operation. Once they were found, the rest was simple. The responsibility of the commander in chief in these circumstances manifestly is great.

How much greater is the responsibility of the soldier? If he is incompetent, he is responsible for the loss of as many men in his own army as he puts out of action in the opposing force. If he is diligent, if he sees clearly, then he may be the chosen instrument by which the lives in modern war of a million of his fellow citizens may be saved and the war aims of his nation achieved. It is said, you remember, that Marshal Foch was a student at Metz when his lessons were interrupted by the thunder of cannon announcing the signing of the Treaty of Frankfurt and the transfer of Metz to German sovereignty. That was in 1871. I believe that thereafter, until the hour of the Armistice, his life was devoted to just one end: to making himself fit to serve when the time came. Could you have any nobler end for your life than that?

One of you is going to be general in chief perhaps. Prepare yourself well for it, and know that by your competence—although you may be charged with the slaughter of your foe—by your competence you may be able to save your nation from ruin and your neighbor's son from death. The higher the professional standards of the army, the more profound its study, the more correct its analysis of its relationship with the political branch of government, the less the cost of men's conflict.

Notes

The stenographic transcript of this lecture is filed in the archives of the U.S. Army Military History Institute, located adjacent to the Army War College at Carlisle Barracks, Pennsylvania.

1. *Division and Reunion, 1829-1889* was originally published in 1893 by Longmans, Green, and Co. (New York, London, and Bombay) as the third and final volume of a series entitled *Epochs of American History*.

2. In connection with Grant's appointment as general in chief, it was decided that he would make his headquarters in Virginia with the Army of the Potomac so that he could personally direct the operation of Union forces against the army of Lee. The position of "chief of staff" was created to facilitate Grant's communications with President Lincoln and with the Union's seventeen departmental commanders. In his excellent study of *Lincoln and His Generals* (New York, 1952), T. Harry Williams noted that Lincoln regarded Halleck as the ideal man for this new position because "Halleck had the happy faculty of being able to communicate civilian ideas to a soldier and military ideas to a civilian and make both of them understand what he was talking about."

3. Otto Eisenschiml was the author of several books on the Civil War, including *Why Was Lincoln Murdered?* (Boston, 1937).

4. J. C. Ropes was the author of *The Story of the Civil War* (New York, 1894-1913; 3 parts in 4 vols.; completed by W. R. Livermore). In the bibliography of *R. E. Lee*, Freeman describes this book as "an admirable study." Oliver Lyman Spaulding was the author of *The United States Army in War and Peace* (New York: G. P. Putnam's Sons, 1937).

5. Although General Scott was not a graduate of West Point (the school was only six years old when he was commissioned into the army in 1808), he had great respect for the professional training provided there. In a celebrated speech delivered three months after his capture of Mexico City, Scott paid tribute to the achievements of West Point officers during the Mexican campaign and declared that were it not for these officers, an army four times the size of his could not have taken Mexico City.

6. The *Deutschland, Scheer,* and *Graf Spee* were the "pocket battleships" built by Germany in the 1930s as commerce raiders. Diesel-powered for long-range operations, these lightly armored ships were heavily armed (six 11 inch, eight 6 inch, and six 4 inch guns) and fast (28 knots). During the Second World War the *Deutschland* sank only 7,000 tons of shipping, the *Graf Spee* more than 50,000 tons, and the *Scheer* more than 137,000 tons. In December 1939 the *Graf Spee* was damaged in an engagement with three British cruisers and four days later was scuttled in the Rio de la Plata estuary; in April 1945 the *Scheer* was sunk by the RAF; and in May 1945 the *Deutschland* was scuttled after being heavily damaged by the RAF.

7. The Act of 1855 expanded the army by two cavalry and two infantry regiments in order to police the frontier (the size of which had increased dramatically as a result of the Mexican War).

8. Max Hoffmann was the First General Staff Officer on the staff of the German army that fought the battles of the Masurian Lakes (September 1914 and February 1915). These lakes are in the northeast corner of Poland.

9. John G. Nicolay and John Hay, Lincoln's private secretaries during his presidency, were the authors of *Abraham Lincoln: A History* (New York, 1890; 10 vols.).

10. Carl Sandburg, the renowned American poet, was the author of *Abraham Lincoln: The Prairie Years* (New York, 1926; 2 vols.) and *Abraham Lincoln: The War Years* (New York, 1939; 4 vols.).

11. Here is the paragraph, taken from *Personal Memoirs of Ulysses S. Grant* (New York, 1885-86; 2 vols.):

> In my first interview with Mr. Lincoln alone he stated to me that he had never professed to be a military man or to know how campaigns should be conducted, and never wanted to interfere in them: but that procrastination on the part of commanders, and the pressure from the people at the North and Congress, *which was always with him*, forced him into issuing his series of "Military Orders"—one, two, three, etc. He did not know but they were all wrong, and did know that some of them were. All he wanted or had ever wanted was some one who would take the responsibility and act, and call on him for all the assistance needed, pledging himself to use all the power of the government in rendering such assistance. Assuring him that I would do the best I could with the means at hand, and avoid as far as possible annoying him or the War Department, our first interview ended.

12. In *Lincoln and His Generals*, T. Harry Williams argued convincingly that this account, taken from Grant's memoirs, gives Grant far too much credit for strategy and Lincoln far too little. However, it does serve to illustrate Freeman's point: the president must have a general in chief capable of formulating and executing a sound strategic plan in support of the war aims.

Part Four
The Naval War College

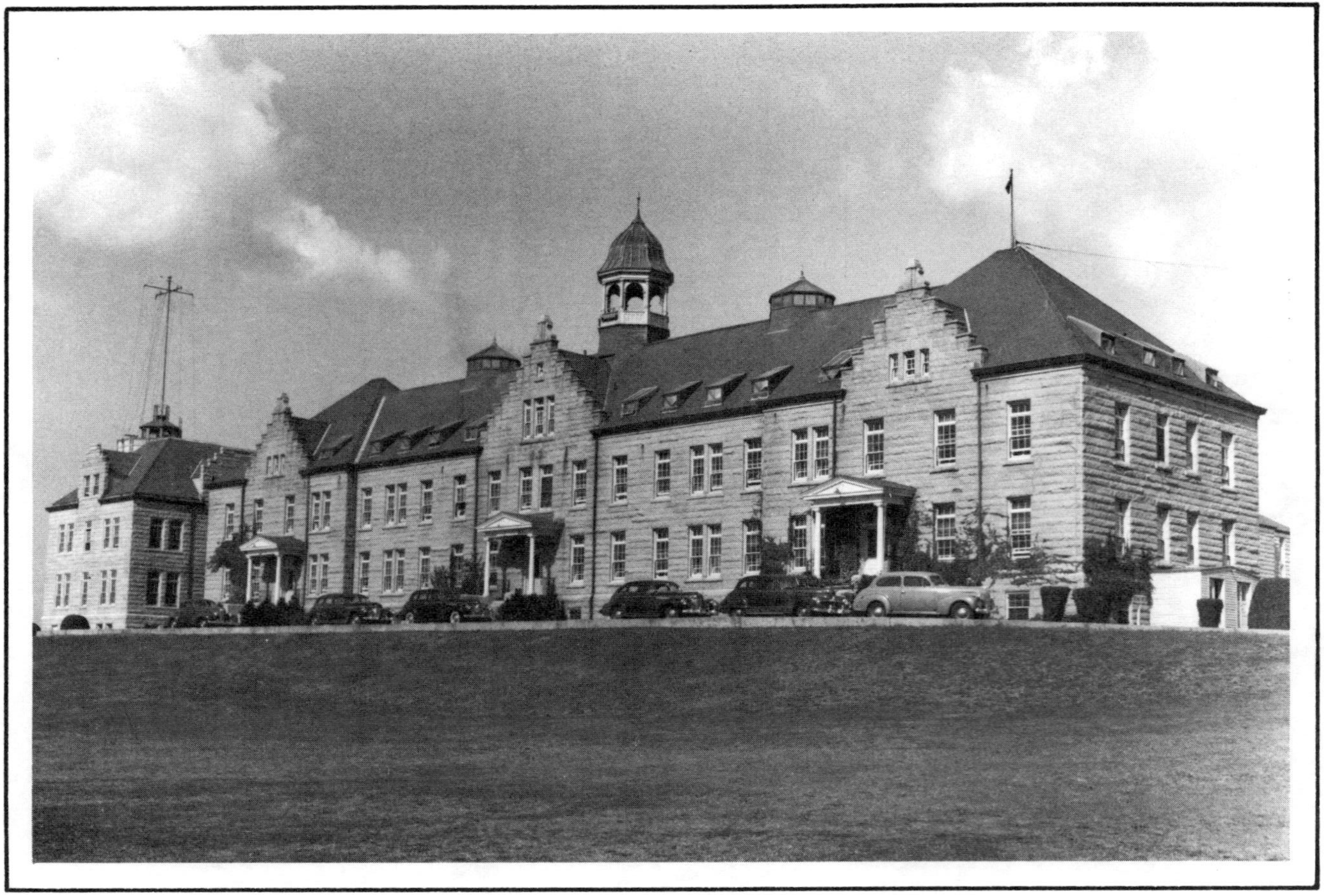

THE NAVAL WAR COLLEGE, NEWPORT, RHODE ISLAND

This photograph, taken in 1947, provides a good picture of what Freeman saw when he lectured at the Naval War College in the late 1940s. On the left is a signal tower that was used to communicate with ships in Narragansett Bay.

With the publication of *Lee's Lieutenants: A Study in Command* during the war years 1942-44, Freeman became very well known and respected in military circles. In the fall of 1945, he served as an adviser to the assistant secretary of war on a worldwide tour of major military headquarters. During this tour, Freeman had the opportunity to meet many of the war's military leaders, including Eisenhower, Nimitz, and MacArthur.

In the eight years following the war, Freeman lectured at many service schools throughout the country, primarily on the subject of leadership. In writing to General Omar Bradley, army chief of staff, on these lectures, Freeman noted, "I certainly am seeking no job, because I have enough to do, but I find as I go from one school to another that the students need a more realistic approach to the study of leadership and they are not getting it, in every instance, from the textbooks and from the abstract classroom lectures they receive." *

These postwar lectures on leadership reflect Freeman's last major historical project: a biography of George Washington, begun in 1944 after the completion of *Lee's Lieutenants.* This biography was published in seven volumes during the period 1948-57 and won for Freeman his second Pulitzer Prize.

The two lectures in this section were delivered at the nation's oldest war college, the Naval War College, established in 1884 in Newport, Rhode Island, and situated on a small island overlooking Narragansett Bay.

---

* Freeman to General Omar N. Bradley, 4 June 1949, Freeman Papers, Library of Congress (Container 95; General Correspondence File).

14

New Leadership in the Light of Old

Lecture of May 13, 1948

Freeman begins this lecture by stating that the great American military commanders have all been men of character, and that they won their battles and wars by superiority of numbers, of equipment, and of morale. When one of these components of superiority has been lacking, says Freeman, the great commanders have made up for it by a transcendent superiority in another.

Freeman then proceeds to analyze in detail the component of morale, which he breaks down into four factors: supply, discipline, command, and victory.

In an eloquent conclusion to this lecture, Freeman recalls the mottoes of several great commanders of the past.

The admiral, gentlemen, is very kind in welcoming me and very tolerant in not giving me what is, in reality, my familiar name at the various army and navy schools in the nation. Whenever I go to one of the command schools, those who know me, and particularly those who through the years have endured my lectures at the National War College,[1] always style me the "Rip Van Winkle of the American armed forces" because I have had the great and distinguished honor, through the years, of living for a long, long time with some of the great men of the armed services of the past.

It's no small thing for a man to live for thirty years of his life while he looks into the private correspondence of such men as Robert E. Lee and George Washington and Stonewall Jackson. It's no small thing to stand, as it were, and look over the shoulder of those men as they are writing their most confidential messages to their chief executive. It's been a great privilege.

It's been a great privilege also for a man to have known, as I have known, some of these great men in the flesh. I can recall, as a little boy, the tottering, bent figure of Jubal A. Early, who was commander of the Second Corps of the Army of Northern Virginia during some of the late phases of the war. We little boys, in the old town where General Early lived, shuddered when we saw him because there was a tradition in that town that General Early ate a little boy every morning for his breakfast. And yet, small as I was, I marvelled at the deference our fathers showed for that old man when he would walk down the street, bent and bowed but still clad in Confederate gray, carrying in his hand an army staff, oftentimes chewing tobacco furiously all the while. He would scowl at the men who would stop and take off their hats to him. The most he would do would be to grunt in answer to their greeting. And yet, when they saw him, they saw not the man that was but the man that had been. As they looked with eyes of maturity, they saw again the vision of that man in youth. They saw him, and that gray coat of his was covered all over with buttons and with braid, and that staff in his hand was a sword of command there on the heights of Fredricksburg or deep in the Wilderness of Spotsylvania. Yes, it's been a great privilege to have known those men. I saw Longstreet in the flesh; I saw Fitz Lee when he still could ride a horse; I saw John B. Gordon, one of the few civilians who ever showed qualities of high command without technical and professional training as a soldier. I knew them all, to my great joy.

Then, having communed with them and in these later years having had the thrilling experience of dealing with young George Washington, I had the great honor, before, during, and after this war, of seeing their young colleagues of America. It was a great thing to go to Vienna and to see Mark Clark for example, when I remembered him as a tall, perhaps the tallest of all men at the war college in 1936-37. It was a wonderful thing to see Eisenhower abroad in Frankfurt, and the last time I had seen him he had been sitting in the outer office of MacArthur, who at that time was chief of staff. It was interesting, and at the same time it was amusing, because quite often when I would go into the offices of these men, whether it was at Frankfurt or whether it was at Tokyo, they somehow would straighten up and become a little self-conscious, as if they said to themselves, "My God, is that man going to take my historical photograph here and now?"

One remarkable thing about them, gentlemen, is that they are all so much alike. I looked not long ago at the magnificent bust of John Paul Jones, and I thought to myself, "That could be the composite picture of the American naval commander. The eyes, the head, the line of the mouth, the poise of the shoulders, the courage, the confidence, and yet with all the good humor of it—that isn't John Paul Jones but that's the American naval commander, that indeed is the American fighting man."

I have seen them. I have seen young George Washington come back at the end of the war in 1759.[2] He wasn't brokenhearted but he was disillusioned. He had given five years of his life under immense emotional strain to the cause of the country, and he was coming back with exactly the same rank that he had when he entered the service. He had been a provisional officer, correspondent of our National Guard officer of today, and when it was all over he came back. Oh, there was applause for him, but there was abuse for him likewise. Think of it: It had been said of him that when he sent in the report of a great alarm on the frontier, he did it because he wanted reinforcements and a higher command; he had seen the people in the colony of Virginia denounce the officers of his regiment as drunken debauchees; there had actually been a time when the commander in chief of the British forces in America had suspected that George Washington was the man who was communicating secretly with the enemy. All that he had to deal with, and yet he came back, typical of hundreds who were to follow him—he came back with wounds of pride and bruises of body and with a reputation far less exalted than he deserved, but he came back with integrity of soul. What's true of him is true of all that long, long company that wore the epaulets and carried the insignia of the American forces. I can say this: I do not know the commanders of the War of 1812 in any detail because I have not studied it; the others, I might say, I am not altogether unacquainted with; and I have not yet seen one great American seaman, one great American soldier, who was not at the same time a great man of character.

That tribute I would like to pay at the very start of my remarks to you gentlemen, as you are here now concluding a year of the most eventful study, of the most fascinating experience you'll ever have in times of peace. Be sure of that: These men who stand out in the annals of our nation are men fundamentally of integrity of character above everything else. Oh, you'll find a wastrel and a rascal who fights a brilliant battle and sometimes wins a chance campaign; but you'll never find one in all the annals of our nation who had the esteem of his country, America, who did not at the same time have self-respect, the justification of an honest character devoted to his nation.

Yes, I say these men have many things in common, and the history of our nation's wars have many things in common. Nowhere, gentlemen, more than in the history of war do we find more visibly, more surely demonstrated the truth of that great observation of George Adam Smith. He is the author, among other things, of that historical geography of the Holy Land.[3] I beg you, if you have the opportunity, to read it, because it will explain to you the basic physical conditions that determine even now the conflict that seems to be progressing toward this grim climax between Zionist and Arab. He says in that masterful book, one of the most fascinating volumes of our times, "History never repeats itself without interpreting itself." You'll never read of your second war without understanding better the first war you ever studied. The first campaign that you have mastered will help you by its repetition thereafter to interpret the second campaign.

It is true of American history, and through the years, generation after generation, the same story is recorded. How did they win the wars? By superiority. That's how they won them—by superiority. Of course, superiority has three aspects: superiority of equipment, superiority of numbers, superiority of morale. That army is invincible which has superiority in all three respects. But oftentimes in the history of our nation, a nation so slow to prepare for its defense, we are not able until the final phases of the war to have superiority in all three of these respects. Wherefore American history and American wars interpret themselves again and again not in terms of only one superiority, but in terms of a transcendent superiority in one particular which makes up for deficiency in another.

Take the navy of the Revolution, shaped as it was, and yet what it lacked in firepower and in number of vessels it made up in morale. Inferiority was ours in many ways in the great amphibious campaigns of the French and Indian wars—a campaign, a succession of campaigns, but gentlemen, a far greater study than they have received at the hands of our public. Read the history of Cartegena in 1741, if never you've read it.[4] Read of the two descents on Louisbourg, how one failed for lack of cooperation on the part of amphibious forces and the other succeeded primarily because of it.[5] Follow the works of that amazing man John Bradstreet and see how one officer, making his own ships, was able to cut the line of communication of the entire French force in order to make possible the victory of John Forbes in western Pennsylvania in 1758. Ah, yes, if we have lacked superiority in one particular, it has been the great service of American officers that they have made it up as far as men might in the other particulars. Are we numerically inferior? Then in morale we must be superior. Have we fewer guns? Then fire them more accurately. That's the story.

On superiority of force and superiority of equipment I need not dwell. That is a story known to you, every phase of it. You have followed it here in your course. May I consequently speak to you of old leadership and new in terms primarily of morale—superiority of morale—and what that means to leadership and what that demands of leadership. I take my text primarily from the Army of Northern Virginia. I do so for two reasons. The first is that this army was hopelessly inferior in numbers and in firepower of the artillery arm, and it was incredibly inferior in all other forms of equipment; what superiority it had was, of necessity, superiority of morale. And I will take it as the basis of my text for the reason that my good Confederate father once explained to me when he said, "My son, as you write of American history, and in particular of the conflict between the states, never depreciate the Army of the Potomac. I fought against it, and I want to say that with the exception of one army, the name of which modesty forbids me to mention, it was the greatest army in America." Modesty no longer forbids me to mention that Army of Northern Virginia. Indeed, my heart beats faster each time I hear its name. And if, as an historical writer, I have come to the great divide, it was not when I wrote this book or that one better or worse than those that preceded it; it was when I stood before a general assembly of admirals and generals and younger soldiers and said, "Gentlemen, I make the great concession. The Army of Northern Virginia has been outdone by the American army of the Second World War." "But," I said, "you have got to admit that it was good because it had so many descendants of the Army of Northern Virginia and the Army of the Potomac in it."

General Lee never set forth his theory of morale. Nowhere did he ever write the basic doctrines; but Lee—and Jackson with slight variation, and before them Washington—laid down certain guiding principles of morale that are of infinite value to leadership. They held that morale depended upon four things: upon the service of supply, upon the nature of discipline, upon the competence of command, and upon the component of victory. The service of supply; the nature of discipline; the quality of command; the component of victory.

You may have to fight a great battle at sea again, which God forbid; sometime you may be compelled to throw out on the line a weary division that has lost half of its numbers; or sometime, God forbid, you of the Marine Corps may have to fight another Iwo Jima. Iwo Jima—I must pause at that name, and I must say to you, if you ever find a man who would depreciate your comrades of the Marine Corps, you ask that man, "Have you ever seen Iwo Jima; have you ever looked down from Suribachi on that far sounding beach?" And if he says no, you then say to him, "Never speak of the Marine Corps until you have seen Iwo Jima." You may be compelled to throw out your troops; we have made the mistake oftentimes in keeping them too long in line. I said in 1939, I shall say in 1949, that we have never yet appreciated the factor of fatigue and its effect on men, fatigue of combat. When you throw men out, above everything else, let them wash, and find for the ragged new uniforms; and above everything else, no matter how heavily you have to call on commissary, give them something special to eat. Read if you will in that connection the story of what happened to the Army of Northern Virginia after Sharpsburg, when only through the blunders of the adversary did the army escape defeat. When Lee drew his army back into northern Virginia, the first thing he did was to increase the ration and the next was to put the army in decent uniforms. The result was the morale that showed itself from the heights of Fredricksburg on the thirteenth of December.

Oh we of America, we students of wars, have never appreciated until this conflict what the service of supply means. You may remember how often in the past we have sneered at the commissary of the old war and the quartermaster of the new. Let me, as a writer of military history, say to you that I never see a quartermaster officer who fought in France that I don't take off my hat to him.

I had the privilege of going over General Patton's diary and of deciding whether it should or should not be published. Boy! That document burned the pages it was written on! Patton did not literally call men by hard names, but he came just as close to it as a gentleman could. And when I read that story of the drive, drive, drive of the Third Army, I said, "Glorious work; fine command of those tank divisions; superb leadership at the top." But don't forget those men who kept those tanks full of gas and those men's bellies full of food. I remarked that once at the ground forces headquarters, and some man said to me, "Don't give all the credit to Patton's service of supply. Just remember, above other things, that if anybody else's tank cars or anybody else's gasoline or anybody else's trucks ever got down in the Third Army area, they never got out again!"

Service of supply—what that means to man!

Discipline. I spoke a moment ago of the battle of Sharpsburg. I've often marvelled at that fight. It was a segmented battlefield, an incredible battlefield. The attack began on the left; Lee was forced to draw it in. The battle shifted to the center, and there came critical operations when it was one little brigade of two regiments that stood out there against a storm of attack—the Twenty-seventh North Carolina and the Third Arkansas. I said, "How did that command ever stand? How did it ever stand?" During the day, when the attack on it was most furious, Old Pete Longstreet sent Colonel Sorrel to ask the commander, Colonel Cooke, if he wanted any help. Colonel Cooke sent back word no, and he added among other glorious observations that Sorrel could present his compliments to the general and tell him that he and his two regiments were going to stay there until every Yankee in front of them had been so long in hell that General Sumner was calling the devil by his first name![6]

How did they do it? I often wondered, until I read the story of that Twenty-seventh North Carolina and found that whatever else had happened, the commander of that little regiment had inculcated discipline by looking after his men—looking after his men. Many years ago, when Confederate veterans were still quite numerous, I made a point of asking them what they thought was the greatness of Lee. They didn't know anything about strategy. They didn't know anything about logistics. (The word hadn't even been used in their war; the first use I've ever found of it was in 1866.) But they gave with surprising unanimity the same answer: "He looked after his men." That discipline they regarded first. The comfort of the men as the prerequisite of the fighting quality of those men is the soundest discipline of all. That little regiment had been engaged in the battle of Malvern Hill. It had come out in the drenching rain. Its commander had ridden back to the rear and had called the cooks and had had them build warm fires for the men and had had hot food ready for those men when they came out. And that, I've said a thousand times, was one of the secrets of the discipline of those troops. They were good because they were looked after and because they had good quality to start out with.

I could elaborate—I have two long lectures on that very question of the relation of supply to discipline—but I hurry on because I must say to you a word about the place that command has in the morale of troops.

Command. We think of command primarily in terms of the relationship between the officer and the enlisted man. What an absurd definition; what a strange limitation! We must think not merely of the man in the ranks but of the young officer and of what must be done to bring forward the young officer of ability, to make him feel that he is a part of the machine and not merely the mouthpiece of the high command. I often say that no matter how great our armies may have been either in the First or the Second World War, we never have invalidated the point of the question that Lee asked at the battle of Mine Run. It was December 1863. All of a sudden, there was a threat on his flank—it was his right flank—and he was facing east. It looked bad for a moment, and the first question he asked was, "What regiment is on that flank, and who commands it?" One regiment, and he knew the value of that one regiment. Woe to that officer who ever gets so high that he doesn't think of his juniors! No man is fit to command who lacks understanding of those who work with him.

You are going to be called on some of these times to deal with incompetent men. Fortunately, now our army and navy schools are large enough for us to take selected material and training. While in the mercy of God we frequently find those men who have material military sense (MacArthur says it is just as definite as the sense of sight and of smell) without having professional training, of course we are going to rely on professional training throughout. But we are never going to be able to say that because a man was trained at Annapolis or at West Point, or had group schooling here or at Washington or

Leavenworth or at Norfolk or the amphibious school or wherever it may be, that he is on that account going to be good. He isn't. He isn't going to be good unless he knows how to make the best of the material he has; he isn't going to be good until he has stood the test of combat; he isn't going to be good unless he shows that he can deal with his companions in arms. To get rid of the incompetent man without ruining him for the future is as great a problem for the commander as to see to it that the soldier or sailor has his chance.

Command means cooperation. Read the story of the two attacks on Fort Fisher and see how in the one instance the lack of cooperation on the part of a political, stupid general denied the Federals the victory which was won easily in the renewed attack because there was cooperation.[7] And it means cooperation with your next in command. How many beautiful stories come to mind as I admonish you to think of the man next below you not as someone who is going to outstrip you but as someone to whom you have an obligation, someone to whom in the true spirit of comradeship you may extend the greatest cooperation. I've seen it. I've seen it at Pearl Harbor. I've seen Nimitz when, knowing that his days as commander in chief of the Pacific were ended and that ahead of him was the high office of chief of naval operations, he called to Pearl Harbor the man of all men whom he trusted, the man of all men whom he wanted to be his successor; and there on the hill looking down on the scene of that great tragedy of December 1941, there on the hill at his headquarters, Nimitz took him in. I was at the house next door, and there wasn't a morning when they did not sit down together at the mess table and walk out together; and never was there a more beautiful example of comradeship and mutual confidence, those essentials of command, than was displayed there. As I looked at them, I said to myself, "Ah, the comradeship of David and Jonathan, which is the most beautiful of all the brotherly stories of Holy Writ, is repeated in the relationship of Nimitz and Spruance."

It was forecast in the story of Lee and Jackson. Turn, if you will sometime, to that story of May 1, 1863, when there at the bivouac, Lee called Jackson to him and said, "Well, how do you plan to get at those people, General?" And Jackson, taking out a crude sketch map, said, "I plan to go around here"—and he drew it with his finger—and Lee said, "What are you going to make the movement with?" Jackson in his muffled voice answered, "With my whole corps, twenty-eight thousand men." That left Lee only twenty thousand. Jackson to go on a movement against a flank that was in the air; Lee with twenty thousand to stand there and take the hammering of the whole of the Federal army—it was an audacious thing! It put a tremendous burden on Lee, and yet what? Such was the trust, such the lofty conception of command, that Lee simply said, "Well, go on."

Ah, the Wilderness of Spotsylvania has lost its terror now. Where was the forest with saplings shattered by fire, there lie now the cornfields. Where one could hear the sound of the whippoorwill, there now is the laughter of children. The odor of earth mold and of pine has given way now to the scent of gasoline on the highways. Where of old there was the rumble of the caisson, now you hear the whirr of the school bus and the honk-honk of the passing motor car. The Wilderness has lost its terror; the Wilderness has become a part of civilization; and yet I think there are times when in the May noon or in the shadows, you hear the voice of Lee saying, "Well, go on."

Morale, depending largely on command. Morale—creature of supply; creature of discipline; creature of command. Morale means your full regard for your comrade and no jealous measuring of the risks you take or the honor that may come to him.

The greatest of all morale perhaps is the morale of victory. I need not enlarge upon it. Oftentimes before the war, I said to classes of the war college, "Gentlemen, don't fool yourselves; you never know what you are until you've come to combat." And I repeated then what I said to General Marshall. I said, "General Marshall, you are a soldier and I'm only a writer on military history, but don't you be surprised if 25 percent of your corps commanders fail you in the first campaign." He didn't like it; he said that the screening process that we had gave us the assurance of a much higher level of successful command than that. Well, maybe he was right. The point is, by reason of superiority in numbers, in morale, and perhaps above all, in equipment, we never had to put that quite to the test because an incompetent man (and we had some), a mediocre man (they were not lacking in our corps command or in our divisional command) can get on so long as there is victory. Had we been repulsed on the line of the Rhine or on the line of the Meuse, there might have been a different story. Then we would have realized that morale in adversity calls for different qualities from command than in victory. We had the morale of victory all the way through. Aye, we were living again those days of the French Revolution. The music of the Marseillaise was in the eyes of men; their ears rang with it; they saw the light of a new world, the hope of a new day; and one of them quoted volumes when he said of the feeling of the French army, "We felt as if we were forever marching into the dawn."

Gentlemen, I am done. I have said to you that the story of the American command is a story of integrity and of superiority. I have said that that superiority was of numbers, of equipment, and of morale;

and I have then tried to explain to you that morale involved adequate service of supply, that with it was coupled the right sort of discipline, the right type of command, and a great component of victory. I have this only to add for you. You are going out, many of you, on Saturday. Wise words will be spoken to you, I have no doubt, by your commencement orator; wise words will be spoken to you by the secretary of the navy. Maybe you'll wear your sword. What is going to be on that sword?

Once while I was in Tokyo, I happened to be in General Fellers' office waiting for General MacArthur to receive me.[8] There on a desk was a great box, and in it, under an exquisite piece of white silk (the very whiteness of the silk was a mockery), was the most beautiful Samurai sword that ever I saw. I asked Fellers whence it came, and he said that as far as he could make out it was the sword of the Ministry of War. I looked at it—I did not have the presumption to touch it—but I thought about my own father's sword, and I thought about the swords of those men of whom I'd written and about the swords of great captains of the past.

What would have been the motto on Napoleon's sword? Surely it would have been those words he had taken from a French statesman: "Audacity, always audacity." What would have been on Washington's sword? Ah, had he written the motto that described his life, it would have been those words he spoke as a young commanding officer, a young colonel: "Discipline is the soul of an army." And on the other side he would have written no doubt, "Preparation for war is the best guarantee for peace." On Jackson's sword, what would have been written? Stonewall Jackson's sword? Ah, the words he spoke on that same flank movement at Chancellorsville: "Push on, push on!" And on the other side, "Take no counsel of your fears." I think of Grant's sword as having written on one side, "I'll fight it out here if it takes all summer." And on the other side, "Let us have peace." Lee's sword? "It is history that teaches us to hope." That would have been his message. And on the other side, "I will take the consequences of my acts."

Great swords these. Some hang on the walls of museums; some are in cases where reverent eyes gaze on them. Some day your children and your children's children will take out your sword. Your motto may not be written there, engraved on steel, but it will be written in the history of the American army and navy. What will be your motto? What is the ideal that you set for yourself? Of all the lessons of old leadership, priceless anew, which will apply to you? On your answer depends not only your service to your nation, but likewise your loyalty to God and your self-respect as a man of integrity.

Notes

1. The National War College was established in 1946 in the building that had housed the old Army War College (at Fort Lesley J. McNair, Washington, D.C.). The National War College has no record of Freeman lecturing there; therefore, he must have been referring to his lectures at the Army War College (1936-40).

2. Washington was appointed an officer in the Virginia militia in October 1753, several months before the outbreak of the French and Indian War. In August 1755 he became the commander of the Virginia militia. On 31 December 1758, with hostilities in his theater at an end, Washington resigned his commission to take a seat in Virginia's House of Burgesses.

3. Sir George Adam Smith, Old Testament scholar and theologian, was the author of *The Historical Geography of the Holy Land* (1894) (completely revised in 1931 for its twenty-fifth edition).

4. In 1741 the British made an unsuccessful attempt to take Cartagena, Colombia, from Spain (then allied with France). The expedition was a disaster: of the 3,500 Americans included in the landing force, only 600 survived.

5. In the summer of 1757 a British force under John Campbell, Earl of Loudoun, failed in its attempt to capture the French fortification at Louisbourg, Nova Scotia (which guarded the main entrance to the St. Lawrence). One year later, in July 1758, this fortification surrendered to British forces under command of Jeffrey Amherst.

6. Sorrel was Longstreet's assistant adjutant general; Sumner, the corps commander of the Union forces attacking Cooke's brigade.

7. On 25 December 1864 Union forces under General Benjamin Butler failed in their attempt to capture Fort Fisher (at Wilmington, North Carolina). On 15 January 1865 Union forces under General A.H. Terry captured the fort. Both operations included the participation of Admiral Porter's North Atlantic Blockading Squadron.

8. Fellers was MacArthur's military secretary.

15

Leadership

Lecture of May 11, 1949

This is the "standard" lecture on leadership delivered by Freeman in the postwar years—a lecture which he fondly referred to as "Old Number One."

In this lecture, Freeman skillfully weaves examples from the Revolutionary War, the Civil War, and the Second World War into an eloquent statement that leadership consists of three things:

1. Know your stuff.

2. Be a man.

3. Look after your men.

When I was a lad I had the great pleasure, the infinite honor, of seeing some of the great men of the War between the States. Strange as it seems, I can remember Jubal Early. What a somber (I almost said a sinister) figure he was as he walked around town, chewing tobacco fiercely and leaning on a long staff. As soon as we little lads would see him we would run away, because it was thoroughly understood among all of us lads of about five years old or thereabouts that General Early ate a little boy for breakfast every day.

I remember John B. Gordon; I remember Fitzhugh Lee; I remember James Longstreet. I knew well a number of the younger staff officers of General Lee and General Jackson. I knew personally and talked often with three of General Lee's staff officers, one of them his assistant adjutant general, and of course I knew the leaders of the Spanish War, of the First World War, and of the Second World War. Many of these men of the Second World War I taught at the war college. And it was amusing beyond expression to go to headquarters immediately after hostilities, to go to General Eisenhower's headquarters or to General Clark's headquarters or to General MacArthur's headquarters, and see some of these men I had known as majors at the war college stand up and say, "My God, am I going to have my historical photograph taken now?" So those are the circumstances that make me feel, as it were, that I am the Rip Van Winkle of the armed services.

But no man can go through this long stretch of years and have the honor of seeing these great men without having an admiration for them, an admiration for the service and a reverence for the leadership that these men exemplify. I have seen a new chapter of it during the last year because I have been studying George Washington after he came to the command of the American army in June 1775. Nothing that he had ever done before showed the qualities that he then displayed. I don't think anybody who studied Washington as he was in 1759 is prepared for what Washington was in 1775. I think strangely enough, that out of his civilian training, out of all the difficulties he had to endure, there developed the patience, the maturity of judgment, the essential sanity that were the hallmark of the remarkable ability of that man.

You know, we look at Washington usually through the silly pages of Parson Weems[1] or as we see him in the portraits of Gilbert Stuart. I think either approach is wrong. Washington wasn't the stupid prig that he is made out to be by Weems, nor was he the embalmed celebrity that he appears to be in Gilbert Stuart's portraits. Of course, many of the portraits of Gilbert Stuart are pretty good works of art of the type and of the age (he made a good living in portraits of George Washington); but personally, except for the one at the Boston Art Museum, I'd like to see all the Gilbert Stuarts of Washington destroyed. I wish they were all burned up, because they give such a false impression of the man. The Peale portraits of him, even the Trumbull portraits, have so much more of the vitality that was Washington—the sanity, the judgment, the humanity that was his. You who are older used to see George Washington presented to you in front of the east portico of the Capitol. Washington, being a modest man, I think would have been very much embarrassed if he had seen how nearly naked he was presented in that statue of him in front of the Capitol, where he sits in a Roman toga which would suit Washington weather in July and no other weather in the world. And he sits there with his hand outstretched, as if saying, as Lorado Taft used to put it, "My body lies over at Mount Vernon; my clothes in the Pension Office."[2]

He exemplified leadership, which is not anything like as complicated as some of the psychologists would make it out to be. Psychology is going to be a great subject one of these days. Now it's just in its infancy; and when we try to apply it in the abstract to problems of leadership, we usually make monkeys of ourselves—we don't get very far. Leadership is fundamentally common sense and mankind. Maybe I'm going to oversimplify it for you this afternoon, because I'm going to say that it consists fundamentally of three things and three only. If a man meets these three conditions, he is going to be a leader; if he fails to meet them, he may be on the roster as the head of a command, but he will never be at the head of that command when it marches down the pages of history—never!

First, know your stuff. Know your stuff, just that. If you are an aviator, know it. And know something else besides. We are entirely too much disposed in the American armed services now to have men who begin their professional career on too narrow a foundation, and they go up and up and up, and the higher they go the thinner their knowledge is. We have to have specialists, but very few of them can afford to be primarily the leaders of men. Our advanced specialists, they must be men who know something about leadership, but they are primarily laboratory men—research men. The leader must have a broad foundation if he is going to keep his position. Know—know your own branch, know the related arms of the service; you can't know too much if you are going to be a successful leader. And know the yesterdays. I have always said, and said many times here at the war college through the years, "Don't rely on us military historical writers too much. We don't know but so much. We can't fight wars." But after all, don't ignore the yesterdays of war in your study of today and of tomorrow.

I always thought that one of the finest things that ever was said about MacArthur was that when he had a period in which he was relieved of active administrative duties and was for three months able to do as he pleased, he took those three months and caught up on everything that he could read in order to bring his knowledge of today into line with the yesterdays of war. The same thing is true of Marshall. Marshall is one of the most avid readers of military history that I know. The same thing is true of Nimitz. Of course, Nimitz sometimes made bad choices of his reading. He said to me one time, for example, "Ah, Doctor, you never will know how grateful I am to you"; and he mentioned one of my books that he had read at Guam while he was in command there. I said, "How is that, Admiral?" "Well," he replied, "every night, after I had finished my duties, I would go to bed and turn on the light and I would read for about half an hour of some of General Lee's problems in dealing with his subordinates. Then I would go peacefully to sleep, because I would reason then that General Lee's problems of command were infinitely greater than mine were, and that I had a far easier time with my subordinates than he had with his." I said, "Admiral, you never were more mistaken in your life. You had cuckoos and some prima donnas with you and I'll not argue with you about that, but what put you to sleep was not peace of mind—it was my style."

Know your stuff—know your specialty, know the background of military history. Know it so that when the man comes to you and says, "What do I do in these circumstances, with this weapon, with this gun?", you can tell him; and if you don't know and want to be a leader, then for heaven's sake tell him honestly, "I don't know." A man very seldom loses the respect of his men if he says he doesn't know something when he can demonstrate that he knows something else, but look out for that man who tries to bluff about his knowledge.

I was dealing one time with a very tough audience, and I happened during the course of my remarks to say something about Iwo Jima. I didn't think I was doing so hot myself; I wasn't getting on so well. But when we came around to the question period, some man way back in the audience said, "Doctor, you have been talking about Iwo Jima. Would you mind discoursing for a minute on what you think of the tactics of small landing parties as they were employed at Iwo." I said, "I don't know a thing in God's world about it." I saw my audience was very much relieved from that minute. If you don't know, say so and try to find out.

Know your stuff. Now that means a lot in the way of the utilization of your time. And it means a lot in the way of utilization of a navy wife or an army wife. You boys think you have a hard life to lead. You don't have any tougher life to lead than the life of a navy wife. And both the navy husband and the navy wife need to learn all they can, when they can. I'd like to give you a little motto on that question. I gave it to one of my historical secretaries. She happens to be the one who came up with me this morning. She said it was the most useful thing I'd ever told her. It came from Oliver Wendell Holmes, a justice of the Supreme Court of the United States, who should have been chief justice. Holmes would get a boy from Harvard Law School every year, and that boy would have one year as Holmes' law clerk, a magnificent training, out of which in their generations have come some of the best lawyers in public service in America. And one of the favorite things that he would tell these boys was, "Young man, make the most of the scraps of time." Now believe me, if you want to know your stuff and know it better than the other man, you've got to spend more time on it; and if you are going to spend more time on it, you've got to make the most of the scraps of time. The difference between mediocrity and distinction in many a professional career is the organization of your time. Do you organize it; do you make the most of the scraps of time? Bless my soul, I don't suppose that the admiral, with his dignity and justice and regard for all the amenities, says no to you about playing bridge; but there is many a man who would have three more stripes on his sleeve if he gave to study the time that he gives to bridge. Don't say that you have to have the recreation. You have to have enough recreation, but diversification of work is the surest recreation of the mind. You don't have to go and forget the whole world. You have to work different brain centers, and that is all you need to do. If you do it you get the recreation, and out of the recreation you will get the training. Write it down, my young seamen, my young mariners (I love the word *mariner*); write it down: "Make the most of the scraps of time."

If we have another war, which Almighty God forbid—and I know not one single leader in the armed services who does not say amen to that—if we have another war, it is going to be a highly technical war; but the older principles of leadership will stand. Number one will remain: Know your stuff.

I have not a record of a single American soldier, a single American admiral who, when all was said and done, was not proficient in the knowledge of his specialty. Don't think the time spent at schools is lost either. Professional training for war is a categorical imperative of efficiency. In history I believe I knew General Lee's brigadier, major, and lieutenant generals pretty well. I think I have written about most of them, however poorly. Of all that company, there were only two who became distinguished division commanders who had not had professional training.[3] This idea of the inspiration of the soldier is nonsense. The idea that out of the great body of our people you are going to get soldiers of high eminence—there is absolutely nothing to it. If you require professional training to save the lives of men in peace and you call the man who does it a physician, are you not likewise called upon to have professional training for war in order to save the lives of men in war? And that man you call an admiral or you call him a general. Professional training is worthwhile. The best money that ever was spent on the navy of this country has been the money that was spent here at Newport. I don't believe any man can contradict that.

Know your stuff. And be a man. That is number two. Be a man. We have had some leaders in American history who may not have been all they ought to have been in their regard for some of the amenities of life, but I never knew a great American seaman, I never knew a great American soldier, or read about one, who was not fundamentally a man. And that means a man of character; it means a man of industry; it means a man of fair play. We were talking at the house of the president of this college a little while ago about the matter of courage. And the admiral said to me, "Doctor, have you ever found in history any process by which you can tell whether a man is going to show courage in action?" I said, "No, you never can; I don't believe you ever will. If we do, it will be thousands of years hence and by that time, please God, we may have sense enough not to fight wars." But this is a fact: The type of courage that keeps a man from turning his back on his adversaries and running away is one thing. That is not so uncommon. But the type of courage that is shown by a leader who will take his part of the load in all circumstances—that's a much rarer type of courage.

What is the coward? Who is the coward in the high rank? He is not apt to be a physical craven, but he is a man who sometimes tries to pass on to the other fellow the more difficult job and won't do his own. You take that great captain of the state from which I have the honor of coming. You can see beautiful stories of the physical courage of General Robert E. Lee. I never go to Washington from Richmond on Highway Number 1 that I don't see the house where he was standing one day on the porch, with a glass of buttermilk between the table and his mouth, when a round shot came within four feet of him and shattered the lintel of the door. You can see the place there today, and it was said that no man observed a quiver when the glass went to his mouth. I have read the story of how he conducted himself on that bloody field of Spotsylvania Court House. That is fine, but if you want to see what courage is, what the real test of the man is, you read Lee's farewell to Jackson on the second of May, 1863. When Jackson, called upon to make the great turning movement there at Chancellorsville, was asked by General Lee, "What troops do you propose to make this movement with?", Jackson said, "My whole corps, sir." Lee then had about fifty thousand men. Jackson wanted to take twenty-eight thousand of them, put them in motion around the flank, and leave Lee twenty-two thousand men with which to face the Federals while Jackson was out of action and making that movement around the flank. Lee could have said, "Why, those are impossible figures! Take fourteen thousand men, and leave me enough at least with which to defend this line against these seventy-five thousand Federals here in the Wilderness." Not so. Lee knew what concentration of force meant; Lee knew the doctrine of superiority of force at the point of contact. Lee had the courage to take his chance in order that his comrade might have superiority of force for difficult offensive operations. In that, gentlemen—and it is repeated gloriously a hundred times in American history—in that you see what I mean by the word courage. What I mean by the words, Be a man.

Aye. Be a man who is disciplined in spirit. Be a man who is observant. How many fine persons there are who go through this world. Never forget and, as God gives me might, I shall never fail on a lecture to mention Cadmus Marcellus Wilcox—Cadmus Marcellus Wilcox and his observation of a string over the shoulder of the Federals in that same battle of Chancellorsville. Remember Cadmus Marcellus Wilcox? What a name! Cadmus had his orders: "You move when the Federals do. You've got one little brigade here; you are holding Banks Ford; and when they move, you move." Cadmus went out the next morning early.

(Every good seaman ought to be out early. People talk about what you ought do for the redemption of the American people. The American people need nothing in this world more than they need to get up earlier and go to bed earlier.) Cadmus Marcellus got up earlier than most men, and he went out and looked—which a great many people never do—and over Banks Ford he saw that Federal sentinel walking his post, and another and another down the line, in plain view. Well, there is nothing uncommon about a sentinel walking his post, is there? But Marcellus wasn't content with that. Marcellus took his glasses and he looked at that sentinel, who may have been thinking about anything under the sun other than his military duties; and Marcellus observed that over that sentinel's shoulder there was a string, and behind that sentinel's left hip as he looked at the end of the string was his haversack. And Marcellus looked at the next sentinel, and he had on his haversack, and the next and the next; and Marcellus said to himself, "Those birds are getting ready to move, because if they were simply in camp they wouldn't have on their haversacks and their haversacks wouldn't be full. They have got their rations on them because they are getting ready to move." He ordered his artillery hitched, got his infantry in position, and within fifteen minutes after those Federals started their withdrawal, Marcellus was in the road; and he hadn't gone three miles before he had the great opportunity of his career to stop a Federal offensive.

Observation! Be a man, not a blind man. Might as well go down in the engineroom and stay there if you are not going to look and see.

Last of all, the third point: Look after your men. Look after your men. What a simple thing you are saying, Rip Van Winkle! Here you have three-fourths of the brass and nine-tenths of the brains of the American navy before you, and you are saying that leadership is three things and you have listed those things so simply. Know your stuff, be a man, and look after your men. We came a long way to hear you, Rip Van Winkle, and is that all you have to say? Yes, that is all, because that is the sum observation of my travels. Look after your men.

I mention to you the fact that as a youth I saw those gray columns moving up the street and I heard the clatter of cavalry forty years after. I saw those men who had thrust through the Wilderness, those men who had stood at Second Manassas, and those who had climbed the hill at Gettysburg and had their red banners with them until twenty-two of those flags were there on one acre in the Federal position. I saw them. I knew many of them, and often I asked them, "Tell me, that great man who is our Southern demigod,[4] this Lee—what was there about him that made you reverence him? What was there in him that made you tell us that next to the love of God and His Son, there had to be reverence for him?" An incredibly simple answer, my friends, they gave me. "Oh," they said, over and over again, "he looked after his men! We knew that when he demanded anything of us, it was because he had to. And when he said, 'Men, you must take that height,' we took it, because we knew that was the cheapest thing to do." He looked after his men.

So did the lieutenants—some of the men to you unknown. Did you ever hear of the name of John R. Cooke? Some of you did. Just a brigadier general in the Confederate army. I remember him well, an old man running a grocery store, an unprosperous grocery store. He had in his head the most beautiful bullet hole you ever saw in your life. He must have been hardheaded: it never cracked his skull. One day when he was in his thirties he was commanding two little regiments at Sharpsburg. On his left early in the morning something had happened. Something had gone wrong, even with Stonewall Jackson, and the flank had been swept back. The Federals were at the Dunker church, and Hood's great Texans, the Grenadier Guard of the Confederacy, were panting in the woods. The tide swept around to the center of that segmented battlefield. There an impression was made, not too deep. Cooke stood there, a little salient—two regiments—and against his fire, with the supporting artillery around the Dunker church, a Federal corps broke itself in vain. During the fight Longstreet sent word to him and asked him if he wanted help, and I am told that of all the classic cussing that ever has been heard in the American army—and the American army sometimes casts reflections on its adversary's ancestry back six or eight generations—there never had been heard such words as those that Cooke sent back. "Give him help! Not until every man he had was pursuing through hell the last Yankee in front of him!" Or words to that effect. I said to myself, "What is in that man? What made that Twenty-seventh North Carolina regiment that way? This Third Arkansas—Arkansas is a good state, good fighters (they have some mighty long-winded politicians among them)—but what made that Third Arkansas regiment do that?" And I took the pains to go back, and I found that from the very time that Cooke had taken over that regiment (he had been a captain in the regular army before the war) he had done everything he could to tell those men, "I am going to demand the maximum of you, and I am going to do the maximum for you." He held them to the highest standards, and he did for them everything that a man could to protect them from casualties.

Look after your men. It means many things; it means many things that you don't think about. It means mail facilities; it means food. General Lee, no matter how much impoverished his commissariat was, never failed to increase his men's rations after they had won a fight. Hot food is one of the greatest builders of morale in the history of war.

Looking after your men means looking after their clothes. I was telling one of the officers today how much emphasis George Washington laid on the cleanliness of person. That great builder of morale, that same Lee, when he got his men out of a dirty campaign always tried to put them by a stream where they could wash. And the most valiant men were the men who, if they needed it, got the new uniforms. Look after your men and your men will look after you. I don't believe there has ever been an exception to that dictum.

I said one day to MacArthur, "You know, I think when I come to write the history of your campaign, there from the Solomons northward, one of the things I am going to find the most difficult to understand is how you did so much with so little." Well, he lighted his corncob pipe for the 453rd time that afternoon and made the seventeeth oration that he had delivered to me that day, and he said many things that were absolutely true and sound. And we talked about his casualties, about how few there were in terms of what was done. I said, "Difficult as it was, you looked after your men." And I quoted him some of the things I told you. He said, "Well, if there was economy of life, it is something for which"—and he dropped all his theatrical manner—"something for which I will be grateful to the end of my days." He said, "When I thought about the number who were killed, nothing could console me except the thought that maybe by God's grace and hard effort we had saved some that might otherwise have been slain." He is a tall man. He got up and walked the floor, as he sometimes did when he spoke; but believe me, he grew taller and taller in my eyes as he spoke those words.

Gentlemen, have I oversimplified this case? I think sometimes we overcomplicate it. I think sometimes we take these books on psychology, we take all the arts of salesmanship, and we try to apply them to the armed services in a manner that is too elaborate. I don't believe I'm oversimplifying when I say to you, Know your stuff; be a man; look after your men.

Remember, you may in God's mercy have had your day of battle. You who were there in the Arctic night; you who flew across the Hump; you who went from South America to Africa; you who fought those submarines up and down our coast; you who went out from Pearl Harbor never knowing whether that submarine would come back again or whether your burial place ever would be known to men; you who were in the supply service; you who were in the battlefield; you who had the immortal honor of serving with Spruance, with Kinkaid, with Halsey—you may have had your day. You may live until over it all comes the glamour of the years, and you may tell the tale so often that you'll hardly be able to distinguish the fabric from the embroidery.

Such things happen. On the other hand, your challenge may lie ahead; the era of atomic warfare may bring us problems vaster than anybody ever faced before.

I covet but one thing for you and that is, if you come to the final day, which must for America always be the day of victory, I covet for you nothing more than that in the day of victory, you can say with a clear conscience what was said by the vanquished as he rode back through those thin gray ranks across the red hills of Appomattox one day in April 1865. The men knew that something had happened because he had been in the midst of the Federal lines. They broke ranks; they thronged the road; they gathered around him; they put up their hands. "General, are we surrendered? General, give us another chance; we'll fight them now!" He said, "No, my men. I've done for you the best I knew how to do." Your nation demands of you no less than that; your conscience should ask no more than that you do your best.

Notes

The stenographic transcript of this lecture is in the Naval Historical Collection of the Naval War College. The lecture has been published twice in the *Naval War College Review*: in September 1949 and in March-April 1979. In a letter to the president of the Naval War College, Colonel J. L. Shanahan, USMC, noted, "During my early years in the Corps most of the senior officers . . . were on speaking terms with this address. Over the years familiarity with it has more or less faded away, possibly because subsequent to Dr. Freeman's address the subject has been so awfully treated that its very title has become anathema to most audiences. (The only other title likely to cause a more desperate rush to the exits is 'Human Relations.') This is a misfortune, because Dr. Freeman produced a work worthy of continued notice. He laid out the subject in three principles consisting of 11 words, all of which have one syllable. They are Greek in clarity and brevity, yet their apparent simplicity provides more questions than answers. Thereby, they serve both as effective guides to everyday action, and as food for reflective thought. Such a work has light to shed."

1. Parson Weems was the author of *The Life and Memorable Actions of George Washington* (1800), the source of several Washington myths (e.g., the hatchet and the cherry tree).

2. Lorado Taft was a prominent American sculptor whose works include the Columbus Memorial Fountain in Washington, D.C.

3. These two were John B. Gordon and Wade Hampton.

4. The word *demagogue* appears here in both the stenographic transcript and the published versions of this lecture. However, considering the context of these remarks, I think Freeman probably used the word *demigod.*

Part Five
Later Lectures

GEORGE WASHINGTON

This portrait was painted by Charles Wilson Peale in 1787, the year that Washington served as the president of the Constitutional Convention.

In June 1949, at the age of sixty-three, Freeman resigned from his post as editor in chief of the *Richmond News Leader* in order to devote himself full-time to the completion of his biography of Washington. On the day Freeman died, June 13, 1953, he completed the draft of the last chapter of volume six, which brought Washington to the end of his first term as president. The seventh and final volume of the biography was written by Freeman's research associates, Mary Wells Ashworth and John A. Carroll, and published in 1957. In 1958 the seven-volume biography of Washington was awarded the Pulitzer Prize.

In these two later lectures, both of which were delivered at the Armed Forces Staff College, Norfolk, Virginia, the dominant figure is George Washington.

16

Leadership in an Enforced Defensive

Lecture of January 1951

In this lecture, which was prompted by the events of the first six months of the Korean War, Freeman examines the requirements of leadership during enforced defensive operations.

During such operations, says Freeman, the leader must:

1. Emphasize the maintenance of discipline.

2. Ensure that the initial stage of a withdrawal is deep enough to permit the men rest.

3. Pay increased attention to the physical comfort of the men.

4. Be alert for the opportunity to shift to the offensive.

5. Remain the master of himself. He must not neglect his dress or his bearing or his sleep. He must avoid blame and bickering. And he must have faith in the justice of a Power beyond himself.

Ladies and gentlemen, whenever Admiral Hall calls on me to come down here, I come. It is a great privilege to visit this school and always an inspiration to see him. I never go away without a renewed faith in American leadership when I have talked with him, with the members of the faculty, and with the noble body of student officers who are here. Going as I do to nearly all the armed forces schools, it is a particular pride to me to realize that three of the best schools of all are here in Virginia. This is one of the preeminent schools of the armed forces; the school at Quantico is admirable; the engineer school at Belvoir is fine.

It is a real privilege always to come and to talk to you, and it will be a great relief to the officers today to know that I'm not going to deliver "Old Number One." At least I'm not going to deliver "Old Number One" exactly in the form in which you are accustomed to it. I have no doubt that Admiral Hall, our distinguished visitors from the fleet, and the members of the staff could get up and give you "Old Number One" just exactly as I would give it, because they've heard it so often. It is very simple, "Old Number One" is. It contains just three maxims of leadership; and one of them is to know your stuff, the next one is to be a man, and the third one is to look after your troops or your crew or your fleet, as the case may be. Now you'll see as I go on this morning that the bones of "Old Number One" are still there, but there are certain circumstances that have prompted me today to take a different approach, and in particular to talk of leadership in enforced defensive operations.

The twenty-fifth of June you picked up the Norfolk paper, which is mighty good, and you saw there a story that the Northern Koreans had crossed the line. You said, "Ah, good God, more trouble with those Koreans!" When I saw it myself, I said, "I never knew why we were there. I never understood why we were there, and now I see we've got another mess on our hands." We didn't realize then that there was no announcement of any change in our strategical policy, but the news of that invasion of Korea ultimately worked out a temporary shift from our traditional doctrine of the offensive to the defensive.

The doctrine of the offensive is fundamentally sound, but adherence to it can be prevented from time to time by circumstances concerning which I think there is no essential disagreement among students of war. First of all, we may be denied the offensive by overwhelming superiority of the enemy in numbers and in firepower or in either. Still again, we may be denied the offensive by the nature of the terrain of operations. Once again, we may be denied the offensive because we lack some essential of transport or supply. Occasionally, too, we may be unable to assume the offensive because of national policy. We've had a touch of that in these Korean operations. History abounds with examples of that sort.

At the Air University at Maxwell Field, we are studying this winter the relationship of strategy to national policy. Next Monday we are going to talk down there about the interrelationship of national policy and military objectives. You'd be surprised to know I'm going to take my illustrations from Spain, because the rich period of Spanish history, more than any other, I think, is an example of the manner in which not strategy alone but tactics also were adjusted to national policy.

Then once more, we may have the offensive denied to us because of the necessity of fighting for time in order that we may develop our weapons and train our armies; or, as happened once in American history, we may do it while we are waiting for an ally to appear and to help us in a day of distress.

Of course, whenever these basic conditions change, our strategy should change also. Even in an unescapable, long-continued defensive, opportunities may be offered to inflict a heavy blow. In short, I think our doctrine of the defensive is sound when we teach at Leavenworth, and here, that our defensive ought always to be an active defensive.

While the doctrine of the defensive remains distasteful, not to say abhorrent, we must never look on defensive war as something always to be shunned, because defensive war sometimes is necessary. Don't ever forget that we owe our independence as a nation to Washington's firm and unhesitating adherence to the doctrine of the defensive war. Over and over again when he lacked adequate force for the mission that he had, Washington deliberately said, "We must fight a defensive war"; and it was by a defensive war fundamentally that he finally defeated the British.

Furthermore, don't assume always that a defensive fails to inflict heavier losses on an adversary proportionately than an offensive does. If anybody were to ask you, "What is the most costly campaign ever conducted on American soil?", you wouldn't hesitate for a moment in your answer. If anyone were to say to you, "What is the most costly month of American warfare on our own national soil?", you would say immediately, "Why, it was from the fourth of May, 1864, when Grant crossed the Rapidan, to the fourth of June, 1864, when he was hurled back in his great attack at Cold Harbor." During that time, by a proper sort of defensive, General Lee inflicted on General Grant losses equal to the total infantry strength of the defensive army. That is a most incredible achievement to be performed in one month, but it was performed.

The defensive makes certain special demands on officers and men, and consequently it ought to be the subject of the most careful study as to strategy, as to tactics, and as to the logistics involved. What's the greatest defensive campaign of modern times? Of all those I've studied, undoubtedly the most brilliant was the withdrawal to, and later from, the Hindenburg line in 1918. What was the worst campaign? Certainly, of all, there never was a defensive campaign worse than that of Napoleon's withdrawal from Moscow in 1812. Next to that, the worst one I've ever studied was the Russian withdrawal from the Dunajec line and the Warsaw salient in 1915—a hideous affair.

What's the difference between the Russians' failure in 1915 to conduct a good defensive and Hindenburg's magnificent success in 1918? Study. Study. The Germans, while they believed in the offensive, nevertheless took some of the best men they had to study the defensive. I don't know whether you've ever run across in our modern studies the name of von Hutier. I think he must have been of Alsatian extraction and originally his name was Hutea; but von Hutier was the "retreat specialist" of the German army in 1918, and I believe he did one of the most brilliant jobs in history.

We need to study defensive methods. We ought never to be ashamed for one instant to have retreat specialists and to have them study all aspects of that subject. There is no more reason why we should refuse to study the defensive than there is that we should refuse to have a fire department merely because we don't like fires. Now please remember that. We don't know what lies ahead of us. We know that the moment we have a force commensurate with our mission we are going to take the offensive. We may be compelled to a long defensive; we must study accordingly. Remember the fire department!

I'm not going to attempt to go into the technical problems of a long defensive. You know infinitely more about those than I do, and I can add nothing whatever to your information regarding them. But there are certain historical elements about a defensive operation that affect leadership most directly, and I think they ought to be reviewed for you this morning. In the first place, please remember that manifestly and hourly discipline is never more surely tested than in a long defensive, and in a defensive operation must never be relaxed for an instant.

Of course, when you apply that, you never can afford to relax discipline at any time. But do you know when I would have said that the Confederate army was doomed beyond all hope of victory? It was in that operation that I just mentioned a little while ago, Second Cold Harbor. What a campaign! The doom of the Army of Northern Virginia was sealed, in my judgment, on the third of June, 1864, when General Grant most unwisely called for an assault on that prepared Confederate line there in the fields around Old Cold Harbor. How in the world he ever did it I'll never know. You can go there to this day and you can see the battery positions almost directly over the heads of the infantry on the Confederate side of the front. Grant called for a general assault on a front of about eight miles, and the men went forward. As they went forward, as they prepared to go forward, a great many of those boys took pieces of paper and on them wrote their names and stuck them in their pockets so that they would be identified when they were killed. Now when that Army of the Potomac was able to make that assault in the face of what the men knew to be certain death, then, ladies and gentlemen, the graybacks were gone and the bluebellies were destined to win. It couldn't be otherwise when discipline had reached that point. I often look at that old battlefield and think of those lines in Browning's "Childe Roland" when, after describing so dramatically the impossible task that was before Childe Roland, he said, "Childe Roland to the dark tower came and dauntless the slughorn to his lips he put and blew." There comes a time when you have to do it, when discipline alone will carry you to the dark tower.

Every campaign in our history has illustrated the truth of that maxim, and if I had my way would be written on the walls of every barracks in the United States, "Discipline is the soul of an army." That, after all, is the foundation stone of the American armed forces; and on that stone, laid by George Washington, the whole structure has been reared. Listen to these noble words of Washington in one of the darkest hours of the Revolution: "Nothing can be more hurtful to the service than the neglect of discipline, for discipline more than numbers gives one army superiority over another." That's the father of your army speaking, gentlemen. What does it remind you of? To those of you who read Desmond Young's recent study of Rommel,[1] it reminds you of a very famous quotation of Rommel: "The best form of welfare for the troops is a superlative state of discipline, for this saves them from unnecessary losses." The defensive is the supreme hour for the military police. It's the supreme hour to keep your men in line. It's the supreme hour for the real test of discipline.

I mentioned a little while ago that the doom of the Army of Northern Virginia was sealed in those operations there at Cold Harbor, and it is true. But when did the army literally go to pieces? When in the days of hunger on the way to Appomattox those men began to forage. They left their lines to forage and they never came back. Of course, some of them have given us classics. Did you ever hear that lovely story? I often refer to it when people give me a very generous introduction that I don't deserve. They remind me of that Confederate who'd been off after a hen or a rooster or a rabbit or a pig or whatever that poor country might offer, and he was going along a worn fence when up came a platoon of Federals, well fed, perfectly equipped, in good uniforms—and he in his rags and hunger—and they said, "Surrender, surrender; we've got you!" And he put his old musket up against the fence and said, "Yes, you've got me; and a helluva get you've got, too, a helluva get you've got!" Well, when discipline goes, you get just that, and there isn't any army left. That's the first thing to remember about leadership in defensive operations.

The second thing is this: Because discipline is to be tested, the initial stage of an enforced withdrawal ought to be deep enough, if practicable, to allow the men thereafter to have reasonable periods of rest. Now there is a maxim that is not accepted with anything like the adequacy it really calls for. You find the average man, when he gets his blood up in a losing battle, is not going to withdraw any more than he has to withdraw. He wants to go just as short a distance to the rear as he can, and having gone, wants to fight back as hard and as fast as he can. In the initial stage of the operation, military history warns you against that very thing. Go back far enough to have a chance to rest your men. If you don't go back far enough, you're going to have your men fighting night and day and very soon you're going to have them broken down.

Don't ever forget the campaign of 1776, from the loss of Fort Washington in November to Washington's return to Princeton on the third of January, 1777. Washington had a dark period in November 1776. Nobody has ever understood it as fully as it ought to be understood; but he came to that point where his judgment wavered and where he, who of all men had insisted most on the concentration of force, consented to the most unreasonable dispersion of force in the whole of the Revolution. It reminded one of that situation that Charles Lee[2] described—the old rascal—when he said, "If certain of the timid Americans had their way, they would place two soldiers at every gentleman's residence and think that the country was secure." Washington dispersed force. But when Washington was forced to withdraw after the loss of Fort Washington, he didn't try to stop on the Hackensack; he didn't try to stop on the Passaic; he didn't try to stop on the Raritan. He retreated straightaway to the Delaware and put a sufficient barrier between him and his enemy to give him time to rest his men.

When Lee was defeated at Gettysburg, did Lee fall back to the mountains and try to come down the way he'd gone up by the Cumberland Valley? Of course not. Lee knew that he couldn't sustain that offensive any longer in Pennsylvania, and he got out and didn't stop until he reached the Potomac River.

You know, the Southerners had invented a name for a rapid retreat. They called it a "manassas." They, of course, had taken that name from the first battle of Manassas, after which the Federals went back on the Washington defenses as fast as they could go. And one of the Confederates who was in the withdrawal from Gettysburg in July 1863 said, "We did a manassas, getting away from Gettysburg."

Well, you don't like to do a manassas, but did you read what Don Whitehead said the other day?[3] Don Whitehead said Sunday morning—and he's a mighty good observer—"If it comes to a choice" (he was quoting an officer in Korea) "if it comes to a choice between saving our face and saving our hide, I'm for saving our hide." Quite often it is imperative that a leader have the moral courage to withdraw far enough.

The related maxim is perfectly simple and so familiar and so obvious that I don't think I need waste your time on it. It is, In an enforced withdrawal of a long-continued enforced defensive, regard for the physical comfort of the men should be increased rather than diminished. Instead of saying, "Well, things are going to pot; we'll just have to make the best of it," we ought in every instance say, "The men need better care now than they ever have had, and we must give it to them."

The Army of Northern Virginia, to cite it once more, was about as badly feared an army as we had had in America after the Revolution, and it certainly was the most nearly naked army that we'd had since the days of the Continentals. You remember when General Lee had his troops on review and the English guest was there; and the English guest saw the men pass by, and there was nothing to their credit in passing, and he said, "General, your troops are ragged in the seat of their pants." "Yes," said General Lee, "but the enemy doesn't see that side of them."

Lee had a rule; he had a rule. When his men came back hungry (as they were always), scant as rations were, he fed them up a little bit. His rule was, On a withdrawal, wash, eat, change clothes, and rest. He didn't use those exact words, but he applied them over and over again. If you want to see a very good example of it, take the operations after Sharpsburg, when the Army of Northern Virginia was almost trapped, and see how Lee proceeded in the course of a very short time to take that defeated army and have that army ready for the campaign of Fredericksburg in December and capable of that immortal classic of Chancellorsville in May 1863. He fed them up; he looked after his men.

During a retreat in depth, the enemy is apt to make mistakes and, in particular, to become overconfident. Watch for the opportunity of shifting to the offensive, even if it is for a short time only. That's a maxim on which it seems to me a good part of American victory depends.

You know, on that famous eleventh of November, 1918, Lloyd George, then British prime minister, came into the House of Commons and had the armistice terms in his hand and to a cheering House—it was the supreme moment of his life—to a cheering House he bowed as he came forward and then he laid the armistice terms on the table; and the House, still cheering, finally sat down to let him speak. Do you remember how he began? He said, "Well, we've won; but my God, how near we came to losing." I asked him after that, four or five years, I said, "Mr. Lloyd George"—you know a newspaperman will ask anybody anything; he'll ask the Lord when the Day of Judgment is coming if he has the opportunity—I said, "Mr. Lloyd George, why did you start out your speech that way, as great an orator as you are?" "Well," he said, "I said that because it was true: How near we came to losing."

How near in America we came to losing in November 1776, when Washington had to make that retreat of which I have just spoken, that retreat in depth all the way across the state of New Jersey. He got behind the Delaware. Ah, never pass on the main line of the Pennsylvania from

Morrisville across to Trenton, never pass without looking up that river and in spirit saluting that Continental army. He had just one week more in the life of that army, just one week more. At the end of that time the men's term of service (except for fifteen hundred of them) was up and they were going home. He found his opportunity in the course of a defensive; he found *one day* when he thought he had a chance. He took advantage of that day, and *that day* in my judgment saved the American cause. If Washington had not crossed the Delaware, Christmas night, 1776,[4] I believe the American army would have been defeated, dissolved, and the American cause for the time lost. Never let the doctrine of the defensive carry you to the point where you shut your eyes and take the enemy's blows. You may have to take the blows, but for God's sake keep your eyes open.

Finally, to do his part in all of this, the officer must be completely the master of himself; and very seldom, ladies, is the officer the master of himself unless he has the full support of his wife. I spoke the other day at Belvoir, and I had been threatening for five years, I reckon, to get all the officers' wives together and just talk to the wives, the husbands not present. And I'd been threatening it up at Belvoir so often—I think I threatened it here once—that General Weart said, "Alright, let's do it; let's get the wives together." They came together and I talked to them. The next day somebody up there wrote me a letter and said, "You'll be very much interested in a difference in the response of the ladies to what you said. The young wives, the wives of young officers, say you were too pessimistic. The wives of those who went through the First or Second World War say they know you are right and you didn't tell the tale even as hard as it was." Well, I have seen the correspondence of many a soldier to his wife. Henry Knox,[5] God bless him, twenty-six, writing to his wife; Nathanael Greene,[6] writing to his; Robert E. Lee; George Patton—those sacred letters. Very seldom is the courage of a soldier, a fighting man of any arm of the service, greater than the courage of his wife.

A man must be, I say, completely the master of himself in the day of trial, in the hour of danger. He must be himself and must never neglect his own dress or his own bearing. His men think he knows more than he does know, and they look to him for the signs of the times. If he is negligent, if he is distracted, if he isn't completely the master of himself, then they are going to be demoralized because he is negligent. You remember that episode of General Lee at Goode's Bridge? He was on his way to Appomattox. The end was near (though he didn't know quite how near it was), and that morning a young lieutenant came up on horseback and dismounted and made his report to the general, and Lee said to him, "Lieutenant, would you mind looking at your britches for a minute?" The lieutenant looked down, and he had one britches leg in his boot and the boot in the other britches leg. "Oh," he said, "General, I dressed this morning in such a hurry that I didn't notice it." "Lieutenant, always notice it; always notice it. Your men are watching you, and if you are negligent they think something is wrong."

The leader must get rest. You remember the famous tale of the Japanese general who said, "We sleep too much. I'm going to cut down on the hours of sleep and reduce them to the absolute minimum." He got down to the point where he was sleeping two hours in the twenty-four, and he said, "I've almost conquered it." "Yes," said one of his companions, "but you don't know what you're doing. If it weren't for your chief of staff you'd be dead now and your division would be ruined." You have to learn, of course, to keep short hours, but you have to rest when rest counts more. Remember General Lee's maxim: One hour before midnight is worth two hours after midnight. Remember the words of his great adversary: "Sleep when you can," said Grant, "because you don't know when you can't." It's a doggone good rule.

A man can keep on his legs and can persuade himself that he has his endurance when actually he has lost it. I suppose here in the library you have a little book by Colonel Charles Marshall describing his experiences as a staff officer of the Confederate army.[7] If it is here, read Marshall's account of himself during the last days of the Appomattox campaign. He hadn't slept any for five nights, hardly, and he said he heard himself speaking and speaking utter nonsense with no relation whatever to the events that were going on around him. Heard himself as if he were a separate ego listening to his exhausted self speak.

The leader at such a time must avoid blame and bickering. Have I quoted to you here at this school that famous American officer of the final campaign in Europe who was talking about the maxim that we ordinarily find 25 percent of our new division commanders who don't really stand the gaff? I told him I had remarked to General Marshall before the war, "General, don't you be surprised if 25 percent of your division commanders and your corps commanders fail you in the first year of operations, because that's been our universal military experience." General Marshall didn't like it. He said with the training our men had and the processes of selection we employed, we wouldn't have anything like 25 percent. This general, who commanded one of the great armies in Europe, said to me, "I think Marshall was wrong." He said, "Where we were led astray in our conclusions was the fact that we were conducting a victorious campaign. It would have been a very different story if we had met with adversity and had been in retreat." Said this army commander, who commanded a group of armies, "If I had two division commanders who were failing, I didn't displace them simply and solely because I knew that we were within two or three weeks of victory and that we might worry along with them and not have to send them back to the United States in disgrace." That's when the bickering begins; that's when you find fault with your buddy; that's the time of every other time when the leader must be a man and be the master of himself.

He's not going to do it unless he has a moral and a spiritual background. Old Noll Cromwell[8] said it all when he looked over those recruits that had been sent him and in disgust turned away from them and said, "Give me only such men as makes some conscious of what they do." Ah, how many of our leaders in the day of danger and in the hour of death have called for men who make some conscious of what they do! Here again the words of Washington: "You ask me how I am to be rewarded for all of this. There is one reward that nothing can deprive me of, and that is the consciousness of having done my duty with the strictest rectitude and the most scrupulous exactitude and the most certain knowledge that if we should ultimately fail in the present contest, it is not owing to any want of exertion in me or of the application of every means that the Congress of the United States or the states individually have put in my hands."

At such a time as that a man needs, and a true man can have, the consciousness of a Power beyond that of the man himself. What said Foch when they asked him about that campaign of the Marne in 1914, when France barely escaped what happened to her in May and June 1940: her back to the Marne; Paris exposed; von Kluck and von Bulow at the point where, if they had coordinated their attack, they could have destroyed the army of Joffre? What said Foch then, as he fashioned that spearhead that penetrated the German line and threw them back in the end to the Aisne? He said, "On the Marne, God gave me clear vision."

Oh, beware of the doctrine of a chosen people, but believe in the doctrine of the triumph of the right! We cannot always apply the maxim, Be still and know that I am God, but we have in our history every assurance, Be right and see that I am God. God is not always, as Napoleon said, on the side of the heaviest battalions; or at least if they are the heaviest battalions, they don't always happen to be in history the heaviest in armament alone but they may be the heaviest in moral power. You can't get away from it. Believe me, Washington spoke for himself but he spoke for all those who have followed after and have stood at the real history of the American army when he said, "Providence, to whom we are infinitely more indebted than we are to our wisdom or our own exertion, has always been displayed in power and goodness when clouds and darkness seem ready to overwhelm us."

Was he speaking of you in 1951 when he said, "The hour is now come when we stand much in need of another manifestation of the bounty of Providence"? Be right in your own life; seek to make your nation right; and take no counsel then of your fears.

You know that the Assyrian king came down once against the king of Israel, and the chief strategist of the king of Israel was a man they called a prophet. His name was Elisha. And the enemy found out where the GHQ of Israel was located, and a column was delivered to a surprise attack on GHQ at Dothan. Horses and chariots and a great host, and they came by night and encompassed the city about. When the servant of the man of God—that is, the aide of the chief of staff—was risen early and gone forth, behold, a host with horses and chariots was round about the city. And the servant said, "Alas, my master, what shall we do?" And Elisha answered, "Fear not, for they that are with us are more than they that are with them." And Elisha prayed and said, "Lord, I pray thee, open his eyes that he may see." And the Lord opened the eyes of the young man and he saw; and behold, the mountain was full of horses and chariots of fire round about Elisha.[9]

Oh, do you say this is mere tradition, beautiful but meaningless to the men there south of Wonju in the mountains of Korea? Never let yourself be misled. If there is one truth in American military history above another, it is that when we have been right, God has guided us. Oh, they are freezing—20° below zero on some of those mountain heights. Very good, very good, because very bad.

There was a day, that same twenty-sixth of December, 1776, when the freedom of this nation was hanging in the balance; and Washington took that little wreck of an army that was to stay with him only one week more, and he crossed the Delaware. There was sleet and there was snow, and it was almost impossible to take even that light artillery and to carry it forward. But they came to Trenton; and in the Providence of God, when the time came for the final test, the sleet was in the face of the foe and at the back of the American soldiers. Oh, even if it is winter in Korea, the sleet will be in the face of the foe!

Notes

Although this lecture was delivered at the Armed Forces Staff College, Norfolk, Virginia, that college has no record of it. The stenographic transcript of the lecture is filed in the archives of Air University, Maxwell Air Force Base, Alabama, and is dated (incorrectly) 10 June 1949. Based on some of the remarks made during the lecture (particularly the reference to "the men there south of Wonju"), I would date it between 4 January 1951 (the Chinese capture of Seoul) and 25 January 1951 (the beginning of the UN counteroffensive). The stenographic transcript of the lecture is not titled; the title that appears here is mine.

1. *Rommel, The Desert Fox* (New York: Harper, 1950).

2. A major general in Washington's army, Charles Lee was extremely critical of Washington and slow in carrying out his orders. Put in charge of the attack at Monmouth, New Jersey, in June 1778, Lee instead ordered a retreat, which was halted only by the arrival of Washington himself. For this Lee was court-martialed and suspended from command. He continued to criticize Washington, and in 1780 he was dismissed from the army.

3. Don Whitehead, a reporter for the Associated Press, was awarded a Pulitzer Prize in 1951 for his reporting of the Korean War.

4. On Christmas night, 1776, Washington's force crossed the Delaware River at a ferry landing about nine miles north of Trenton, New Jersey, where a Hessian force was garrisoned. At 8 o'clock the next morning the Americans attacked this garrison, taking the Hessians by complete surprise. By 10 o'clock the battle was over: more than 900 Hessians were captured, with 22 killed and 84 wounded; a few Americans were wounded, but none were killed.

5. Henry Knox was Washington's chief of artillery.

6. A major general in Washington's army, Nathanael Greene commanded the left wing of the American force at the battle of Trenton, served as the army's quartermaster general from 1778 to 1780, and was then assigned to command of the army in the South.

7. *An Aide-de-Camp of Lee, Being the Papers of Colonel Charles Marshall,* edited by Major General Sir Frederick Maurice (Boston, 1927). In the bibliography of *Lee's Lieutenants,* Freeman describes this book as follows: "Although incomplete as a military memoir, this contains much useful material." Marshall served on Lee's staff from March 1862 until the end of the war.

8. Oliver Cromwell, leader of the parliamentary forces in the English civil wars and "lord protector" of England, Scotland, and Ireland from 1653 until his death in 1658.

9. This biblical story is taken from the sixth chapter of The Second Book of the Kings.

17

Leadership in Allied Operations

Lecture of August 26, 1952

In this lecture, Freeman turns his attention to the requirements of leadership during allied operations. To illustrate these requirements, he tells the story of the joint operations of the American and French forces in the United States in 1778-81.

From this story emerge six rules of leadership in allied operations:

1. *Know the language of your ally.*
2. *Establish personal contact with allied leaders as soon as possible.*
3. *Ensure that the commanders assigned to cooperate with allied forces are men who will cooperate.*
4. *Establish unity of field command.*
5. *Criticize your ally only when absolutely necessary, and ensure that such criticism does not fall into the wrong hands.*
6. *If the command rests with you, do not assign the most difficult task to your ally. Take it for yourself.*

It is a great privilege to come here and to discuss this new phase of your work, the training that you are to receive in preparation for the duties that you must discharge hereafter more or less in the realm of diplomatic service. This does not mean that this is going to be turned into a school of diplomacy. God forbid! It does not mean either that you are to regard the prime function of a fighting man as being that of a talking man. Again, God forbid! You are going to have, on the other hand, a new relationship of the American armed forces with those of the rest of the world. In past wars, certainly down until the Second World War, when we cooperated we were the minority, and we were moving into the ambit of large, organized forces that had their staff work perfectly oiled and operating efficiently. We became the minority, in a sense, and at the same time we became the students during the First World War. For example, we had to borrow so much in the way of experience and staff equipment from the French. They were admirably schooled, and they were good teachers. But now I suspect, were the situation reversed, we would find that the French would be helping us and that in all likelihood—with no disparagement to the fine work done by the French in their staff instruction and in their Ecole de Guerre—we would have to do a good deal of the teaching, and that certainly the heaviest part of the burden would be ours, not theirs.

It has occurred to me that to illustrate the type of duty you may be called upon to discharge, I would do well to confine myself to a single succession of operations. I think diffused study of military operations can become superficial. As I remarked to the general and his guests this morning, I'd rather study one campaign thoroughly, if it is a good campaign, than to study a dozen campaigns superficially.

I used to carry the Army War College over some of the battlefields of Virginia; and I quit, quit cold, and almost contemptuously, because I said it was impossible even for the finely trained soldiers of that outfit to learn anything that was usable in the brief time that was given them. How can any man, for example, take in Fredericksburg, Chancellorsville, and Spotsylvania Court House in one day and then come down and expect to do the operations of the Seven Days and Second Cold Harbor in another day? It just can't be done. Sometimes the war college did not proceed that fast. I think in one instance they attempted to cover all of the campaigns of the War between the States in Virginia in a week. How perfectly absurd an enterprise! I beg you, do not neglect the study of any period, but work on the sound principle that it is better to know everything of one campaign than to know something of every campaign. If you know everything about one campaign, you will find that then you are able to understand those contingent factors, those elements of personality that may mean in the end as much as the strategy or the tactical dispositions of the opposing generals.

So this morning, with your permission, I am going to try to describe for you the joint operations of the American and French forces in the United States in 1778-81. A part of this is, I have to admit, an almost new story, and some parts of it, as you will see in a few moments, are almost on the ground where you stand. Certainly some of the operations that are to be described briefly here are operations the echo of which rolled across Willoughby Spit and over to this site in 1778 and 1781.

You will remember that the operations of 1778 began almost immediately after that hideous winter that the American army had spent at Valley Forge. That was the winter of 1777-78. It was not, as many have thought, the worst winter of the war. The winter of 1779-80 at Morristown was worse in every respect than the year 1777-78 at Valley Forge. But after Valley Forge had come the evacuation of Philadelphia by the British and that bold, daring, almost contemptuous movement of the British to carry their full army and their wagon trains from what is now Camden, New Jersey, up to the region of

Navesink, which is not far from South Amboy. They went clean across the state of New Jersey with their wagon train and their column that occupied twelve miles of road. For a variety of reasons, Washington was almost unable to strike them at all until he tried to strike their rear guard at Monmouth on the twenty-eighth of July. That ended the operations, it was thought, for the year. Washington was prepared for other eventualities, but he thought they would not develop in the region of New York. Actually, they did not.

But, that very next month after July 1778, word came that a French squadron had reached the mouth of Delaware Bay. This squadron was described in very exaggerated figures as consisting of a very large fleet that included about a dozen capital ships (that is, ships of sixty or more guns) and as having aboard five thousand troops. Actually, it had no troops aboard and not a great many marines. This was the fleet of Comte d'Estaing. He was an army officer who had become a fleet admiral, and he was bringing over this force to cooperate with the Americans. Until that time we had suffered from a hopeless inferiority of force, and it did not look as if the fleet that he brought was going to be strong enough to be of any real help. The fleet went from the mouth of the Delaware to a station off the region behind Sandy Hook, roughly the region that now bears the name of Raritan Bay. The British were behind the bar, and d'Estaing came up and was going to attempt either to get behind the bar and hurt the British or if possible to drive into New York. Here, then, was the first contact between the Americans and the French as armed forces.

There had been numbers of French officers in the United States—some of them very bad, some of them bums, some of them whiskeyheads—who had been driven out of the French army and thought they had a chance to make careers for themselves over here. They were so bad that Washington said at one time that with the exception of Lafayette, he would be glad to get rid of all of them. I think when he made that observation he had forgotten the French engineers who had come over. Those were competent men. They were Duportail, Gouvion, Radiere—excellent men. I think Washington must have forgotten them. But the others were bums, and our experience with them was anything but satisfactory. Now comes a French fleet under high command of qualified professional naval officers. This is the first opportunity we have had for cooperation.

Now what does d'Estaing need? He needs, first of all, of course, pilots. He needs accurate intelligence. He doubtless needs water, and he needs easy communications with the American commander in chief. It is not easy to give him any of these, but Washington, after a fashion, is able to provide him with pilots. The pilots say that the French ships draw so much more water than the British ships that it is impossible for the French fleet to get behind Sandy Hook. So far as water is concerned, d'Estaing tries to get it for himself, and he doesn't make a very good job of it. As for intelligence, Washington had to admit at the very outset that he did not have an exact report even of the strength of the British fleet that was then in New York waters. Here comes your ally, and you are unable to tell him the strength of the enemy in your immediate front! As for easy communications, Washington suffered then from that which was a positive affliction to him for many, many months, namely, the short force he had of men who were qualified to communicate with the French in their own language. Actually, Washington had in his immediate staff only two men who had a good speaking knowledge of French. One of these was a young fellow, a cocky little artillerist, who later became rather famous in America. He had been born down in the West Indies and had learned French and spoke it quite well. His name was Alexander Hamilton. Washington had another boy on his staff in his twenties, a young aide who had been educated at Geneva and who spoke French admirably. The boy was named John Laurens. These were the only men Washington had who could establish contact with the French in their own language.

Now this brings us to the first of the many rules that have to be applied in the type of duty that you are called upon to discharge. First, learn at least one of the languages that you are going to have to use. Learn at least one.

Just think of the contrast, gentlemen, between the duty that lies before you compared with the duty that was represented by young officers in the 1870s and 1880s, less than a century ago. General Bruce and I, and perhaps some of the other seniors here, can remember when General Hugh Scott was chief of staff of the United States Army. That for which General Hugh Scott was most renowned was the fact that he could use the sign language of the Indians. Scott learned the language (even if it was a sign language) that was required for dealing with the allies and the enemies that we had in the West. Now it is for you to learn Japanese, to learn Russian, to learn Rumanian, perhaps Hungarian—a number of those far dialects and languages; and they can be learned. It was said with great pride that by 1785 the number of Americans who were teaching French in the United States had reached twenty-three. There were twenty-three French teachers in the United States at that time. Now, of course, you can get yourself a phonograph and one of these training courses, and if you have good ears and will make the effort, you can learn excellent French in a far shorter time than ever seemed possible to your elder brothers. Learn one of these languages. It will prove to you invaluable.

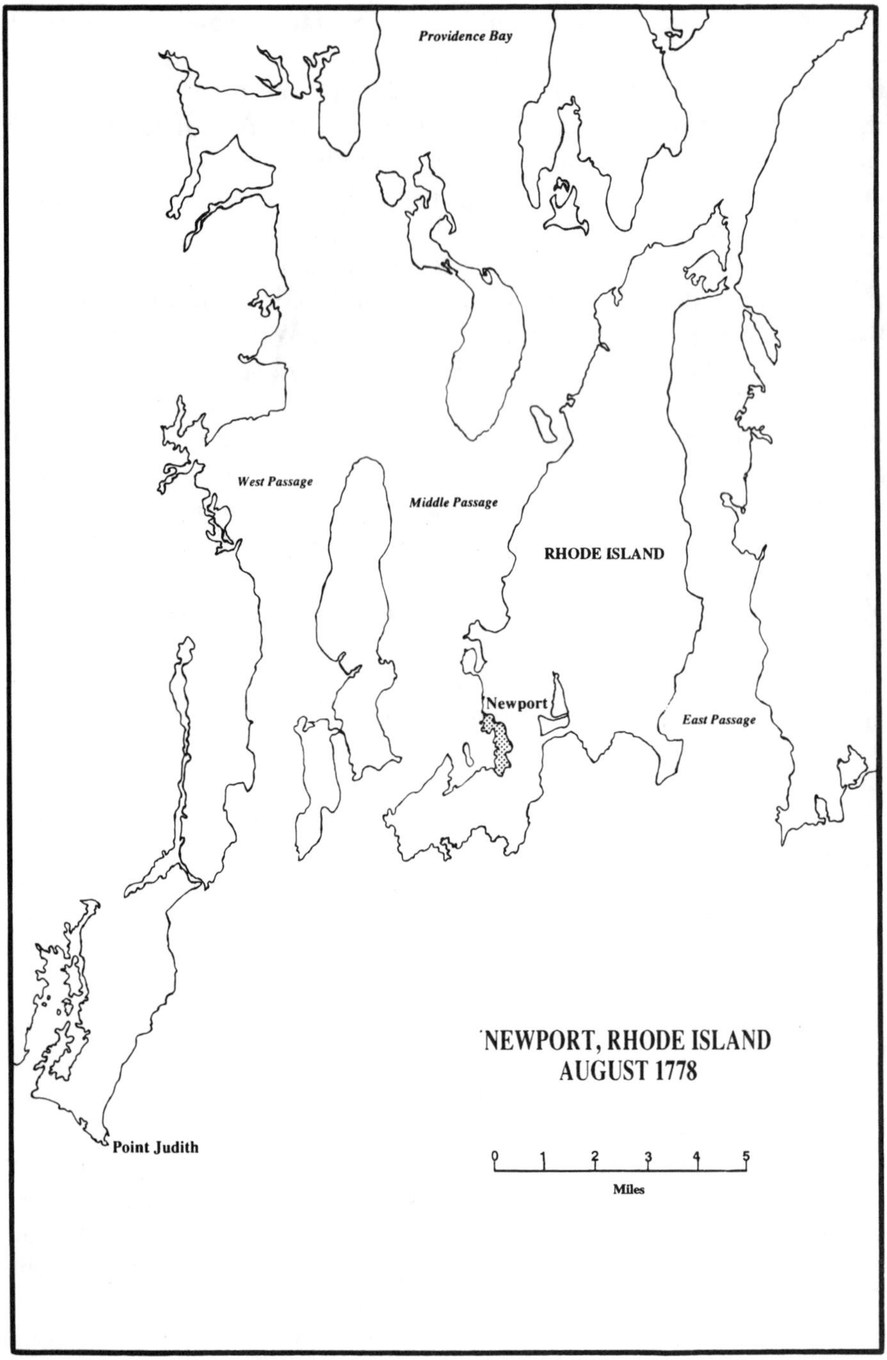
Providence Bay
West Passage
Middle Passage
RHODE ISLAND
Newport
East Passage
Point Judith
NEWPORT, RHODE ISLAND
AUGUST 1778
0 1 2 3 4 5
Miles

Well, nothing could be done in front of New York. D'Estaing, therefore, is sent from New York up to Newport, Rhode Island. There is a little British squadron off Rhode Island, and there is a British force on land there under General Pigot. It was thought by Washington and his French associates that it would be possible to send this fleet of d'Estaing up there and, with the reinforcement of the American troops around Newport, to bag the British army that was there and to take this little British fleet, merely a small squadron. That seemed a practical thing to do because, among other things, it would give the Americans that admirable port. At the time, they had no good port except Boston, and Boston wasn't good in winter. They had Philadelphia after the evacuation, but Philadelphia was upstream and difficult. New York wasn't theirs; Newport wasn't theirs; Charleston and Savannah were easily assailed by the British whenever they wanted to take them. Newport seemed to be an excellent place to take. Washington thought a good thing to do would be to send Lafayette up there because Lafayette, being a Frenchman of high rank, would certainly be acceptable to d'Estaing. In addition, he decided that he was going to send up there General Nathanael Greene, who was his ace combat officer, a native of Rhode Island, and a man who could be relied upon for admirable service there. Washington, however, did not change the commander at Newport. It was assumed that good relations could be established between the commanders there and that this officer would be the man to do it.

We cannot afford, in actual fact, to fail to have the earliest possible direct contact with our allied leaders and with those civil authorities that we must see. Washington, if possible, should have gone to Rhode Island himself and talked with d'Estaing. Actually, Washington felt that he was too busy. He sent the best men he could, but d'Estaing had to deal with the American commander already in position there. That commander was John Sullivan. Sullivan was a fairly good combat officer. He lacked that which Napoleon said was necessary for a man to be successful in war, namely, he was not lucky. Napoleon, you remember, said a man had to be as fortunate as he was able to be a good soldier. Sullivan was not lucky.

Well, what a grand plan that is now, whether Sullivan is lucky or not. Here is Sullivan with about four thousand troops; here are two columns coming under Lafayette and under Nathanael Greene. They will have about eight or nine thousand American troops there to go against the British, who are estimated at about four thousand, maybe less. Here are these comparatively weak British frigates in and around the waters of Rhode Island. Here is coming d'Estaing.

A plan is worked out very promptly under which d'Estaing is to force the entrance. He is going up what is called in that region the Middle Channel. He is going to force his way up there on the eighth of August, and on the tenth he is going to land a force on one side of Rhode Island and General Sullivan is to land an American force on the other or east side. It will be possible for d'Estaing to destroy that little British squadron, to bombard and destroy the British batteries, and then the French from d'Estaing's fleet, most of them sailors, and the American force can come down Rhode Island and wipe out the British. Fine! Good plan! Nothing wrong with it—except John Sullivan. And John Sullivan had made up his mind that he was going to show this damn frog that he knew something about military operations on his own account.

On the eighth of August, d'Estaing's fleet comes magnificently up the Middle Channel, firing on the British force on land. The British frigates by that time had been burned up. On the morning of the ninth, word came to Sullivan that the British had withdrawn from the northern part of the island. Now the plan was for operations to begin on the tenth. Sullivan jumped the gun for his own glory and came ashore on the ninth and then sent word to d'Estaing that he was there and expected d'Estaing to cooperate. D'Estaing's plans had all been made for the next day.[1]

Then presently word comes to d'Estaing, "There is something out at sea; what looks like a fleet has been sighted." They go down to Point Judith as quickly as they can, send officers down there, and when they get there the faces of the lookouts are long and alarmed. "Yes, two hours ago we saw ten white dots down to the east and southeast; and since that time the number has increased steadily and they are getting closer; and we can't make out the colors as yet but it doesn't look good." A few minutes later they counted thirty-five ships. And when they got within sight and they took their glasses and studied them, they shook their heads. "They are the British." This is Lord Howe's fleet, that has come up here to capture the French fleet that was to capture the British fleet; and now d'Estaing is himself blockaded in the Middle Channel. Well, that's a pretty kettle of fish, isn't it?

The next day d'Estaing says, "I'm going out and meet them." He is a queer man, but when he got his blood up he'd fight. He is a long time in getting it up, but when he got it up he'd fight. He went out. Lovely sight to see those French ships going out to sea. And to his great surprise and delight, the British made way and seemed to withdraw—their object, of course, being to maneuver him into a favorable position.

The day after that, save one, there came up a terrible storm that dismasted the French flagship and also one of the other French ships of the line. That badly crippled d'Estaing. D'Estaing said, "I promised Sullivan I was coming back to Newport, and I'm going back." As soon as he could he went back off Newport, and he said to Sullivan, "I can't stay here." Sullivan raised hell. There he was on Rhode Island, cut off, the British in his front, the French fleet going to withdraw. He sent everybody he could to the French fleet to urge d'Estaing to stay. D'Estaing said, "We can't repair these ships here; we've got to go to Boston." And he went. Sullivan issued an order in which he said in effect, "We must fight this battle alone because we are not going to have support from the force that we had a right to expect would support us in these operations."

Now of all the things that old fool could have said, that was the worst. What's the matter? You have here one of the most important of all the things to remember. The personality of cooperating officers is of the greatest importance. If Greene had been put at Newport in the place of Sullivan, this would never have happened.

Well, d'Estaing never came back. You hardly could blame him for not coming back. But he was a professional soldier, and queer as he was, he stood his ground and as a fine naval officer he did everything that was expected of him at Boston. By and by, without a word to anybody, good-bye, he's gone—got to go down to the West Indies—and there we are as before. Whatever chance we had of equality at sea, to say nothing of naval superiority, is lost.

Now I beg you, one of these days take that story and follow it out step by step, and you will see that it has developed these three points: first of all, you must have acquaintance with the language if you are going to know the people; second, you must have contact with the leaders as early as possible; third, you must be sure that the officers who are to have cooperation at the higher level are men who will cooperate.

I remember once saying to Foster Dulles, when he came back from Russia, "Did you make any progress?" "No, none." I said, "Couldn't you get any cooperation?" He said, "How are you going to cooperate with people who won't cooperate?"

You'll find some men of that sort. Sullivan jumped the gun because he wanted to have the credit of victory, and the price was a very narrow squeak. His army got off safely, much more readily than he thought, but it was a close call.[2]

Seventeen seventy-nine brought a serious development in that in the fall, d'Estaing went down and tried to take Savannah, Georgia. He did not succeed. The next year, 1780, in March, the British took Charleston, South Carolina, which left us in reality no port except Philadelphia and Boston and what might be or might not be the result at Newport.

That situation was relieved very soon by the announcement that here now is coming another force. This time the French are sending not merely a fleet, but they are sending troops; and on the tenth of July, 1780, the French fleet and the French force arrive at Newport. The fleet consisted of seven or eight ships of the line with their auxiliaries, and the troops a few more than four thousand tip-top French troops under the very cream of the French professional officers.

Now, notice how Washington has done what every other man ought to do. Notice now how the French, when they come, come prepared on the basis of their experience for dealing with the Americans. Here comes Rochambeau, a small man, fifty-five years of age, a first-class soldier, a man very little disposed ever to put anything in writing, a man who believed in military diplomacy to the nth degree but a man whose heart was absolutely faithful to his instructions, a man who was devoted completely to the cause, and a man who had, in addition, the most important instruction that could be given him: "You are to be subordinate to General Washington." In other words, we have here that great rule of success in the operation of allies: unity of field command. It has often been said that Washington was made a marshal of France. That's not true; but he had the authority of a marshal of France in dealing with this army, and he had in Rochambeau a man whose spirit of cooperation was simply magnificent.

The head of the naval force was an admiral by the name of Ternay, a tough old bird but a loyal, stout man. Pretty soon this little French fleet was blockaded in Newport, and it was generally thought that Ternay was so much disappointed by the result of it that he lay down and died. In his place there came into the command of the French fleet an officer by the name of Chevalier Destouches, a man about whom very little is known. It was not expected that he would command the fleet.

Now comes an opportunity. Benedict Arnold and some British troops have gone down into Chesapeake Bay and have landed at Portsmouth, Virginia. They have established a base of operations there. The British based in Charleston, South Carolina, have driven a little American force through South Carolina up into North Carolina and close to the Roanoke River in northern North Carolina.[3] The British may send forces down to strengthen Arnold at Portsmouth. If they do, then Cornwallis, moving northward, and Arnold or his British opposite number, Phillips, coming down from the north, can catch Nathanael Greene between them. On the other hand, Arnold has scarcely any naval support in the Chesapeake. If, therefore, Destouches will come down and strike vigorously at this force of Arnold's, then, by Jove, we may relieve the northern pressure on Greene and at the same time wipe out

Arnold—this traitor. Can it be done? Can it be done? Can Destouches break his way out (the British having a very feeble patrol at that season of the year, winter, 1781)? Can he break his way out and come down there and trap Arnold? Tight question. But then, in the mercy of God, it looks as if the big chance has come.

On the twenty-second and the twenty-third of January, while the French fleet is riding easily off Newport, well havened, the British fleet at Gardiner's Bay suffers a tremendous storm. One of its capital ships is sunk; one of them is dismasted; one of them is driven to sea, and I don't know what happened to it. Now Destouches has superiority of force. Can he get down to Virginia now, knock Arnold out, and get back in time to protect the force at Newport? It is a daring thing. Washington says, "Try it." Destouches says, "It is too big a risk to take my whole fleet. I'll send one '64' and two frigates and will try." He tried it and didn't succeed. He couldn't carry his heavy ship up the Elizabeth River; he couldn't reach Arnold's batteries, which were south of Portsmouth; and the whole situation was one of obscurity. Destouches came back. Washington said, "Ah, now, if only he had taken his whole squadron instead of sending a part of it."

Washington was a very careful man in what he said. He very seldom let himself be in any way indiscreet in criticizing anybody. But in this instance he thought that such a big chance was lost that in a letter to his manager at Mount Vernon, a letter in which he wrote this paragraph and marked it on the side "Private," he said, "I think you ought to know that Destouches went down there with these few ships when I advised strongly that he go with his whole squadron; and if he had gone with his whole squadron, he would have captured this whole force. It was a mistake for Destouches to have gone down there with so small a force." He wrote that in several letters, but the one to Lund Washington, his manager, was the most explicit. Well, there you are. They are back. What are you going to do about it now?

One morning Washington asked what newspapers had come from New York, and someone said to him, "Here's Rivington's paper of the fourth of April." "Ah, let me see it." Washington sat down to read it, and there at the foot of one of the columns was an extract from his letter to Lund, and the extract contained his criticism of Destouches and that movement. What had happened was, the letter most foolishly had been entrusted to the general mail, and a British sympathizer on the west side of the Hudson (which was known as Smith's Clove) had captured the letter and carried it on to New York, and there it had been made public, made public ostensibly because of the effect it was certain to have on Franco-American relations. Now that is a devil of a mess for you, isn't it? An operation undertaken by your allies and the

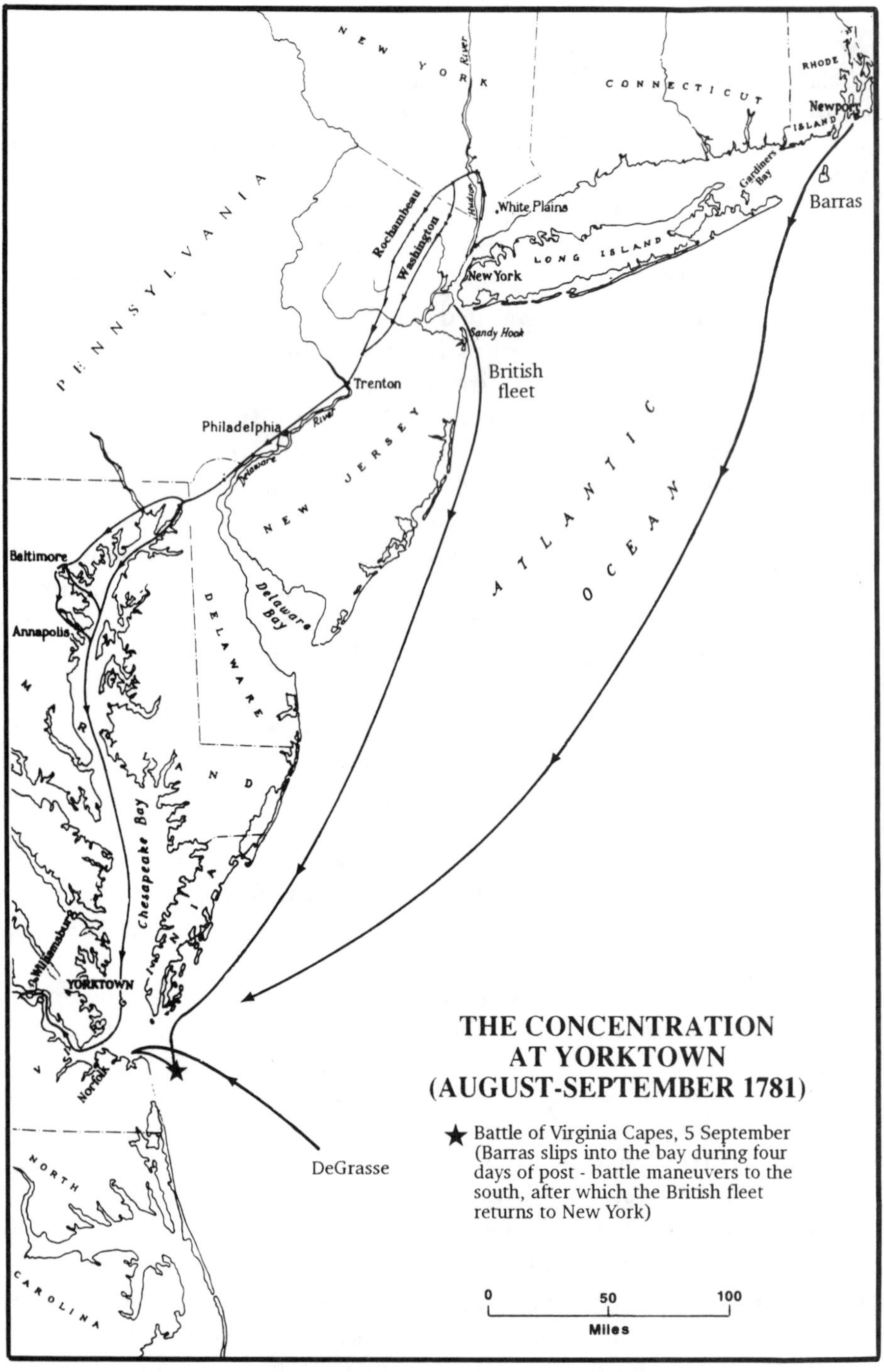

Adapted with permission of Charles Scribner's Sons, an imprint of Macmillan Publishing Company, from Atlas of American History, Second Revised Edition, edited by Kenneth T. Jackson. Copyright 1943, 1978, 1985 by Charles Scribner's Sons.

American commander in chief publicly listed as critical of it in a letter to the manager of his farm!

Of course, the lesson that applies here is quite obvious. Never criticize your ally unless you must, and then never criticize him in anything that's got any chance of falling into hostile hands.

Well, what are you going to do about it? Here you are, and you put the question to yourself, Mr. Student. Here you are. You have written this criticism of the French. It is printed. What are you going to do about it? What are you going to say? Got any excuse? Any extenuation? Anything you can say?

By and by, Washington got a letter from Rochambeau, and Rochambeau said, "I've seen this thing in the paper, and I think you ought to know that the reason Destouches sent those few ships was twofold. In the first place, Destouches didn't have many supplies; and in the second place, he was asked by the Congress and by the state of Virginia to send just about that strength of ships south."

Washington hadn't been told any of that. So he sat down and wrote a letter to Rochambeau, and he said, "I wrote this letter. I can't remember whether I wrote that exact language or not because I didn't keep a copy of the letter, but that is substantially what I said. It was a private letter. It was not intended for publication, and it was written when I frankly didn't understand what your situation was. That's all. I just have to leave the rest to your generosity."

Rochambeau replied, "You can do it. I just inquired to know what the facts were. I don't believe Destouches has seen the letter. I'm going to say nothing to him about it. But if he says anything to me, I'm going to tell him exactly what you have said." And with that, the generosity of Rochambeau saved what otherwise might have been a terrible situation.

A few months passed. Washington undertook to carry the French from Newport over to New York and to deliver an attack there. There again he made a mistake in that in order to get a surprise attack on New York, he took these French cavalry and gave them too long a march for a hot day. He had as commander of the cavalry the Duc de Lauzun, a bird who always boasted that he was a sweetheart of Marie Antionette. He was a big faker and a big liar but a right good soldier (they are not always incompatible). Lauzun came over and he couldn't make it, and Washington learned another lesson there. In cooperation, if the command rests with you, never put the toughest job on your ally. Take the toughest job for yourself.

Well, the great day is coming. The French are going to make a deliberate effort now to get superiority of force. Word comes to Washington on the thirteenth of August that Admiral de Grasse is coming to America with a fleet, a big fleet, and is coming to Chesapeake Bay. Now, is there any chance to save Greene? Is there any chance to trap the British who are still there? Cornwallis has entered Virginia. He has been to Portsmouth. It is said that he has gone over to establish a base on the peninsula of Virginia at a place named Yorktown. Is there any chance of catching him? "Yes," says Washington, "with naval superiority, we can do it." Is de Grasse going to the Chesapeake? "We'll go to the Chesapeake."

And on the fourteenth of August began what was one of the greatest moments in American history, the decision of Washington to effect a change of base and to establish a new concentration in the Chesapeake Bay area. See what he had to do. Here he is in New York. Barras, who has succeeded Destouches, is at Newport with six ships of the line and with all of Washington's salt provisions (his bacon and his pork and his salt beef) that are needed in Virginia for the army. The British are in New York in considerable strength; they are in Virginia and they are around Charleston. Washington will leave a little force to bait the British in New York. He is going to take the whole of the American force that he can spare, two thousand men. He is going to tell Barras, "You go to sea with my salt provisions and come to Virginia." He said to Rochambeau, "Will you march with me to Virginia with your whole force?" "Most heartily," said Rochambeau. Washington takes his two thousand men, puts them under Benjamin Lincoln, and starts out.

Now, what has he got to do? He has to hold Cornwallis at Yorktown with a little force that is there under Lafayette and the Virginia militia. Greene must maneuver all he can, but Greene can't do a great deal—he's too weak. Barras has got to escape the British, who, if they learn of his departure, may seek to intercept him between Newport and Chesapeake Bay. While that is happening, Washington and the French, with the heavy artillery, must come down all the way from New York to Yorktown. In addition to all that, ships must be found aboard which can be put the French reserve heavy artillery at Newport that must be brought by water down to Virginia. The thirteenth or fourteenth of August those decisions are reached. Washington begins his march.[4]

On the fourteenth of September, Washington is in Williamsburg, and he has then this news: "De Grasse is in Lynnhaven Bay with thirty ships of the line. Barras has not yet been heard from; he is probably at sea."[5] With de Grasse came three thousand French troops under Saint-Simon. They are landed and they are in camp in Williamsburg. Lafayette has held Cornwallis in Yorktown. Here is Rochambeau's army, just behind Washington. Here are the Continentals, marching by a different route and coming down.

On the twenty-ninth of September, Washington is able to say, "Barras has arrived; the heavy artillery is soon to be landed. Rochambeau's forces, my own troops, Lafayette's command, Saint-Simon's troops—all these are ready. De Grasse is at the mouth of the Chesapeake. Let us close on Cornwallis."

As you well know, August to September to October, two months and three days after that concentration was ordered, Cornwallis surrenders. What did it? Willingness to learn how to deal with the other man; learning to cooperate, if by no other method than trial and error; integrity of leadership; the application of every lesson. Gentlemen, if that is not a challenge to you, in the larger aspects of the diplomatic service of your careers as officers of the armed forces, then believe me, I am unable to shape for you what a challenge would be.

Notes

The stenographic transcript of this lecture is filed in the archives of the Armed Forces Staff College, Norfolk, Virginia. The transcript is entitled "P-6: Leadership"; the title that appears here is mine.

1. This paragraph and the one preceding it have been edited to conform with the account of these operations given by Freeman in his biography of Washington.

2. D'Estaing's ships departed Newport for Boston on the night of 21 August. One week later Sullivan withdrew his force to the northern end of Rhode Island; and on the night of 30 August, Sullivan's force made an uncontested withdrawal to the mainland. Thirty-six hours later the British fleet returned with a large landing force, only to discover that Sullivan was gone.

3. The British force was commanded by Cornwallis, and the American force by Nathanael Greene.

4. On 19 August.

5. This account is not entirely accurate. The following chronology, taken from Freeman's biography of Washington, is provided for clarification:

21 August - Barras' squadron is scheduled to depart Newport. (Although it does not actually depart until 25 August).

26 August - De Grasse arrives at Chesapeake Bay.

5 September - Washington is informed of De Grasse's arrival.

12 September - Washington is informed that De Grasse has left the bay to engage a British fleet off the Virginia Capes.

14 September - De Grasse reports that he has returned to the bay after a favorable (though incomplete) engagement with the British fleet, and that Barras has joined him without meeting the British.

Appendix

1.

Lincoln's Second Inaugural Address

In the first speech of this collection, Freeman sees the key to Lincoln's greatness as his self-mastery of mind and spirit. Nowhere is this self-mastery better illustrated than in Lincoln's second inaugural address. In this address, which was delivered on 4 March 1865, Lincoln provides a concise explanation for the cause of the Civil War and sees in the war the justice of God. Five weeks after this address, Lee surrendered to Grant at Appomattox. Six days later Lincoln was dead, the victim of an assassin's bullet.

Fellow Countrymen:

At this second appearing to take the oath of the presidential office there is less occasion for an extended address than there was at the first. Then a statement somewhat in detail of a course to be pursued seemed fitting and proper. Now, at the expiration of four years, during which public declarations have been constantly called forth on every point and phase of the great conflict which still absorbs the attention and engrosses the energies of the nation, little that is new could be presented. The progress of our arms, upon which all else chiefly depends, is as well known to the public as to myself, and it is, I trust, reasonably satisfactory and encouraging to all. With high hope for the future, no prediction in regard to it is ventured.

On the occasion corresponding to this four years ago all thoughts were anxiously directed to an impending civil war. All dreaded it, all sought to avert it. While the inaugural address was being delivered from this place, devoted altogether to *saving* the Union without war, insurgent agents were in the city seeking to *destroy* it without war—seeking to dissolve the Union and divide effects by negotiation. Both parties deprecated war, but one of them would *make* war rather than let the nation survive, and the other would *accept* war rather than let it perish, and the war came.

One-eighth of the whole population was colored slaves, not distributed generally over the Union, but localized in the southern part of it. These slaves constituted a peculiar and powerful interest. All knew that this interest was somehow the cause of the war. To strengthen, perpetuate, and extend this interest was the object for which the insurgents would rend the Union even by war, while the Government claimed no right to do more than to restrict the territorial enlargement of it. Neither party expected for the war the magnitude or the duration which it has already attained. Neither anticipated that the *cause* of the conflict might cease with or even before the conflict itself should cease. Each looked for an easier triumph, and a result less fundamental and astounding. Both read the same Bible and pray to the same God, and each invokes His aid against the other. It may seem strange that any men should dare to ask a just God's assistance in wringing their bread from the sweat of other men's faces, but let us judge not, that we be not judged. The prayers of both could not be answered. That of neither has been answered fully. The Almighty has His own purposes. "Woe unto the world because of offenses; for it must needs be that offenses come, but woe to that man by whom the offense cometh." If we shall suppose that American slavery is one of those offenses which, in the providence of God, must needs come, but which, having continued through His appointed time, He now wills to remove, and that He gives to both North and South this terrible war as the woe due to those by whom the offense came, shall we discern therein any departure from those divine attributes which the believers in a living God always ascribe to Him? Fondly do we hope, fervently do we pray, that this mighty scourge of war may speedily pass away. Yet, if God wills that it continue until all the wealth piled by the bondman's two hundred and fifty years of unrequited toil shall be sunk, and until every drop of blood drawn with the lash shall be paid by another drawn with the sword, as was said three thousand years ago, so still it must be said, "The judgements of the Lord are true and righteous altogether."

With malice toward none, with charity for all, with firmness in the right as God gives us to see the right, let us strive on to finish the work we are in, to bind up the nation's wounds, to care for him who shall have borne the battle and for his widow and his orphan, to do all which may achieve and cherish a just and a lasting peace among ourselves and with all nations.

2.

Lee's Farewell to the Army of Northern Virginia

Lee's farewell to his army was drafted by Colonel Charles Marshall, revised by Lee, and issued to the army on 10 April 1865 as General Order No. 9. In his biography of Lee, Freeman noted that when Lee revised this document he "struck out a paragraph that seemed to him calculated to keep alive ill-feeling." This was characteristic of the generosity of spirit displayed by both Lee and Grant in connection with the surrender of Lee's army.

After four years of arduous service marked by unsurpassed courage and fortitude, the Army of Northern Virginia has been compelled to yield to overwhelming numbers and resources.

I need not tell the brave survivors of so many hard fought battles, who have remained steadfast to the last, that I have consented to this result from no distrust of them; but feeling that valor and devotion could accomplish nothing that could compensate for the loss that must have attended the continuance of the contest, I determined to avoid the useless sacrifice of those whose past services have endeared them to their countrymen.

By the terms of the agreement, officers and men can return to their homes and remain until exchanged. You will take with you the satisfaction that proceeds from the consciousness of duty faithfully performed; and I earnestly pray that a Merciful God will extend to you his blessing and protection.

With an unceasing admiration of your constancy and devotion to your Country, and a grateful remembrance of your kind and generous consideration for myself, I bid you all an affectionate farewell.

R.E. Lee
General

3.

Washington's Resignation of His Commission

On 23 December 1783 Washington appeared before Congress, then meeting in the State House at Annapolis, Maryland, for the purpose of formally resigning his commission. This account, taken from Freeman's biography of Washington, serves to illustrate two of Washington's most significant qualities: his conception of his commission as a public trust, and his respect for civil authority.

The General arose and stood in front of his chair. He bowed; members took off their hats momentarily but did not return the bow. Out of his pocket he drew the text of his address, and held it in a hand that shook visibly. He began: "Mr. President: The great events on which my resignation depended having at length taken place; I have now the honor of offering my sincere Congratulations to Congress and of presenting myself before them to surrender into their hands the trust committed to me, and to claim the indulgence of retiring from the service of my country.

"Happy in the confirmation of our independence and sovereignty and pleased with the opportunity afforded the United States of becoming a respectable Nation, I resign with satisfaction the Appointment I accepted with diffidence. A diffidence in my abilities to accomplish so arduous a task, which however was superseded by a confidence in the rectitude of our Cause, the support of the Supreme Power of the Union, and the patronage of Heaven.

"The Successful termination of the War has verified the most sanguine expectations, and my gratitude for the interposition of Providence, and the assurance I have received from my Countrymen, increases with every review of the momentous Contest.

"While I repeat my obligations to the Army in general, I should do injustice to my own feelings not to acknowledge in this place the peculiar services and distinguished merits of the Gentlemen who have been attached to my person during the War."

Thus far, he had controlled himself, but now his emotion rose at the thought of his officers, and he had to grip the paper with both hands to hold it steady enough for reading. He went on: "It was impossible the choice of confidential Officers to compose my family should have been more fortunate. Permit me Sir, to recommend in particular those, who have continued in Service to the present moment, as worthy of the favorable notice and patronage of Congress.

"I consider it an indispensable duty to close this last solemn act of my Official life, by commending the Interests of our dearest Country to the protection of Almighty God, and those who have the superintendence of them, to his holy keeping."

He was able to complete the sentence, but he choked and knew he could not go on immediately. A pause followed as he fought to recover his voice. If he could scarcely follow his manuscript, there were many spectators who could not see him through their tears. A moment more and his voice came back strongly: "Having now finished the work assigned me, I retire from the great theatre of action; and bidding an Affectionate farewell to this August body under whose orders I have so long acted, I here offer my commission, and take my leave of all the employments of public life."

Index

This is an index of the personalities, events, and themes which relate directly to the book's main topics: Freeman and leadership. Unless otherwise indicated, all place names are in Virginia.

About the Editor

Lieutenant Commander Smith attended Yale University on an NROTC scholarship, graduating in 1971 with a B.A. in History. A surface warfare officer, he has served in the destroyers *Laffey* and *Cone* and in the helicopter carrier *Tripoli*. His service ashore includes a three-year tour as the Executive Officer of the U.S. Naval Weapons Facility, St. Mawgan, England. Commander Smith is currently assigned as the Managing Editor of the Naval War College Press. He lives in Portsmouth, Rhode Island, with his wife Carol, his son Matthew, and his daughter Merryn.